GLORY DEAD

BOOKS BY ARTHUR CALDER-MARSHALL

Two of a Kind
About Levy
At Sea
Dead Centre
Pie in the Sky
A Date with a Duchess
The Changing Scene

The desolation of a palm-fringed beach at sunset

ARTHUR CALDER-MARSHALL

GLORY DEAD

> Glory Dead
> Glory dead!
> Glory dead when backra come.
> Glory dead!
> Glory dead when white man come.
> *West Indian Song*

INTRODUCTION BY BRIDGET BRERETON

PEEPAL TREE

First published in Great Britain in 1939
by Michael Joseph Ltd
This new edition published in 2022
Peepal Tree Press Ltd
17 King's Avenue
Leeds LS6 1QS
England

Copyright © 1939, 2022 Estate of Arthur Calder-Marshall

Introduction © 2022 Bridget Brereton

ISBN13: 9781845235314

All rights reserved
No part of this publication may be
reproduced or transmitted in any form
without permission

CONTENTS

Bridget Brereton: Introduction — 9
Foreword — 25

Part I
A Portrait of the City — 33

Part II
1. The Tourist's Trinidad — 75
2. Where's Mr. Ganges? — 81
3. Medicine and Magic — 98
4. Cultural Evenings — 111
5. Still Waiting For Lefty — 133
6. Fight! Fight! Black is White! — 138
7. Liberty Costs Eighteen Pounds — 143
8. Moscow Agent — 158

Part III
Some Observations:
On Patriotism — 179
On Trinidad's Industries — 187
On Crown Colony Government — 199

LIST OF ILLUSTRATIONS

The Desolation of a Palm-Fringed Beach at Sunset	*Frontispiece*
Frederick Street is Port of Spain's Regent Street	32
Barracks, Hovels and Model Dwellings	90-91
Andre Louis Gambier Wonders Shall He Sail?	147
Two Desperate Characters – Mr. and Mrs. Percival	153
East Indian Leader, the Honourable Adrian Cola Rienzi, né Krishna Deonarine	169
Your Colour is God's Colour	178

To Tony De Boissière

whose help made the writing of this book easy
and whose company made it a pleasure.

BRIDGET BRERETON

INTRODUCTION

The English writer Arthur Calder-Marshall visited Trinidad in 1938. Born in 1908, he had already published at least six books, the first appearing in 1933 when he was in his mid-twenties, and was well known in Britain as a precocious literary talent. He had joined the British Communist Party, and was a member of the London based, left-wing Writers and Readers Group in the 1930s. Calder-Marshall seems to have been a correspondent or writer for the London *News Chronicle*, a British daily founded in 1930 which supported broadly left-wing policies at home and abroad (especially with respect to the Spanish Civil War); he mentions articles he wrote for the paper while in Trinidad. "I was only in the island for about three months", the young author wrote, "but by the end of that time I think I had come to an understanding of the place and people as good as any outsider could achieve".[1]

Glory Dead was apparently written in Mexico City, and published in 1939 by Michael Joseph.[2] It is not clear why Calder-Marshall decided to write a book about Trinidad, but if we can believe the account given by V. S. Naipaul in his lightly fictionalised essay about him, it was Graham Greene who suggested it. Greene was an early admirer of Calder-Marshall's novels, and had recently published a book about Liberia; he thought a similar one on Trinidad, populated by the descendants of enslaved people from West Africa, would be a good idea.[3] In any case, given the young writer's politics, it was clear that this would not be a typical "travel book" or tourist guide from the Caribbean, but would instead try to probe the situation of ordinary Trinidadians and critique the effects of British colonialism and capitalist exploitation.

Calder-Marshall's main guide while in Trinidad was Jean Antonio "Tony" de Boissière, to whom his book is dedicated; his influence on the book can be detected at several points, as will be noted. Tony de Boissière – not to be confused with his mixed-race cousin Ralph – was born in 1906 and was a member of one of Trinidad's aristocratic white French Creole families, the grandson of Poleska de Boissière (1836-1927), a locally famous *grande dame* – he published a typically malicious portrait of her in 1942. He was more or less an outcast from his snobbish and prosperous family, living as he did a "Bohemian" and homosexual lifestyle; he was a famous drinker, raconteur, conversationalist and cook. By 1938, he had returned to Trinidad after sojourns in New York and other travels, and was making a precarious living by writing and editing. In the 1940s, de Boissière published several short books or pamphlets, most of them mocking Trinidadians of all groups, including his own French Creole community, and he edited a short-lived literary magazine, *Callaloo*, in the early part of the decade. He was a bitter critic of British colonialism and of the lifestyle and attitudes of British expatriates in Trinidad.[4]

The historical background
The history of Trinidad in the 1920s and 1930s has been well researched, with a focus on politics, labour organisation, and socio-economic conditions. The brief survey that follows will help to delineate the colony's situation at the time of Calder-Marshall's visit.[5]

Trinidad had been a crown colony, without an elected legislature, since its absorption into the British Empire in the early 1800s. But following labour unrest in 1919-20, and persistent agitation by middle-class reformers, limited constitutional change was enacted in 1924. The legislative council, hitherto consisting only of officials and nominated "unofficials", would now include seven elected members. The first elections were held in 1925, and they brought Captain A. A. Cipriani, a white Trinidadian who was the colony's main labour leader, into the council. But the electorate was small, perhaps six per cent of the total population, because of high property and income qualifications for the franchise; a few women, who could meet the qualifications in their own right and were over the age of 30, were enfranchised along with qualified men over 21. The qualifications for membership were even higher, and only men could be elected. The governor and his group of top officials retained ultimate control over legislation, and the vast majority of the population had little or no say in the colony's governance. By 1938, there had been no further constitutional changes of any significance.

Nor had the island's traditional social structure undergone much change. An upper class, consisting mainly of families of European descent (white Creoles), or British expatriates, dominated social life as well as economic activities. An expanding middle stratum consisted of people of mixed descent (African/European), along with upwardly mobile Afro- and Indo-Trinidadians, who had acquired middle-class status through education, command of British culture, and (less often) successful engagement in farming, skilled trades, or small businesses. The majority of the people, mainly of African and Indian (South Asian) descent, constituted the rural and urban working classes, involved in estate labour, peasant farming, and urban waged jobs. Though the upper class was still very much in control of the economy, and still claimed the traditional deference to whiteness, it faced significant challenges to its ascendancy by 1938. These came both from politicised members of the middle stratum, especially well educated professional men and (less often) women and young progressives, and from the new labour organisations of the period.

Trinidad's economy still featured plantation agriculture as the main employer of labour. The cocoa industry, which had flourished between around 1870 and 1920 and had for a time replaced sugar as the colony's leading export crop, was hard hit by the collapse in world prices in the early 1920s. It entered into a period of decline which continued all through the interwar period and beyond. Sugar struggled on, enjoying modest prosperity for the mainly British companies which increasingly controlled the industry, and it was the largest single employer of wage labour. Wages were notoriously low, however, and seasonal underemployment was the norm; the housing provided for resident workers, mainly Indo-Trinidadians, usually consisted of crowded and insanitary barracks.

But the most striking feature of Trinidad's interwar economy was the emergence of the oil industry after 1912. It rapidly expanded with the onset of the motor car and oil-dependent ships, planes, machines and heavy vehicles world-wide. By 1938, the oil companies, mainly owned by British and American investors, already contributed the largest amount to the colony's revenues and provided good dividends to their shareholders. Though a small producer in absolute terms, Trinidad was the largest oil exporter within the British Empire at the start of World War II.[6]

For the majority of the colony's people, the interwar years, and especially the 1930s, brought "hard times". There were some advances in public health, and the death rate did slowly decline in this period, while birth rates remained high, so that the population increased even with the end of indentured Indian immigration in 1917. (The censuses recorded the population of Trinidad & Tobago as 365, 913 in 1921, 412, 783 in 1931, and 563,222 in 1946 after the end of the war.) But living and working conditions, for most of the colony's rural and urban poor, remained appalling. Wages never kept pace with post-World War One inflation, not even in the prosperous oil industry. Unemployment was a serious problem, but even more insidious, perhaps, was the seasonal underemployment so marked on the sugar estates, still the largest employer. The decline of the cocoa industry also negatively affected the thousands of estate labourers and peasant farmers, of many ethnic groups, connected to that crop.

A great deal of evidence in the 1930s, much of it in official reports and surveys like the 1938 Forster Report (an important source for Calder-Marshall) and the more famous 1939 Moyne Report, pointed to an alarming prevalence of malnutrition, grossly inadequate sanitation, poor health, and preventable morbidity and mortality among the working classes. The housing of the poor was appalling, whether in rural cottages in the villages, the unplanned slums springing up around the oil fields, the notorious barracks of the sugar plantations, or the tenements in Port of Spain, the capital, and its environs. Rural underemployment, retrenchment and low wages pushed migration to Port of Spain, creating the infamous "barrack yards" of the eastern districts where the poor crowded – they were mainly African while the residents of the plantation barracks were mainly Indians. Even "respectable" middle-class residents of the city, coping with low and static salaries, inflation, and often very large families, faced great difficulties in maintaining a suitable lifestyle; a good example is provided by the childhood experiences of the future prime minister, Eric Williams, born in 1911.[7]

In the face of all this, and stimulated by world events like the rise of socialism in Europe and the Labour Party in Britain, the Russian Revolution in 1917, and the consequences of World War One, serious labour organisation began in Trinidad, as in the British Caribbean as a whole. In the interwar period, the leading organisation was the Trinidad Workingmen's Association (TWA). It had been founded in the 1890s, but it really came into prominence in the labour unrest of 1919-20, when its leaders represented the many different groups of striking workers. In 1923, Cipriani, who had become a public figure because of his defence of the returning soldiers of the British West Indian Regiments, accepted the presidency of the TWA, lending his considerable personal prestige, and his gifts of oratory, to the labour cause. Cipriani and the TWA secretary, William Howard-Bishop, made the TWA the most important labour body in the colony, with many sections, and branches all over the island. In 1934, the TWA was renamed the Trinidad Labour Party (TLP) when Cipriani refused to register the TWA under the 1932 Trade Union Ordinance, which lacked basic protections and rights for unions. In any case, the TWA/TLP functioned as a combined umbrella union and political party both before and after the 1934 name change. In 1925, as we saw, Cipriani entered the legislature as the elected member for Port of Spain, a seat he held until his death in 1945; he was also active in the City Council and served as Mayor of Port of Spain for many years. He consistently tried to use his seat in the legislature, and his involvement in city government, to defend the workers' interests, but he achieved few tangible gains in the face of the indifference of the colonial government, and of most of his colleagues (nominated and elected) in the Legislative Council.[8]

Though Cipriani's TWA/TLP was unquestionably the leading labour group in the interwar years, it faced challenges from younger leaders from the mid-1930s. They grew impatient with the Captain's insistence on "constitutional" methods of protest and his autocratic leadership style; they were also more closely in touch with workers' conditions on the ground. In Port of Spain, the Negro Welfare, Cultural and Social Association (NWCSA) was formed, a socialist body with a genuinely working-class leadership, including women such as Elma Francois (spelled "Francoise" by Calder-Marshall) on the front line.[9] In the south, oil workers and others responded to the agitation of T. U. B. Butler, a former oil employee of Grenadian origins who was also a Baptist preacher and an inspiring speaker.[10] Another former member of the TWA/TLP who broke away was A. C. Rienzi, a socialist Indo-Trinidadian lawyer also based in the south, who challenged Cipriani with a new grouping there.[11]

Parallel to the emergence of the new labour organisations – and closely related to them – was the rise of racial consciousness on the part of Afro-Trinidadians. Marcus Garvey's United Negro Improvement Association (UNIA) was immensely influential in Trinidad in the 1920s and 1930s; most of the leaders of the TWA/TLP were Garveyites, UNIA branches were to be found all over the island, and the UNIA newspaper circulated widely, despite attempts to ban its importation. When the Italian Fascist dictator invaded Ethiopia in 1935, this unprovoked attack on the ancient and independent African nation, and the subsequent failure of Britain and France to support the exiled Haile Selassie, powerfully stimulated race consciousness in Trinidad and throughout the Caribbean colonies.[12] Racial consciousness among Indo-Trinidadians was stimulated by the struggles for self-rule in India led by Gandhi and Nehru, but was still in its early stages in the pre-World War II period.

In June 1937, a strike by oil workers in the south led by Butler (without Cipriani's knowledge or support) escalated into an island-wide labour protest, involving workers in rural and urban Trinidad, of Indian as well as African descent. The authorities used traditional methods to suppress it – fatal shootings by armed police and volunteer forces, the arrival of two British naval ships with sailors and marines – and it was more or less crushed in a few weeks, with Butler in hiding from the police. But it was a watershed event in the colony's history. In its aftermath, new trade unions, including the important Oilfield Workers' Trade Union (OWTU), were established, led by Rienzi and a few others. Moreover, the colonial government finally recognised it would have to modify its policies to address labour grievances and demands, as recommended by the Forster Commission, whose 1938 Report was frequently cited by Calder-Marshall. When similar widespread protests broke out in other British West Indian colonies in 1937-38, the Moyne Commission was sent to the region to investigate the situation and make recommendations. It had just completed its famous Report when World War II began (and after Calder-Marshall's book appeared).[13]

Tobago, the much smaller island which was joined to Trinidad in 1889, was essentially a peasant economy in 1938. Its population was 25,358 in 1931 and 27,208 in 1946, according to the censuses. Most of the people were farmers and agricultural workers, overwhelmingly of African descent. Though there were a few estates employing wage labour and growing cocoa and coconuts (estate based sugar production had ended), own-account peasant farmers were dominant both numerically and in terms of output. Tobago's people were overwhelmingly rural, living in close-knit villages; wage-earners were relatively few. As a result, Tobago was less influenced than Trinidad by the industrial conflicts and labour mobilisation of the 1920s and 1930s, though TWA/TLP did have branches there and Garvey's movement had some adherents on the island.[14] Calder-Marshall did not write about conditions in Tobago, though he and his wife apparently visited the smaller island and attended a dance at Mason Hall there.

Glory Dead

Calder-Marshall divided his book into three parts. The first, titled 'A Portrait of the City', narrates "imaginary, but typical incidents" (p. 29, page references to this edition) during 24 hours in the life of Port of Spain, Trinidad & Tobago's capital city. Employing a racy, novelistic technique, he presents many anecdotes, or vignettes, to build up an impressionistic portrait of the dynamics of human relations in a colonial town. In Part II he abandons the fiction/novelistic mode; it consists of eight essays, more or less straight factual reportage, on various subjects. In Part III, titled 'Some Observations', Calder-Marshall sets out his views on patriotism in Trinidad, the island's industries, and crown colony government.

The anecdotes narrated in Part I, which resemble in style and format the kind of short essays that Tony de Boissière would publish in some of his pamphlets and journals in the early 1940s (and he was no doubt the source for many of them), are engagingly written, lively, and often amusing. Calder-Marshall tried to include vignettes about all the social and ethnic groups living in the city to illustrate the range of occupations, classes and races to be found there. Inevitably, perhaps, the people who feature in them tend to be one-dimensional 'types' rather than fully realised human beings, often doing or saying the kind of stereotypical things popularly associated with their class and/or ethnicity . The author is sympathetic to most of them, especially the city's poor, but the format encourages a sometimes dehumanising approach, rather like the postcards of colonial 'types' so popular with tourists in the early 1900s.

City people of every ethnic and class background populate Calder-Marshall's anecdotes: upper-class white men and women, homeless vagrants, barrack-yard Afro-Trinidadian residents, Portuguese rum shop keepers, policemen, American sailors, prostitutes (many!), a Syrian pedlar, a black lawyer, brown suburban householders, volunteers on parade, newspaper men, an oil driller from the southern USA quarrelling in a bar with a Cockney and an Irishman. He juxtaposes the lifestyles of the very poor and the prosperous, as when he writes about three Port of Spain women living in three very different districts: an impoverished washerwoman in East Dry River, a middle-class landlady in Woodbrook, and an upper-class lady holding a bridge party in Maraval (pp. 41-43). Calder-Marshall has a good grasp of the spatial and social dimensions of the city, no doubt thanks largely to de Boissière's guidance, and many of these vignettes are very convincing.

One striking feature of these anecdotes is the salience of American sailors and marines on shore leave, misbehaving in Port of Spain (pp. 33-34, 43-44, 65-68, 70-72). Clearly, they were a major presence in the city in 1938, long before World War II brought about the 'American Occupation' when huge naval, army and air bases were established on the island after 1940.[15] So, of course, were prostitutes, whose struggles and trials are salient in Part I; the view persists in Trinidad that it was the invasion of American servicemen after 1940 that made prostitution a significant issue.

Calder-Marshall's sympathy for the city's poor is evident in Part I, as in the portrayal of the strains on family life in the urban barrack yards when the man is unemployed and desperate (pp. 68-69), as is his contempt for the racism and callous indifference of the upper class men and women he writes about. There are places where he veers perilously close to stereotypes about tropical life – "Life is slower... Men move like turbot in a tank, whose breathing seems a major occupation" (p. 40) – and about the various 'types' he writes about. But, on the whole, Part I offers a lively and generally convincing picture of life in Port of Spain.

In Part II, Calder-Marshall is the sober reporter, probing key aspects of Trinidad's social, political and economic situation in the year following the major labour protests of 1937. In 'The Tourist's Trinidad' (chapter 1), he writes about his negative first impression of the capital city: "I have met no one whose feeling on landing in Port of Spain is not one of repulsion. It is not prepossessing." This first impression "of evil and corruption", he writes, "is partial, but not untrue" (p. 77). The average tourist, however – the opposite of Calder-Marshall – need see none of this, and this chapter outlines the typical tourist circuit of the day. By contrast, Calder-Marshall 'tours' the barrack yards and slums of the city in the company of the medical officer, reporting on housing and sanitation in chapter 2. His descriptions of the city barracks and tenements, based on his tour and on the recently published Forster Report, constitute a valuable source, comparable to those by James Cummings, who was a young man living in Port of Spain in the 1930s, and by C. L. R. James in his only novel, *Minty Alley*.[16] Calder-Marshall briefly leaves the capital city in this chapter to comment on housing on the sugar estates and around the oilfields in the south of the island, based on the Forster Report.

Chapter 3, 'Medicine and Magic', deals with the abysmal public health situation in 1930s Trinidad and the many inadequacies of the government medical service, which of course encouraged many to seek help instead from traditional healers and 'obeah' practitioners (Calder-Marshall is taken by de Boissière to visit a healing ritual by an 'obeahwoman' in Laventille, a working-class district east of the city). He notes that the governor in 1937, Murchison Fletcher, had expressed sympathy for the plight of the poor in a famous speech in the island legislature just after the strikes and riots in June of that year; he was rewarded with dismissal, while the acting colonial secretary, Howard Nankivell, who had also tried to help the workers, was transferred out of the island. This had taught the lesson "that caution and not enthusiasm is the highest virtue of a colonial servant and that the policy of the Colonial Office is not progress but quiet" (p. 101).[17]

In the following chapter (4), Calder-Marshall introduces several personalities from the island's intelligentsia, starting with de Boissière (pp. 111-113), and including the writer, trade unionist and cultural activist Rupert Gittens and his Club L'Ouverture (pp. 113-119), and the writer, politician and unionist Albert 'Bertie' Gomes (pp. 114-115, 131-132). Calder-Marshall pokes fun at both these men, who were part of the small circle of Port of Spain progressives advocating cultural regeneration and self-government for Trinidad & Tobago and the British Caribbean generally.[18] He writes interestingly about calypso, which was to enjoy great popularity in the wartime years, and reproduces the lyrics of several (pp. 125-130) – without, however, identifying their composers! Calder-Marshall's forays into the city's artistic set culminate (in chapter 5) in a strange attempt, along with de Boissière, to stage a performance of *Waiting for Lefty*, a play written by the left-wing American actor and playwright Clifford Odets in 1935, revolving around a group of New York cabbies planning a strike. The effort to put on the play founders because of the deep colour and class feelings of the potential actors, most of whom decline to perform with people of darker colour and lower class status than themselves. The extent of black/white, dark/light divisions and passions are similarly revealed when Calder-Marshall attends amateur boxing fights in Port of Spain (chapter 6); the crowd noisily and passionately supports the darker-skinned fighters. The bouts are presided over by Captain Cipriani, "wearing khaki with the dignity of a labour leader in whom the capitalists have the fullest confidence" (p. 139), an unkind comment reflecting the reality that, by 1938, the Captain had lost much of his earlier ascendancy as Trinidad's premier labour leader.[19]

Chapter 7 tells the story of André Gambier, a *libéré* (ex-convict) who had escaped from the penal colony in French Guiana (Guyane) and fetched up in Trinidad; Calder-Marshall managed to save him from being deported back to Guyane by writing an article for his paper, the *News Chronicle,* and getting readers to donate money so that he could be sent to Martinique instead. He attended a meeting of the left-wing, proletarian NWCSA in Woodford Square, the main public space in Port of Spain, and writes with obvious admiration of the struggles and courage of the little group of working-class men and women who led it: Elma Francois, Bertie Perceval and his wife (Christina King, though Calder-Marshall does not name her), Clement Payne and Jim Barrat. The heavy-handed police treatment of the speakers only enflames the crowd, as Calder-Marshall noted.[20]

It is only in chapter 8, the last one in Part II, that Calder-Marshall leaves the city scene to write about the labour situation in the south of the island, where the oil industry was located. His account of the events of 1937 is mainly based on the official Forster Report (though he is critical of its findings on some points) as well as on what he was told by participants he met. With Butler still in jail during the first half of 1938 – he was tried and convicted of sedition in late 1937, and not released until after Calder-Marshall's visit – the new oil union, the OWTU, was led by the Indo-Trinidadian socialist lawyer, A. C. Rienzi. Calder-Marshall's assessment of Butler and Rienzi (pp. 163-173) is both sympathetic and astute, and he ends this chapter with a sincere tribute to the new trade unionists, "the finest people that I met in Trinidad", earnest, trustworthy, efficient, and "not fanatical in any sense" (p. 173).[21]

In Part III, Calder-Marshall offers his 'observations', and opinions, on three broad themes. First, in a section titled 'On Patriotism', he sums up what he sees as Trinidadians' attitudes to Britain, British expatriates on the island, and Americans, on the eve of the outbreak of World War II. For him, negative attitudes towards Britain, a lack of Empire 'loyalty', were perfectly understandable, granted all the failures of the colonial regime and the plight of most of the islanders. Moreover, Britain's refusal to aid Ethiopia after Mussolini invaded that country had provoked widespread outrage; in a remark which has been much quoted, Calder-Marshall wrote "Britain's betrayal of Abyssinia is nearly as much to blame for the riots in Trinidad and Jamaica as the high cost of living" (p. 186).

Calder-Marshall is harsh in this section on the British expatriates living in Trinidad, remarking (and the mild snobbery is unmistakeable) that "they are mostly drawn from the petty *bourgeoisie*, and lack both the virtues of the better public school type and the common decency of the worker" (p. 179). Perhaps the influence of de Boissière, who loathed the British, can be detected here. In any case, his analysis of the island's elites lacks the clinical precision and insider knowledge of that provided by C. L. R. James in his 1932 book about Cipriani.[22] It is odd, too, to read that "there is no [local] upper class" (p. 179). Of course, there was indeed an important locally born upper class of European descent, the white Creoles, who seem to have escaped Calder-Marshall's attention. His friend de Boissière belonged to this class (so did Captain Cipriani) and perhaps he persuaded Calder-Marshall that it no longer had much clout or status in Trinidad, which was far from the truth.

It is also clear that for Calder-Marshall (and for de Boissière?), Trinidadians could safely be equated with "the negro" or "the negro people"; this is made explicit in the analysis at pp. 180-181 and again at p. 186. Indo-Trinidadians, who made up close to one-third of the total population in the late 1930s, are almost completely out of the picture; Rienzi is the only Indo-Trinidadian to receive significant attention in Calder-Marshall's book. Of course, this in turn reflects one of the weaknesses of *Glory Dead*: it has a pronounced urban bias. It is nearly all about life in and around Port of Spain, with very little attention to the countryside, where most Trinidadians, and nearly all those of Indian descent or origin, still lived in the 1930s. The oilfields were in the south, but even here, the vast majority of the workers, and of the members of the new OWTU, were Afro-Trinidadians, or people of African descent originally from the neighbouring islands, like Butler. This bias means that *Glory Dead* gives only a partial picture of Trinidad in 1938 (and none at all of Tobago).

The second section of Part III, 'On Trinidad's Industries', is a well-informed and sober analysis of the situation of the sugar, cocoa and oil industries in 1938, based partly on the Forster Report but very much from the point of view of the welfare of the workers and peasant farmers. Calder-Marshall calls for radical reform in the colony's skewed tax system, which featured heavy tariffs on imported basic foods and other goods, but very light taxes on income and on the profits of the oil and sugar companies.[23]

Glory Dead ends with a section 'On Crown Colony Government', which can be usefully compared with James' 1932 book on Cipriani, which is subtitled 'An Account of British Government in the West Indies'; Calder-Marshall may have read it.[24] He attended meetings of the Legislative Council several times, and felt contempt for its members and proceedings, except for Rienzi who at least tried to represent the interests of ordinary Trinidadians in his speeches (as Cipriani had also tried to do, though Calder-Marshall does not acknowledge this). "The Legislative Council is a farce", Calder-Marshall concludes, and crown colony government is "a failure" (p. 203). Only a greatly extended franchise, and the removal of property qualifications for Council membership, could make the legislature an agent for useful change. Only a united labour movement could take Trinidad forward. As things were, Rienzi represented the interests of 90%

of the population, yet appeared to the authorities "a freak, a red, an agitator when he spoke in the Council" (p. 206).

After *Glory Dead*
Calder-Marshall came to Trinidad in 1938 and his book was published in 1939, not long before World War II began. The wide-ranging consequences of the war years, along with the effects of the events of 1937 and their aftermath (the subject of *Glory Dead*), transformed Trinidad & Tobago.[25] Adult suffrage was enacted in 1945 at the war's end, and a series of painfully slow constitutional changes brought the colony closer to internal self-government in the 1950s, culminating in formal Independence in 1962 after the Federation of the West Indies was dissolved in that year.

As far as I know, Calder-Marshall did not publish anything else about Trinidad, or the Caribbean, among his prolific output in the postwar years. But he did keep up a connection with the British Caribbean through his work with the BBC's *Caribbean Voices* radio programme, which played such a significant role in encouraging new West Indian writers in the years after the war. According to Glyne Griffith, *Glory Dead* had considerable influence on Henry Swanzy, the Irishman who ran this important programme between 1946 and 1954, in shaping his sympathy for British West Indian writing. Calder-Marshall, as a prolific, published author who had written a book about Trinidad, served as a "critic-at-large" for the programme during Swanzy's tenure. He was perhaps the most active member of the "Critics' Circle" which Swanzy put together in 1947; it met and critiqued previously aired poems and stories, and Calder-Marshall frequently broadcast these critiques as a regular part of the programme. In a 1948 broadcast, for instance, Calder-Marshall called for West Indian writers to develop a regional consciousness and looked forward to the emergence of a writer who could "capture your common destiny".[26]

It was at the BBC, through *Caribbean Voices*, that the young Trinidadian aspiring writer V. S. Naipaul met Calder-Marshall in the early 1950s. In his *A Way in the World*, Naipaul includes a chapter titled 'Passenger: A Figure from the Thirties' which is a lightly fictionalised account of his relationship with the British writer. He calls Calder-Marshall Foster Morris and *Glory Dead* is renamed *The Shadowed Livery*, but there can be no doubt who he is writing about. Naipaul says he admired the book for its originality and for the way it wrote about Trinidadians "with the utmost seriousness", as if they had "social depth and solidity and rootedness". But he found it "well intentioned but wrong" because it lacked a sense of the absurd which "we all lived with" in Trinidad. In any case, meeting Calder-Marshall just after he had left Oxford and was floundering in his attempts to write, Naipaul saw him as "an important figure from the past" because of his book. So he asked the older man to read the manuscript of the novel he was struggling with; Calder-Marshall told him to abandon it immediately. "He was right. I knew that", Naipaul writes; he dealt with his anger and hurt, abandoned the novel, and immediately started work on *Miguel Street*. "I blessed the name of Foster Morris, this unlikely figure from the past who had set me free" – and he loved *Miguel Street* when it appeared.

The rest of the chapter chronicles the deterioration of the relationship between the two writers, one on his way to success and fame, the other "fading" who "gave off a gloom". Calder-Marshall disliked *Biswas* and wrote a bad anonymous review of it; this marked the end, and Naipaul says he felt only "relief that I could set this disciple-guru relationship aside". He concludes by conceding that the 1939 book "was incomplete but not bad"; it was original "in its direct presentation of subject people as a whole, belonging to themselves". It had a definite place, between the "decadent imperial cruise books and the books of post-colonial writers" like Patrick Leigh Fermor (or, he might have added, Naipaul himself, who was to write many literary "travel" books). It is interesting to think that Calder-Marshall, the "figure from the Thirties", may have played a crucial role in making the young Naipaul into the writer who was to win the Nobel Prize a decade after the older man's death.[27]

There is no doubt that *Glory Dead* was an original kind of travel book, or that it remains an important primary source for Trinidad in the 1930s, as well as an engagingly written and highly readable account. It takes its place as an illuminating source along with the official documents like the Forster and Moyne Reports, the local newspapers, magazines and journals of the period, autobiographies like that by Bertie Gomes, accounts of social conditions in Port of Spain such as the work by James Cummings, and analyses of social and political conditions such as the 1932 book by C. L. R. James (and the classic postwar study by the Trinidadian sociologist Lloyd Braithwaite). It should be read alongside novels which depict the island in the 1930s: James' *Minty Alley*, Ralph de Boissière's *Crown Jewel*, and Alfred Mendes' *Pitch Lake* and *Black Fauns*.

Glory Dead was an illuminating and original work, despite some flaws, when it was published in 1939, and it remains a book of great value which combines high seriousness with an engaging style. This edition should introduce it to the new readership which it deserves to have.

NOTES
1. Arthur Calder-Marshall, *Glory Dead* (London: Michael Joseph, 1939), p. 26. All subsequent in-text page references are to this new edition.
2. The title came from a "West Indian Song", according to Calder-

Marshall; its refrain appears on the book's title page. Dr John Cowley, an expert on West Indian music of this period, believes Calder-Marshall was thinking of the 'Shouter' Baptist song or hymn with the refrain "Glory Day when the Morning Come". This was recorded in October 1933 by Trinidadian singer Wilmoth Houdini in New York City, and a slightly different version, with the same refrain, was recorded by Melville and Frances Herskovits in Toco, Trinidad, in July 1939 (Cowley, personal communication, 9 January 2020). The lines actually quoted on the title page, however, are not heard in the two recordings, and Calder-Marshall may have made them up, having heard the "Glory Day" song on his visit to a shouter Baptist meeting.

3. V. S. Naipaul, *A Way in the World* (London: Heinemann, 1994), pp. 90-91.
4. For Tony de Boissière, see *Glory Dead,* pp. 111-113; M. R. Pocock, *Out of the Shadows of the Past* (Hastings, UK: The Author, 1993), pp. 375-377, p.572, note 77. His publications include: *Trinidad: The Land of the Rising Inflexion* (n.p., n.d.; ?Port of Spain, 1942); *Picong An Anthology of Creole Humour* (Port of Spain: The Author, n.d. ?1942/43); *Cooking Creole* (Port of Spain: Paria Publications, 1992; orig. pub. 1948).
5. This section is based on: K. Singh, *Race and Class Struggles in a Colonial State: Trinidad 1917-1945* (Kingston: University of the West Indies Press, 1994); R. D. Thomas (ed), *The Trinidad Labour Riots of 1937* (St Augustine, Trinidad: University of the West Indies, 1987); S. Basdeo, *Labour Organisation and Labour Reform in Trinidad, 1919-39* (Port of Spain: Lexicon, 2003); J. Teelucksingh, *Labor and the Decolonization Struggle in Trinidad and Tobago* (New York: Palgrave MacMillan, 2015); D. Alleyne, *Export/Import Trends and Economic Development in Trinidad, 1919-1939* (Kingston: Canoe Press, 2010); R. Reddock, *Women, Labour and Politics in Trinidad and Tobago A History* (Kingston: Ian Randle, 1994); S. Craig, *Smiles and Blood* (London: New Beacon, 1988). Shorter accounts can be found in: S. Ryan, *Race and Nationalism in Trinidad and Tobago* (Toronto: University of Toronto Press, 1972), pp. 28-69; B. Brereton, *A History of Modern Trinidad, 1783-1962* (Oxford: Heinemann, 1981), pp. 157-191; H. Neptune, *Caliban and the Yankees* (Chapel Hill, NC: University of North Carolina Press, 2007), pp. 19-77.
6. A detailed account is in Alleyne (note 5).
7. See E. E. Williams, *Inward Hunger* (London: Andre Deutsch, 1969), pp. 11-39.
8. See C. L. R. James, *The Life of Captain Cipriani* (Durham and London: Duke University Press, 2014; orig. pub. 1932).

9. See R. Reddock, *Elma Francois, the NWCSA and the Workers' Struggle for Change in the Caribbean* (London: New Beacon, 1988).
10. For Butler, see W. R. Jacobs (ed), *Butler versus the King* (Port of Spain: Key Caribbean, 1976); D. Figueira, *Tubal Uriah Butler of Trinidad and Tobago Kwame Nkrumah of Ghana* (Lincoln, NE: The Author, 2007), pp. 1-17; and the works cited in note 5.
11. For Rienzi, see K. Singh, 'A. C. Rienzi and the Labour Movement in Trinidad, 1925-1944', *Journal of Caribbean History*, 16, 1982, pp. 10-35; and the works cited in note 5.
12. In addition to the works cited in note 5, see K. Yelvington, 'The War in Ethiopia and Trinidad 1935-1936', in B. Brereton and K. Yelvington (eds), *The Colonial Caribbean in Transition* (Kingston: University of the West Indies Press, 1999), pp. 189-225.
13. For 1937, see especially Singh, *Race and Class*, pp. 158-185; Thomas, passim; Jacobs, passim; Craig, passim; Trinidad and Tobago Disturbances, Report of the [Forster] Commission, Cmd. 5461, 1938; West India Royal Commission [Moyne] Report, Cmd. 6607, 1945 (the Report was presented to the Secretary of State in 1939 but was not published until 1945, as London feared its revelations would be used as propaganda by Germany).
14. For Tobago in this period, see S. E. Craig-James, *The Changing Society of Tobago* (Arima, Trinidad: Cornerstone Press, 2008), Vol. 2, especially pp. 3-35.
15. The best account of the 'American Occupation' is Neptune (note 5).
16. J. Cummings, *Barrack-Yard Dwellers* (St Augustine, Trinidad: University of the West Indies, 2004); C. L. R. James, *Minty Alley* (London: New Beacon, 1971; orig. pub. 1936); see note 13 for the Forster Report.
17. See Singh, *Race and Class*, pp. 158-185; Thomas, passim; Craig, passim; B. Samaroo, *The Price of Conscience Howard Noel Nankivell and labour unrest in the British Caribbean in 1937 and 1938* (Hertford, UK: Hansib, 2015).
18. Gittens was a poet and essayist; a co-founder of two Port of Spain based unions and of a left-wing political party (in 1942); and an editor and contributor to *New Dawn*, a progressive monthly of the early 1940s. Gomes' career can be followed in his autobiography, *Through a Maze of Colour* (Port of Spain: Key Caribbean, 1974).
19. See note 8 for Cipriani; and the works cited in note 5. Calder-Marshall returns to consider Cipriani in chapter 7, pp. 155-156.
20. For the NWCSA, see Reddock, *Elma Francois*. See also Gomes.
21. See notes 10 and 11 for Butler and Rienzi.
22. James, *Cipriani*, pp. 39-49.

23. A detailed account of Trinidad's economic history in the interwar years is in Alleyne (note 5).
24. Or he might have read the short pamphlet, *The Case for West Indian Self Government*, an excerpt from the longer *Cipriani*, which was published by the Hogarth Press, London, in 1933. (Both the longer book and the 1933 pamphlet are included in the 2014 edition.)
25. For the war years in Trinidad, see Neptune; K. Eccles and D. McCollins (eds), *World War II and the Caribbean* (Kingston: University of the West Indies Press, 2017); B. Brereton and K. Eccles, *Islands at War: Trinidad and Tobago During World War 2* (Port of Spain: Paria Publications, 2019). For shorter accounts, see Singh, *Race and Class*, pp. 186-232; Brereton, pp. 185-195.
26. G. Griffith, *The BBC and the Development of Anglophone Caribbean Literature, 1943-1958* (Cham, Switzerland: Palgrave MacMillan, 2016), pp. 28-32, 45-69, 83-84.
27. Naipaul (note 3), pp. 69-102. *The Shadowed Livery* was the title of Naipaul's novel manuscript which Calder-Marshall read and then told him to abandon, which he did; it was never published. See P. French, *The World Is What It Is* (London: Picador, 2008), p. 465.
28. L. Braithwaite, *Social Stratification in Trinidad* (Mona, Jamaica: University of the West Indies, 1975; orig. pub. 1953); Ralph de Boissière, *Crown Jewel* (London: Picador, 1981; orig. pub. 1952); A. Mendes, *Pitch Lake* (London: New Beacon, 1980; orig. pub. 1934); A. Mendes, *Black Fauns* (London: New Beacon, 1984; orig. pub. 1935).

FOREWORD

A NUMBER of writers have written of Trinidad, but none of them find favour with the Trinidadians, except Charles Kingsley. Kingsley visited the island as an old man on a holiday. He left behind him the social conscience, which led him to write *The Water Babies* and turned his eyes exclusively to the countryside.

He found the countryside beautiful and he wrote of it with great sympathy and charm. This is the quality that Trinidadian admire in *At Last,* and their admiration is well founded.

I could have followed in Kingsley's footsteps, and written the most distinguished prose about the sunsets over Savory's Bay. I could have described the delight of bathing in Narangpool, where you can swim naked in cool river water beneath the waterfall, and small fish dart up and nip your flesh. The natural phenomena of the tropics should excite any writer: how, for example, sometimes at sunset in the valleys there will be silence and then a cicada will shrill and suddenly the whole valley is filled with the high voices of a hundred others, like the noise of children pouring from school into the street.

It will prickle the silence like needle rain the surface of a pool for a minute or more. And then it stops as abruptly as it began. Or the foam at Manzanilla. Manzanilla is a long straight beach running for fifteen miles. The sea strides in from the Atlantic, breaking far out. At one time you will see five lines of waves, rolling in and piling foam upon the shore. This froth, like queen of puddings or the head on stout, mounts high, and then is whipped up the sand by the wind and there it melts. But there is always a rope of foam along the sea's edge taken back and forth by ebb and flow, but slower than the water. When you walk in it, the foam clings to your feet and ankles. You look as if you were wearing tart's bedroom slippers.

I could have made a delightful book, describing the flora and fauna of the island, the tropical fish, the parasites that even grow on telegraph-wires, and oysters on the roots of trees. There could have been a chapter on the badjack ants and some fine writing on the different ways that coconut palms look and grow, the desolation of a palm-fringed beach at sunset, the slack neck of a zebu, drooping in long waving frills.

But I have not done so, because the study of the people living in Trinidad interested me more and seemed more important. The plan of life, the medley of different races, the conflict of economic forces baffled me at first. But gradually I came to see clearly the system underlying what at first seemed pure confusion. I was only in the island for about three months, but by the end of that time I think that I had come to an understanding of the place and people as good as any outsider could achieve.

Trinidad itself is a small island. In world affairs it is not of great importance. But the problems which arise in Trinidad arise everywhere in the world where there is white domination of subject races. It is the problem of Great Britain in the West Indies, in Africa and India. It is the problem of the United States in the Black Belt, in Puerto Rico and Hawaii.

Setting out to describe the life of the Trinidadians, I was struck by an immediate difficulty. To describe a different civilisation is an easy matter compared with a hybrid mixture such as Trinidad presents. In Trinidad there is no indigenous culture. The Caribbeans were stamped out of existence by succeeding conquerors. Their arts, craft, religion and civilisation, which were similar to the Venezuelans on the mainland opposite, were utterly destroyed. In the place of that civilisation, a varied tradition has been imported by the different settlers who have come or been brought to the island.

Trinidad was held by the Spanish up till 1797. The tradition of the Spaniards survives, however, only in those few houses which escaped the great fire of 1808. Under the Spaniards there were a number of rich French planters who had emigrated with their slaves from Haiti and other French islands. These planters have exercised more influence on the present culture. The native patois is a decadent form of French, and it has survived until the present time because it is not understood by the majority of whites. It forms, therefore, a secret language, useful to the coloured people.

Most of the islanders are Catholic. The Catholic religion was introduced by the Spaniards and continued by the French. Its survival to the present time is due firstly to its adaptability to the Negro temperament, and secondly to the fact that it is not the official religion of the British Empire. Priests were formerly recruited from Spain and France; now the majority are sent out from Ireland. The rebellious Irish tradition appeals to the Negro. His priest, a Negro feels, comes from a country which has also suffered from the oppression of the English. Therefore his teaching will not be a spiritual version of British Imperialism.

The Negroes, when they were brought to the island, had lost their original culture. Raped from different tribes in the hinterland and along the coast of Africa, they had no common bond except the slave plantations in which they were herded. The old culture died, because the old life was dead. But, as in the United States, a new culture began to grow around the plantation.

In 1834 slavery was abolished, as a means of dispossessing the French planters of their slaves, without paying for them.[1] The culture of the slave plantation was broken up, and it survives today chiefly in the shango dances (Trinidad's form of voodoo) and in certain primitive songs which are sung at wakes and fetes.[2]

As soon as the Negro was given his freedom – but as usual no land – he revolted from agriculture. Even to this day they speak with great contempt of working on the land, as a sign of slavery: and the majority seek work in the towns, the oilfields and the refineries. As the island becomes industrialised, they are forming a self-conscious proletariat and evolving a new culture along working-class lines.

To supply the increasing demand for cheap labour, indentured labourers were imported from India in 1845, a practice which continued into this century until the supply of labour began to exceed the demand. The conditions under which the East Indian labourer lived were little better than slavery: but they were also little worse than India. And because the East Indians were introduced more or less legally, they brought with them their language, religion, dress and customs. The Hindu and Moslem religions both flourish in the island. In many of the country districts the peasants wear native Indian dress. Indian films are shown in cinemas and the dream of many Indians is to return to their native land.

The East Indian culture has not influenced the rest of the island, however. It is a relic rather than a formative influence: and the most progressive members of the East Indian community have dropped their religion, dress and customs and become Europeanised.

Just as there were waves of immigration for manual labour, so there were waves of commercial immigration. At first the Portuguese came from Madeira and gained control of the retail business. The Chinese followed and won from the Portuguese the little general stores all over the island and most of the 'parlours', which are shacks where you can buy mineral waters, condensed milk, butter, eggs and the like. The Portuguese remained entrenched in the rum business.

---

1. *The cost of each slave was around twenty-five pounds. With all credit due to the name of Wilberforce, the motive for the abolition of slavery was the undermining of the economically entrenched French planters. This can be seen from the fact that after the abolition of slavery within the Empire, the British came out for the South in the American Civil War. Here the economic struggle was between Great Britain and the Northern States for the economic domination of the South.*
2. *These songs, like all the music of the island, are musically uninteresting. It is the words that are important. The tune is usually that of some old hymn and the words are words of revolt. The theory advanced by Rupert Gittens to explain this is that the planter listening from the big house would hear the tune and think: "Oh, just singing hymns again. That'll keep 'em out of mischief."*

The last wave comes from Syria. A Syrian merchant, Sabga, puts up a guarantee for his countrymen, who come out and work for him as pedlars of cheap dresses and notions. Their prices are higher than the town shops', but lower than the town price plus the fare a peasant would have to pay to go to town.

In addition to these elements, there are British business men, a mulatto *bourgeoisie,* a small number of Jews and rather more Latin-Americans. In the oilfields, there are also South Africans and a number of drillers from the States. The Government Service is mainly recruited from Trinidadian, but all the key positions are given to members of the Colonial Service from abroad.

About a third of the population is East Indian, the remaining two-thirds is predominantly negroid with admixtures of practically every other blood in the world. The number of people from the United Kingdom in 1931 was 1454.

For reasons with which I shall deal later, this mixed community has developed no culture of its own. The predominant culture is a pale imitation of the British. Yet, running through the whole life of the community, there is something essentially Trinidadian. It is a quality very difficult to analyse, a deviation from the norm, sometimes exasperating and often comic. However good intentions may be, something always goes wrong morally, aesthetically or mechanically.

And if we can judge from the affair of the portraits of Sir Ralph Abercrombie and Sir Thomas Picton, this essential quality existed as strongly in the last century as in this.

During the great fire of 1808 the Cabildo Hall was burnt down, but the portraits of these two early governors were among the things saved. The portraits had been done in crayon by John Russell, "an eminent portrait painter... known by the title of 'Painter to the King and the Prince of Wales,'" as *Franklin's Year Book* describes him.

But though saved, they had suffered from the climate and the fire. So the Cabildo, the equivalent of the present Legislative Council, voted to have the portraits sent to England and copied in oils. The Cabildo had already commissioned Sir Thomas Lawrence to paint the portrait of a later governor, General Hislop, and they decided that he was the best person to do the two copies as well.

Sir Ralph Woodford's private secretary, a Mr. Philip Reinagle, was in London at the time, and he was asked to approach Sir Thomas and arrange the business. But Mr. Reinagle, again in the words of Mr. Franklin, "belonged to a highly artistic family. His grandfather, Joseph Reinagle, was a musician of repute; his father, Philip Reinagle, was a well-known animal and landscape painter. His brother, Ramsay Richard Reinagle, was a portrait painter of merit, who had attained to the dignity of President of the Society of Painters in Water Colours, which he held for many years."

Mr. Reinagle undertook the commission. But he decided that the charges of Sir Thomas were too high and, without reference to the Cabildo, he gave the commission to another artist. "And, as would be expected, he selected his brother, Ramsay Richard Reinagle."

The dismayed Cabildo found themselves presented with two Reinagles instead of two Lawrences: and the two originals by Russell entirely disappeared.

They were scarcely more fortunate with General Hislop's portrait. It was voted in 1811. In 1815 there is a record that Sir Thomas Lawrence had been commissioned to do the portrait and that the fee had been sent to a Mr. Gardiner who had since died. But no portrait arrived in Trinidad.

Two years later, our same Mr. Reinagle made inquiries and was told by Sir Thomas Lawrence that he had painted the portrait and he presumed it had been duly delivered. Mr. Gardiner's executors professed complete ignorance of the whole matter.

Six years later, that is to say twelve years after the picture had been voted, Sir Ralph Woodford, then being in London, took up the search which Mr. Reinagle had abandoned in despair. And at last he ran the picture to earth.

It was hanging in the house of General Hislop.

On his retirement, the gallant General lodged a claim for nine hundred pounds with the Cabildo. The claim was disputed and referred to the Secretary of State for the Colonies, Lord Bathurst, who disallowed it.

So the General swiped his portrait.

This anecdote is more than a crumb of history. It contains the quintessence of Trinidad, an island in which the Government can accuse a man of putting into circulation a vast quantity of notes that should have been destroyed and yet takes no legal action against him: and in which while he is awaiting trial for manslaughter, the Acting Solicitor-General can continue to prosecute his fellow-citizens for sedition and murder.

I have tried to convey something of this spirit in the first section of this book. Out of imaginary, but typical incidents, I have tried to build up a portrait of the capital, which will give the reader that strange and yet familiar atmosphere that is so difficult to define in abstract words. There is one important respect in which life in Port of Spain differs from life in the rest of the island. Port of Spain is centred round the waterfront, from which come all the island's imports and a crowd of tourists. So there are many more of the undesirable urban types, touts, pimps, prostitutes, contra-bandists, sell-outs and tricksters, than you find elsewhere in the island.

To counterbalance this and other false impressions, I have written the second section, dealing with my experiences and the conclusions which I drew as the result of going about keeping my eyes open and asking awkward questions.

By the conclusion of this section, the reader will have a good superficial impression of the island. But there will be certain general questions that have arisen in his mind and not been answered. The third section, Some Observations on Patriotism, on Trinidad's Industry and on Crown Colony Government, attempts to deal with these questions very briefly, not in terms of the distant future, but of the present and near future. The suggestions made are immediate palliatives, not final solutions of the problems presented by Trinidad and other subject countries.

Before finishing this Foreword I wish to acknowledge my debt to The Commission's Report on the Trinidad and Tobago Disturbances, 1937, from which permission to quote has been obtained from the Controller of H.M. Stationery Office; to *Franklin's Year Book* and to *Empire,* June 1938. And I wish to thank all the many friends that I made in the island for their generosity, their unfailing kindness and the help that they lent me whenever I needed it.

A. C.-M.

PART I

Frederick Street is Port of Spain's Regent Street

A PORTRAIT OF THE CITY

A CAR drives up to the quay by the customs. Under the lights there is a group of American sailors, waiting with the Shore Patrol for the last launch. A dozen Negroes are standing round a soft drink stall. They are talking in low tones, but the Americans shout at the top of their voices. One of the sailors is ragging an S.P. and the others chip in with wisecracks.

The car stops and the sailors break off talking. "Who the hell they got there?" asks a voice.

The door of the car opens and two sailors get out: then they catch hold of something and pull it out of the car. It is limp, and lies on the quay without moving.

"Christ!" says another voice. "It's Tomkins, the great brain, the master intelligence."

The master intelligence does not stir.

"Out like a light! And there's the guy who wouldn't drink near beer."

The launch draws up to the quayside and some of the men go aboard. The great brain rises and stands swaying, his fair hair glistening in the light. "I been robbed!" he says. "Show me the bastard took my box of perfume."

He staggers towards the Negroes standing around the stall, but two arms take him and lead him to the launch. "Lemme get at that bastard took my perfume," he shouts. But he makes no attempt to get away, and immediately he is aboard he lies down, goes to sleep and starts to snore.

The church clock strikes midnight, and before it ends the clock on the cathedral begins to echo it. The last sailor gets into the launch and they cast off. The bunch of Negroes still stand there, watching the lights recede.

There is no wind and the city is silent. The moon is full and its deceiving light softens the hard lines of ugly buildings, composes their colours, so that galvanised iron roofs, protruding galleries and even barrack yards look beautiful.

In Woodford Square men are sleeping. Men and women are lying on the pavement by the church. They do not stir. They lie like sacks flung down against a wall. They are so wrapped in rags, so huddled in dead slumber, that head and hat, rags and feet are often indistinguishable. Most of the sleepers are here. But dotted in doorways, lying on the threshold, there are others. Their bare, dusty feet have white soles.

To the west two streets, down St. Vincent Street, marches the relieving squad of the police. Black uniforms, black faces and white belts. A single file of vultures, marching in step, waking the street with the noise of heavy boots.

The black squad marches as soldiers, not police. Their discipline is military. On duty, they live in barracks like a regiment. They must be trained, isolated from the public they were drawn from. Even at midnight they must march. At the corner of St. Vincent and Queen's they wheel. They are the enemies of the sleepers in the open. To have no roof, a bed of newspaper beneath the trees or on a door-step is an offence against the law. Awake, they are paupers, but criminals when they sleep.

To the east three streets there is another group upon the pavement. But these are not utterly destitute and do not lie full length in unbroken sleep. Most sit with backs against the wall of the new market. Round them are baskets, full of produce, covered with cloths. There are a few men, but most are women, with bright bandannas knotted round their heads. One or two have children with them. Some are asleep, but most wait in a state of semi-watchfulness. Every now and again the silence is broken by the voice of one speaking in patois. Another answers slowly. And then silence.

There are still a few cafes open, such as the Bon-Ton and the Lucky. The Bon-Ton and the Lucky are run by rival Chinese. They were built as one shop, but a thin wooden partition divides them now. This division is twelve feet high. They both sell the same things – cigarettes, minerals, sweet cakes, matches. They each have a small counter, three feet from the pavement, and behind each counter is another wooden partition sheltering the alcove, where you can eat. In the alcove of the Bon-Ton there are two tables, covered with oilcloth. One is empty, and at the other sit two 'rats' with their 'sweet men'. They are drinking coffee at three cents a cup. One of the girls is a tall, sulky-looking Negress called Netti, and her man is a buck in white trousers with a thin black stripe and a straw hat at an angle. The other girl, Rita, is a mulatto, and her man, Charlie, is a thick-set, medium-sized Negro without the style of Netti's Francois, but strong and virile.

The two girls have been at the 'Cambridge,' the 'Oxford' and the 'Midland'. They have walked along the arcades all the evening. But times are bad. Netti has made nothing, she has pawned the two straw-bottomed rocking-chairs, and another month's rent will be in arrears tomorrow. She is afraid that Charlie will go with some other girl. Then she will pounce on him, bust his hat, tear his coat up the back in the open street. But she won't get him back.

Rita has made a dollar fifty from two pick-ups. Fifty cents of this she has given to Netti. They live in the same barrack yard and sometimes sleep together.

They are having a coffee before they take their men back to the yard. They talk about Eulalia's luck. She is upstairs with a rich planter. They are drinking champagne. She will get five dollars, and maybe more if he's drunk enough.

A taxi drives up and stops outside. Sambo gets out and goes into the alcove. Rita is one of the girls he pimps for. He tells her he has a German outside, a tourist just here for the night, who wants some fun.

Rita looks at Netti. "I'm tired," she says, "why doesn't Netti go?"

Charlie is annoyed with her, but after an argument Netti goes out with Sambo. As she walks to the car, the door is opened. "Hello, darlin'," she says.

"Excuse me, please," a voice says. "I can not Engleesh gut spik."

"You know where, Sambo," Netti says.

"But, lov," goes on 'the voice. "I can very gut lov. Darrling, I lov you. And you lov me, yes, no, just a bit, please."

There is a mosquito in a net in Woodbrook and no Flit gun. From the savannah the rising snores of the righteous rejoice the God of Thunder. John John is quiet. In St. Clair two that were one are two again.

But in Belmont there is a party.

In the centre of the room there is a card table. A mulatto and his Negro wife, the host and hostess, are playing romey with another mulatto and a Chinaman. There are five other guests sitting round the room, with their chairs against the wall. Every now and again they talk. They are tired, the rum has come to an end and they want to go home. But the hostess will not let them, because of the Portuguese who is sitting by her side. He is very drunk and he has looked in on the invitation of the mulatto. But the hostess is furious, has told him he isn't wanted and asked him to go.

He won't go. His drunkenness has made him obstinate, but not aggressive. In the best humour in the world, he lets every rudeness pass him over. He tries to lean over his hostess' shoulder and instruct her how to play. When she turns round and swears at him, he sits back with his hands folded in his lap and a benign smile on his face.

Someone gets up and leaves, but with grimaces she urges the others to stay on until the Portuguese goes. And, knowing that, the drunk man makes no attempt to go. He gets up and goes out of the room, and comes back five minutes later wearing a bowler hat three sizes too large for him. Only one arm is in his coat, the other down inside his shirt and trousers. Everybody laughs when they see him with the hat over his ears. Everybody, that is, except the Negress.

Suddenly one, and then all, see that this was not the real joke. The real joke is the Rabelaisian skill of his prehensile thumb grasping a walking-stick. The laughter changes to a bellow and at last the hostess laughs too.

Relieved, the remaining guests get up and go. They say good night and urge the Portuguese to come with them. But he shakes his head good-naturedly.

As they feel their way down the steep path to the road, from the house comes the high voice of a woman raised in ungovernable anger. And as they stand under the tall trees, looking at the lighted room, they hear a crack, the crash of a fallen table and a thud. They shake their heads and slowly walk away, until they can no longer hear the woman weeping.

Now the moon is hidden by clouds and a sudden squall strikes the city. The royal palms wave their plumes and the noise of fronds shaken is like the fluttering of birds' wings against glass. Lightermen loading cargo from a freighter in the bay look up and curse, as the derrick slowly swings and stops and drops the cradle in the lighter. Stevedores on nightshift feel the sudden gust, the wind from nowhere tearing through the warehouses. On the mudflats, which are being raised three feet for the new harbour scheme, most of the nightshift is asleep in the hut. But the gang of five is working under the carbide lights at the end of the pipeline. There is a Dutch foreman and four Negroes. They handle the outflow.

The suction dredge is half a mile away. The green light is hoisted as a sign to pump. And down the great pipe flow seventy cubic metres of water a minute bearing great clods of clay.

These clods of clay pile up at the mouth of the pipe and the five men stand there with shovels to ease it off and prevent the flow being blocked. The foreman has no shovel, but he often bends down with his sleeves rolled up and uses hands for spades.

The water comes out, a muddy mass flush with the pipe. It boils up as it strikes the pile of clods. And then, force spent, it flows out over the mudflats.

The squall abates and in two minutes the rain comes. The lights from the harbour are screened, but the first rain is a light drizzle, scarcely denser than dew. This for thirty seconds. Then suddenly, like the noise of innumerable insects scrambling through grass, the heavy rain sweeps across the mudflats and strikes the men working on the pipeline.

Their sweaty shirts are sopped in a second. It is like a pail of water flung on each of them. The great drops burst on their backs and wash the sweat from their faces.

There is no shelter for these men. Their master is seventy cubic metres of water a minute, gushing from a pipeline.

Fivepence an hour, ten hours a day, time and a quarter overtime, time and a half Sundays. Nightshift, dayshift, night-shift. Ten hours on, fourteen off. Unskilled labour, shovelling the clods away, knee high in water. The noon sun blazing, rain like gravel on the back, the sudden cold, the steam of drying.

The rain reaches the houses. At first, before the rain is full, the noise above others is the dripping of water from eaves, the splash of raindrops in puddles, tricklings. But when it grows dense, those sounds are drowned by the thunder of the rain on the roofs, the drumming of drops on galvanised iron. It is like being in a tube station when a non-stop train is coming. First the far noise of the train echoing down the tunnel and then it passes through with a roar and gradually the noise of it recedes. Until, after the downpour, there is just the individual drip and splash from trees and eaves, a shower as a gust fans a palm.

The rain is over. The men working on the pipeline are still working on the pipeline. There is no difference except that they are drenched and shivering.

The Dutch surveyor comes over. He has a bottle of rum and a small glass. He pours a double for each man in turn. "Drink," he says, and the man puts back his head and pours the spirit down his throat. "Goot?" he asks. The man nods, smiling. His gullet is burning. A fire has been lit in his belly, and the flames spread through his body. He draws his hand over his forehead and picks up his shovel.

As soon as the first rain started in the square, the people sleeping on the grass and pavements picked up their beds – the *Trinidad Guardian* or the *Port of Spain Gazette* – and walked to cover.

Now they are standing on the pavement in the shelter of the Town Hall Arcade or beneath the galleries in Frederick Street. They stare at the water running down the tram-lines, pools collected in hollows. They listen to the drip-drip from roof-gutters.

In groups they begin to drift towards George and Charlotte Streets. It is after four and life has begun again there. Some parlours have opened for the market people. Coffee goes for a cent. There are basins of 'souse', pigs' feet in vinegar.

And in the street there are barrows, lit by crude oil lamps. Piles of green coconuts and grapefruit ready skinned. The vendor takes a coconut and with his cutlass slashes off the top. He hands it to the customer, who puts his finger in the hole and works it round. The meat of the coconut is not yet firm and it comes off in a sort of thick juice. Then he drinks, with his lips to the hole, sucking down the thick juice as it trickles out.

When he has finished, he throws it in the gutter, littered with empty husks.

The rain drummed on the roof of the Superb Bus Company Garage so loud that some of the conductors woke up. They were sleeping on benches in their clothes. They thought it was time to work, but the clock struck four and they knew that they had another half-hour of sleep. So they lay down and went to sleep again. The benches were hard, but the fact that some of them had been working till ten the night before and the thick petrol fumes of the garage brought sleep quickly.

At half-past four the cashier arrives and sits behind the desk. The conductors get up one by one and make their brief toilet. They are yawning, and when they have finished their toilet, they go and sit down on the benches and try to sleep more.

Passengers begin to arrive. Each blinks in the light as he comes from the darkness of the street. The conductors look up blear-eyed. "Buy your ticket before you get in the bus, please," says the cashier.

The passenger starts and turns towards the cashier.

She repeats what she has said.

If the passenger knows his onions, he gets into the bus. A conductor gets into the bus after him and argues with him. He sits there and says nothing. The conductor argues further and waves his hands. The passenger crosses his legs, hums 'Nettie Nettie' and looks out of the window. The conductor looks out of the window, shrugs his shoulders and shakes his head towards the cashier. Then he goes out.

But if the passenger is either a sucker or a millionaire, he buys a ticket from the girl at the cash-desk.

Gradually the bus fills up. It is a quarter, half, three-quarters full. The time is now five. Passengers look wistfully at the blackboard on which is chalked 4.30 a.m., 4.50, 5.10. No bus has gone yet, because the driver has not yet arrived. But the argument among the conductors and the garage staff as to who should have arrived begins to become heated.

Suddenly another bus appears outside. It drives very slowly down the street and two-thirds of the bus-load, those wise enough not to buy tickets, rise to their feet and scramble out of the bus. The pirate, which, like a cruising tart, has halted by the next lamppost, makes the journey for twenty-four cents. The charge of the Superb Bus Company is twenty-eight cents. The economic conflict is waged between three classes of buses. Class A is uncomfortable. Class B is very uncomfortable. And Class C is very, very uncomfortable. For price, most people prefer Class C.

As soon as the pirate bus has driven off with two-thirds of the passengers the bus-driver arrives and the remaining third of the passengers get out of the bus and demand their money back. After some argument they receive their money back and they stand in the entrance of the garage waiting for another pirate bus.

There is a hurried discussion, and the driver climbs into his seat and sounds his horn. Everybody comes running back to the bus and gets in. But the bus does not start for another fifteen minutes. Then with a toot and a grinding of gears he lets her in, and with half the number of passengers there were in the bus twenty minutes before he starts on the first run of the day through the cool dawn.

It is half light, and from the passageways come sleep-mazed lovers into main streets. Some are still drunk with rum, others with love. They falter, seem staggered like men from caves coming to sunlight, they lift their eyes and stare into the branches of a flamboyant tree.

The woman who last night was working till midnight sewing a dress is already up. She is emptying her chamber-pot. The other women in the yard look in awe at her. She is a symbol of toil, but the mark of death is already on her. Years after, the others will look back at her. Her early death through overwork will then be as much a justification of sloth as a cause for reverence.

The market is open, and when the stall-keepers file in, the flies rise to welcome them. Dr. Marcano has said: "When by some mechanism which I saw in a paper somewhere some instrument is installed which by suction draws all the flies out through the roof, the Port of Spain market will be among the finest of the world."

There is a bustle as they go in through the open gates. There is indignation when those who have waited all night find themselves supplanted by late arrivals with longer purses. There are protests, high words. And then, once more reconciled for a day to the injustice of a corruptible world, they settle down to make the best of it.

They unpack their goods and stack them. In the cool morning they dress their stalls. They throw out vegetables that are too bruised or rotten. They tie a cock by the leg to the top of a crate of chicken. They cut meat into strips and chunks and give the flies the first feed. They sit by their merchandise and some sometimes fan it with fans.

The cocks are crowing. The birds stir. The nightshift is over on the harbour scheme and the new crew comes on. The taxis come out one by one from their garages. Buses go backward and forward. Ducks rise and shake themselves and start waddling round the yard. Bats retreat beneath roofs.

Twenty-three men stir, open their eyes and turn over. A woman fills a pail at an open tap. The noise of the bucket dredge on the harbour scheme is a grinding groaning. Fifteen men fall asleep again. But hundreds begin to get up. They go to the shower which, if they are well off, is along the gallery, and if they are poor, is across the yard. Some have towels, others have lengths of rag and others have nothing. These last believe 'it dries off'. There is another group which does not go to the shower. This group is already in the closet and, if rich enough, smokes a cigarette.

Just before dawn is the most active time. It is not cold, because here it is never cold. But it is possible to feel active, feel you could run for a bus or climb perhaps a mountain.

Dawn comes late. The hill of Laventille gives one more hour of darkness. Dawn is not the sun's orb rising on a skyline. Dawn is broad shafts of light crossing a dark valley.

With the sun rise servants, yard boys and washers. Men walk from the presses of the *Guardian* and *Gazette* with bundles under their arms for house delivery. Indian boys in small blue cricket caps run to the waterfront, their white teeth glistening as they call the morning paper by the Custom House, along the docks.

From a George Street parlour a gramophone blares forth a calypso. The street starts up. The air is awake. Listless lollers at street corners move their stance from foot to foot.

This is reveille. Those snatching minutes of sensual wakefulness, lying on backs, swing their legs to the ground and go to basin, shower or tap. Day has begun. Work or seeking work. Buying or selling. The visit to the hospital, Mass in the Cathedral, the funeral of a respected citizen whom death has robbed of what he robbed others of.

Dawn and the calypso wake the city like a cutlass slicing through an ants' nest. Except that Port of Spain has no activity with that purpose, speed or devotion to common good, which is the characteristic of the termite. Life is slower. So many difficulties arise in accomplishing the simplest task that no one with the vision to foresee the vast expense of energy involved will attempt anything. Men move like turbot in a tank, whose breathing seems a major occupation.

Dawn comes and they rise, already armed against the futility of endeavour. They see a little food, a little work, a little love and then a little sleep. For most creoles one day is not connected with the next in the construction of long-term purposes. Today is a miraculous conception. This day is not born from last and denies the parentage of tomorrow.

Before they leave for work they take a drink – coffee, cocoa or tea. Sometimes they eat a biscuit, a slice of bread or some fruit. Then they go to work on foot, by bicycle, tram, bus or car. The streets suddenly become full. The doors of shops are thrown open, gates are rolled back, shutters are put up. The pedlars in Frederick Street and Marine Square lay out their notions – pencils, combs, sun-glasses, lengths of cheap lace or ribbons. The barkers come out and stand in the crowded street and shout: "Take your chance, take your chance, ladies. A million yards of linen at twenty-four cents. Don't miss it, don't miss it, don't miss it."

The trams stop at every corner and wait for a minute. At every fourth block they stop longer for the other tram to pass on the double line. They rattle and crash, with people swaying on the hardwood seats. Four cents is the flat rate for trams, three cents for buses. Clang, clang, clang goes the bell, and the conductor swings along the outside step to collect the fares. He pulls different straps, which clock up how many fares he has taken and how many transfers.

In the trams are white and black, coffee and mauve, the full colour range. You can ride on a tram without losing caste. But the whites lose caste if they travel in buses.

Shabby buses rattle down the streets hooting perky little horns, even though the noise of loose parts is warning enough. The drivers are East Indians, wearing dark caps and khaki drill suits.

It is eight o'clock, the sun is shining and there are clouds on the northern hills. A tourist boat is in the harbour. The tender is coming over and the taxi-drivers are lined up outside the customs. The hotel touts are standing in the courtyard of the customs where there is a tank of fish and turtles. The biggest turtle is called Barton, because it moves like the Chief of Customs.

All these men are waiting for their prey. There is no hurry in their slow movements, no antagonism in their gestures. But as soon as the tender arrives they rush forward: "Taxi, sir?" "Hotel, sir?" "See the island, sir?"

One by one the tourists – gawky, befuddled suckers – are snapped up and whirled off, some to do the drive around the Saddle, others to shop, to make love, to eat and drink. They are like a handful of crumbs to starving birds. The birds swoop down and in a moment crumbs and birds have disappeared.

It is nine and the children are in school. They are sitting on benches, three to four classes in each room. Round the walls are slogans – 'United we stand, divided we fall.' 'Never go to bed without cleaning your teeth.' 'God Save the King.' 'God is love.' 'To work is to pray.'

The noise of one class blends with the noise of the next. The voice of the masters is a fused droning, the background for children's jokes. Outside the gates the ice-cream man is waiting for the break. He has water ices for a cent.

In a shack facing the East Dry River an old woman is sitting on the doorstep smoking a pipe. She does not know when she was born, but it was 'before the cholera'. Her daughter is behind her. She is scrubbing the table. There are three seats in the room. One is a rocker, one is a deal kitchen chair without a back and the third a packing-case.

She hears a whimpering from behind the newspaper screen. She ignores it for a moment, remembering the washing before her. But when it does not stop she goes behind the screen, where there is a brass double bed and a crazy washstand with a broken jug. A child of six is lying on the bed, her son. He sees her and begins to cry.

She puts her hand on his forehead. It is burning. This is the second day. Last night as he lay beside her he was like a live coal-pot against her body.

"Eh, eh," she says and goes to the corner where some rags are lying. She takes one and washes it out in the tap outside. As she passes her mother she shakes her head. "Still got de feber. Like a glowin' coal, man."

"Eh, eh. Thaht's baad," says the old woman, and draws at her pipe.

The daughter goes back to her child and lays the wet rag on his forehead. "There, doodoo," she says. "You feel better."

When she goes back into the front room the old woman says: "Why you no take him to de doctor?"

"Me?" she says. "Me take him to de doctor, pay twenty-four cent, stand all day negotiatin' an' then he do nothin'. Me with all de clothes in Port of Spain to wash. Why you don't take him yourself, eh?"

Mrs. F. in Maraval is having a bridge party with three friends. They are playing for a cent a hundred, and between hands they retail their gossip. Nobody is too humble to be the subject of their scandal. Their servants' paramours and bastards are subjects as succulent as the peculation of the late Governor of Carrera, the colony's prison, or the manslaughter charge which the Solicitor-General is facing.

"He'll get off," they say, "just because he's a black man. Now if he was white he'd've been suspended until the trial came up."

At ten o'clock the bridge party will have a rum punch or two, Mrs. F. bawling at the maid for being slow to answer her call, being slow to make the drinks and then for making them wrongly. This subject will so stimulate the party that even the play will be held up, while the latest stupidity of coloured maidservants will be related in front of the coloured maidservant.

In Woodbrook Mrs. Ranji is sitting rocking on her gallery, and each time she comes forward her *alpargatas* click on the floor. She is vexed over a business problem. She wishes to sell the property which she bought in Alfredo Street for twelve hundred dollars two years ago. Mrs. Pompignan, a creole lady, came round yesterday with her brother-in-law and his mother to discuss the purchase terms. She does not want to buy the house for herself, but for a certain party who will pay her a commission fee of two and a half per cent. Mrs. Ranji has demanded 1400 dollars, and Mrs. Pompignan said yesterday that that was all right. But she wanted a little for herself, too, so why not say 1460 dollars and then Mrs. Pompignan can get sixty dollars for herself. Yesterday Mrs. Ranji was satisfied because she never thought to make two hundred dollars profit on the house. But overnight she has grown ambitious. Why let that Mrs. Pompignan get that sixty dollars when she has two and a half per cent as well.

So early in the morning Mrs. Ranji rang up Mr. Gonzales to tell him he can have the house for fourteen hundred and fifty dollars. But Mr. Gonzales wasn't at his office. And now a dozen worries fret her as she sits rocking in her chair.

Will Mrs. Pompignan close the deal before Mr. Gonzales comes in? If she tries to, would it be better to stall her till tomorrow or to close the deal straight away? Would... oh, would... oh, would a hundred things?

A good Catholic, Mrs. Ranji keeps a candle burning constantly before the German oleograph of Our Lady in her bedroom. But now she goes into the kitchen and fills a small brass bowl with glowing charcoal. As she sprinkles incense over it she sniffs the heavy blue smoke.

God, one or other of them, will provide.

She stands back smiling, then, turning, she shoos Floss, her mongrel bitch, out of the best chair and resumes her seat on the gallery, rocking to and fro, waiting for the telephone to ring.

Six hundred and forty-two women are sewing from eight in the morning till five at night for sixty cents.

Two lines of carts are drawn up outside the customs sheds. The first is being loaded, backed against the pavement. A Negro sits on a dais checking the loadings. A cart is full. He shouts, and a cart from the waiting line moves out and backs into its place.

The floors of the carts are battered planks, with narrow uprights stuck around for sides. They rest on wobbly wheels, are drawn by mules, horses or donkeys and carry fourteen, fifteen sacks.

From the sheds the carts branch to the warehouses, carrying the imports of the colony to Huggins, Alston, Gordon Grant. On South Quay, Chacon Street and Broadway, all around the block, Negroes unload them, plastered with flour and sweat.

A wrinkled old woman stops with a basket of mangoes on her head. "You filt'y nigger trash," she bawls, "who I see you goin' wit' down Henery Street las' night?"

The man she's bawling at props up a wall some forty feet away. He shows white teeth, laughing, and two girls standing on the kerb turn round and giggle. The old woman clenches her fists. Her aged face contorts with the world-shaking rage of a child of four. The basket woggles, but remains upon her head. The Negro smiles, the two girls clutch one another.

At last words fail her. She is played out. "You... you nasty man," she bawls. She rises to full height and stalks away.

As a stranger walks down the steps of the hotel a dapper Negro comes up. "Excuse me, sir," he says, "A minute of your time, sir," he says.

"You get hell out of here," says the stranger,

"I'm sorry, sir," says the Negro, "some time when you are less busy, sir." He smiles as he looks after the stranger. He knows his business. "Some time when you've got a few more drinks in you," he says to himself.

Like the Yankee sailors in the bar across the way. They've been tossing it back hard, since they came ashore at eight this morning. Now two are arguing what the name of the first Fred Astaire film was, a subject into which they put a passion Savonarola kept for God. Two others are talking to an Englishman leaning against the bar. One is a pie-faced guy, sweating like the outside of a glass of iced water. "What did your Lloyd George say when the War was over?" he is asking. "Tell me, what did he say?"

"What'll you have?" asks the Englishman.

"Hell he did," says Pie-face.

"I did," says the Englishman.

"Hell," says Pie-face, "you're getting me mixed up. Now I'm asking you, what did Lloyd...?"

"I heard you."

"Well, what...?"

"I don't know."

"I'm telling you," says Pie-face. "He said: 'Gimme the goddam British Fleet and gimme the 'Merican sailor an' I'll lick the goddam world'."

"Uh-Uh."

"Well?" says Pie-face.

"What'll you have?"

Pie-face clutches his arm. "Limey," he says, breathing Scotch in the Englishman's face, "you think us 'Merican sailors is just a pack o' lowdown bums, becos you see us ashore. But it ain't true. I'm tellin' you it ain't true. Becos... becos what Lloyd George said himself."

Pie-face's friend has been staring moodily at his glass during this conversation. Now he looks up and sees painted on the mirror opposite a sailor sitting on a keg of rum. He raises the glass and flings it at the mirror. The glass smashes, splinters on the floor.

He looks round. A smile lights his face. He is happy.

Everybody stops talking. A boy sweeps up the fragments and empties them in a bin on the gallery. Pie-face turns to the barman, beckons him to the far end. "Doan argue with Lofty," he whispers. "I'll pay the damage. Just tell me what it is. But don't argue with Lofty. That boy's got a punch in him'd knock you this day week. Doan argue."

The black barker stands at the corner of Frederick Street and Marine Square, shouting: "Ladies, ladies, don't miss your chance this bright morning. Step right in. Buy your shoes now, ladies, roll in, roll in. Six thousand shoes for thirty-six cents. Dollar shoes, ladies, goin' fast, goin' cheap."

And as he shouts, the shoppers move slowly past, like stream of treacle. Their eyes rove the windows, the dark interiors piled deep in 'seconds', the throw-outs of the home industry.

Sometimes they go inside, poking in bargain trays like fowls in straw.

Sometimes they stand in the centre of the pavement talking, rocks in the stream.

Here in Frederick Street at this time gather women from St. Anns and Woodbrook, St. Clair and Laventille. Here black and white mix, yellow and chestnut, as nowhere else at no other time. Indian women wearing *saris,* Chinese schoolgirls, high-brown mistresses.

They walk down Frederick Street, bent on the same errands, food for the belly, clothes for the back. In the purses they have the same currency, some more, some less. They all wear dresses, most hats and shoes, though different in their quality. As their arms touch, passing, their hearts are beating close. Under different skins, the same organs digest the morning's food, restore the blood, make nails and hair grow, temper the body's heat, urge procreation.

Yet here where Hindu walks with Anglican, Catholic with Methodist, Negro with Indian, Portuguese and half-caste, most feel not the similarity of human beings, but the difference. The essential facts, birth, copulation, death, are hidden by differences in clothes, wealth, pigmentation.

Mrs. Wilson, Government official's wife, stops and chats with Mrs. Tournevant. Her smiles, she feels, are like Royalty's, a cheap largesse. These days, the late inhabitant of West Kensington reflects, we must be democratic. She gives her patronage to octaroons and lighter shades: and, daughter of a retired captain R.N., feels worthy pride because she is not the standoffish colonial official's wife that everyone makes fun of.

Mrs. Tournevant's great-grandmother was freed from slavery when she bore her master's bastard. As she talks to Mrs. Wilson, she is torn in two directions. Being seen talking to a white woman raises her prestige among neighbours and that gives her pleasure. But she knows that behind Mrs. Wilson's affability is contempt and maybe hatred. The pretence of equality is a mask for white superiority: it is like a millionaire wearing dungarees. She is being patronised and she is submitting to being patronised to gain caste with neighbours. So Mrs. Tournevant, laughing and smiling, hates Mrs. Wilson from West Kensington, and hates herself for talking to her.

"You must come and see us sometime, Mrs. Tournevant," the white queen smiles. "Any time. We're in the book. Just ring."

"That's very nice of you," says Mrs. Tournevant, "I'll make a point of it." As they part she vows: "Never. Never." And then the recollection returns that Mr. Tournevant, whatever his ancestry, makes from his commission agency and his slum property three times as much as the white queen's husband. As she goes into Canning's to buy her groceries, she is humming to herself.

César de Montfort owns three-quarters of his Ford V8. His last instalment falls due in four months time. He is waiting on the Queen's Park Hotel rank, when the American lady picks him up.

The American lady is about forty-five, not slim, but still attractive. She looks at him twice before she gets in. Then she smiles and says: "I wanna go up Lady Chancellor Hill. Do you know the route?" An odd question, because Lady Chancellor Hill is just across the savannah and everybody knows it. But César merely nods and smiles back the way she smiles at him.

The American lady gets in the back and sits so that she sees César's face in the driving mirror. He is a mulatto with a warm brown skin. Though his nose is negroid, his lips are not everted. He keeps his eyes on the road.

" What's your name ? " asks the American lady.

"César, Madam."

"Says ah," she repeats, "that's a handsome name. That's French, isn't it?"

César knows the conversation from now on. He shows his teeth, smiling.

"Says ah," says the American lady, "do you like spending all your time, driving a cab around. I mean don't you ever want to get away from it all? Somewhere gay, somewhere where you can make something of yourself."

"I drive de cab," says César, "make a little. Maybe not much, but somethin'. How I go away?" He turns up the hill by the Botanical Gardens.

"Don't you ever feel you'd like to get to a big city? Like New York."

César looks at her flushed face in the driving mirror. She is leaning forward with her eyes fixed on him.

"How I go to New York?"

"It could be managed easy enough, s'posing someone was interested in you." The car turns swiftly round a corner and she falls to one side. When she recovers, she says: "You could learn a trade, a profession, something would bring you in real money."

César brings the car to a stop. The road is ended. The city is laid out below. He turns off the engine. "But," he says, looking at her in the mirror, "no one interested in César.'

The American lady shakes her head. "Someone might be," she suggests.

The Indian drives his cart up to the pavement and unloads his sacks. He drags them into the dark weigh-house, where they are weighed on the scales and then emptied on to the central pile of copra. He is given a chit.

There is a line of men before the cashier's desk. He waits at the end of the line with the chit in his hand. One by one the men edge up and go away until it is his turn.

He hands his chit to the cashier. There is 600 lbs. marked on it. The clerk gives him seven dollars fifty.

He looks at the money, counts it and then slams it down in a rage. "What you doin'?" he says. "Copra dollar fifty, you give me seven-fifty six hundred pound, what you thinkin'?"

The cashier shakes his head. "Copra's a dollar fifty dry," he says. "You see this W. That means wet, man."

He turns on the other men waiting for their money. "See what they doin'," he says, "impositin' on me. It'll be you next." The men stand waiting, saying nothing, fearing that they will be cut too. "Gimme back my copra," he shouts. "I go somewhere else, where they doan rob poor man. Gimme my copra back."

"Get along, man. Get along, man. Can't you see there's others waitin'?"

The Indian rushes back to the weighman. "Why you say my copra wet? When you say that, you lie." He shakes his fist in the man's face. "Gimme my copra back."

The weighman points to the pile of copra. The Indian's copra lies buried with the rest. He can't take it back. He can't prove it dry. He looks back to the file of men, cashing their chits at the desk. He is desperate, hysterical. He pushes his way to the cashier. "Pay me my nine dollar, man," he shouts. "I'll bring a case. I'll bring a case."

The cashier plumps down the seven dollars fifty he has laid aside. "Take it," he says, "before they put you behind prison bars."

A constable is passing. He has heard the noise and he stops. The cashier calls him. The Indian sees the black figure coming, snatches his money and runs into the street, the others laughing.

A group of men is centred round a bench in Woodford Square. Near them lie bodies sleeping in the grass and a scrawny-necked hen scrabbles at the earth, calling her chicks.

The centre of the group is a tall Negro in a tattered shirt and patched khaki trousers. He is barefoot. He stands, facing the bench as he talks. He flings his hands out with the natural ease of oratory. "De name of Uriah Butler shall live in Treeneedahd till perpetuity," he says. "As long as human memory. In de schools dey will teach his name and de great days of las' June."

The men round nod their heads. "Dat is true, man, what you say. All de wide worl' over, dat day they hear of Treeneedahd and Uriah Butler, his glorious name."

A third man breaks in. He has been sitting on the bench. He wears the dirty centre of a felt hat that has lost its brim. "Treeneedahd is a rich island, man. All de riches of de earth, we have in dis land. But we is poor. Who get de riches? This is profoun' question I'm askin'. Who get de riches, when we starve, when we go walkin' de street bare-foot wid no work, not a cent for a bit saltfish put wid de rice? Who get de riches then?"

The man by his side nods. "Dat is true word, man. You dam right what you sayin'." He nods and looks around. He earns a few cents a day, informing the police what the men are saying in the square. He has to keep talk going or he has nothing to report: and besides, he wants to establish sympathy with the others.

The first speaker thrusts his body forward. "You askin' me who takes de riches of dis land. You askin' me and I tellin' you and mark dis plain. Who you see ridin' in de rich saloons, who you hear hootin' de horn, get away nigger trash, you get out o' my way, you no good. It de white folks come from abroad to take de good jobs, rob de coloured folk dis island belong to. And mark dis now, and mark dis plain. Dese white folks we see here in de island, makin' style like they own de whole dam' worl'! They go back to England and dey ain't nothen'. In dere own country, dey ain't de lords and masters. Dere's others, more richer far, more pompous, wouden have 'em in dere houses and dose folks too draw de riches from Treeneedahd. Folks never saw de island, never heard of Port of Spain. Think Treeneedahd in de middle of de Pacific Ocean maybe, think San Fernando is in Spain or Fyzabad in India, but deir monstrous riches derivate from de sweated blood of niggers, like you an' me."

"Dat," says the police spy, "is very well and truly spoken, man. Coulden put it better myself."

On the grass plot opposite the custom house, tethered goats and donkeys crop the grass. They have been brought for sale from smaller islands.

The goats bleat constantly and every so often a donkey bares its teeth, stretching its neck forward, and for a minute bellows to the world the protest of the ass. But the Negroes sitting on their haunches in the shadow of the arcade take no notice. For they have heard the sound so often and they know it has no meaning.

A crowd of stevedores is fighting outside a warehouse in Chacon Street: three hundred men, waiting, pushing, shoving for sixty jobs. The doors are still closed. They have waited more than an hour. They shout for someone to open. They catch the doors in their hands and rattle them. One climbs up the doors, which are made of wooden slats, and crouches poised on the top, uncertain what to do.

Each house has its regulars and takes a few extras every time. That keeps the regulars and the extras up to scratch.

Regulars for other houses are standing round watching. They have no work today, but they are drawn by professional interest. They watch the excitement, the shouting and the animal scramble, with a cool detachment, as they draw their Anchor cigarettes. Their pleasure is to see others in that hectic struggle for work, which yesterday was their own.

An East Indian peddler runs beside a sailor with bracelets of beaten alloy in his hand. "A present for a lovely lady. Three dollars."

"Go away."

"Two dollars. I let you have it cheap."

The sailor keeps on walking, with the peddler at his side.

"A dollar," says the peddler.

"I don't want the darned thing."

"I broke. I sell nothin' this morning. Give it you fifty cent."

"I wouldn't take it for nothing."

The peddler thrusts a bracelet in the sailor's hand. "I give it you for thirty-six."

The sailor takes it and pays over one and sixpence. "Two for fifty cents," says the peddler.

"You done me once," answers the sailor. "Not a second time." He wraps the bracelet in his pocket and goes into the Regent tearoom for ham and eggs.

The handsome young shopwalker is standing at the entrance of the store, watching the girls walk by.

A woman of thirty-five, wearing new black, comes down the street and smiles at him.

"How you doin', Julia?" he asks. "Sorry I coulden come to the funeral."

"You shoulda been there, Tony," says the widow. "Everyone was there. Went in great style. Sixty personages beside the grave. And very formal."

"He'll be a loss," says Tony. "He was a good man."

"Eh, eh. But a jealous man, a very jealous man. You know that, Tony." Tony nods.

"Now I'm free," she says, "free to follow the dictates of my heart, as the sayin' is."

"Get a little fun out of life."

"We're only young once," says the widow. "Maybe you've got a chance now."

"When?" asks Tony.

"There's no time like the present," says the widow. "And I'm goin' home presently."

"But the shop…"

"Of course, if I'm not worth leavin' a silly shop two three minutes."

"Wait," says Tony. He goes inside and speaks to one of the other shopwalkers. Then he comes out again. He nods, smiling.

"I always had a feelin' for you, Tony," she says, "but I always afraid with boys maybe they got somethin'."

"Uh-uh," says Tony, "that's the same goin' with women."

"I'm clean," says the widow. "You would tell me, if you had anythin', wouldn't you?"

Tony colours. "Would I be goin' with you otherwise?" he asks, congratulating himself that he hasn't told a lie.

Eleven-thirty, breakfast time in the Union Club, rendezvous of business and professional men, who do not want to lunch at home.

The Union Club, situate on Marine Square, pretentious in conception, in execution shoddy, but with that subfusc atmosphere, that dingy comfort, those piles of periodicals that make a club a club.

Here gather local magnates, tradesmen, oilfield executives, lawyers, business men, coming from Europe, South America, the West Indies. There are no black men, no Government officials, seated at the tables. But this is a section of the upper crust, swallowing lager, eating crab-backs, pepper-pot or steak. A disunited group of men, bridging the gaps in their common interest with badinage, sly references to private lives, made by convention inordinately raffish. Others are drinking cocktails on the gallery overlooking the garden where salmon flamingos stalk proudly above the guinea-fowl.

This club exists for those contacts falling between business and domestic intercourse; relations that cannot be cemented into friendship through lack of sympathy, but are worth maintaining in hope of future business. A cocktail, billiards and cards, a joke between the calalou and fish, these are club currency.

Leave them at lunch, walk west to St. Vincent Street and enter the parlour beside the *Trinidad Guardian* offices. Here the reporters eat their lunch for ninepence or a shilling, a half-a-dozen crude tables shut from the street by the soft-drink counter. These are East Indians, Negroes, half-castes earning eight to ten dollars a week. They are the intellectuals, the news-hawks, grubbing next lightermen who earn the same salary or maybe more. They are the live wires, fetching a lower price than a dead ox.

But they are brain workers, members of a privileged class. They sit aloof – it pays to be aloof – swallowing their pastelles. Each knows that one day he might be a sub-editor, if he does not offend editors Hitchens or Ambard. Proper behaviour, a nice sense of position, the realisation of where the bread is coming from and who may later add some jam, a pat of butter – these are the qualities needed to scale the ladder; the qualities that prevent promotion, initiative, independent judgment, sympathy with the lighterman eating at the next table, dangerous radicalism are all suspect.

So even in their own parlour they talk with low voices, look across at strangers and whisper. The smallest challenge to authority satisfies the desire for independence. Like sand-crabs venturing from their holes, they scan a small horizon with long eyes, and scuttle to their holes at the shadow of danger.

Leave the intelligentsia for the Salvation Army Hostel. Here for a penny, sometimes for nothing, a group of men are having soup, bread, salt-fish. They are the destitute. They would be unemployed in any other country; but in Trinidad the Government has decreed that there are no unemployed.

Buses and trams are crowded with clerks and shop girls hurrying home for 'breakfast.'[1] Then for a spell the streets are empty, except for those who have no breakfast to go to. And even these do not move, but sit on steps or lie in the shadow of trees, finding in sleep a peace denied in wakefulness.

---

1. In Trinidad, 'breakfast' means 'luncheon,' just as 'presently' means 'now' and 'just now' 'presently'.

Only the police are upright, wakeful. Under white topees their dark faces seem black as they stand directing traffic. Even during this lull two road cops are directing the traffic at the Four Roads intersection. One directs it east and west, the other north and south. Each pursues his duty with absorption.

A Ford V8 is coming from the north, a Morris Minor from the west. Each car is motioned on.

They meet in the centre of the crossroads. The Ford V8 stoves in the rear fender of the Morris, tears its bumper off. A woman screams though she is not hurt.

The two police, without a word, approach the cars, get out their notebooks and lick their pencils. "How this happen?" asks the first policeman sternly.

A stout young man in three-dollar white ducks is walking down Ariapita Avenue. Behind him walks a Negro, carrying on his head the white man's burden, a suitcase filled with dresses and knickknacks. The stout young man enters each gate, walks up to the gallery and waits till he can attract attention.

When a maid comes he says: "Nize dresses. Anybody here want nine dresses?"

He turns and goes 'psst,' pressing tongue forward, jetting air through clenched teeth. This is the crucial moment to hold attention for the black porter to appear and open the suitcase. That done, the sale is as good as made.

This stout young man is Syrian. Trinidad is his land of plenty. He has come here to make his pile. In order to land he has to deposit two hundred and fifty dollars or find a guarantor. Sabga, the Syrian merchant on Frederick Street, has put up a bond for him. Now he is repaying his debt by peddling Sabga's merchandise. He and others comb the island, selling in remote villages articles at above Frederick Street prices.

The young man's ambition is to rise from peddler to petty shopkeeper and step by step to reach the position Sabga holds today, in his turn to hire more peddlers who finally will wrest from the Chinese the commercial ascendancy they wrested from the Portuguese before them.

In the eyes of the ignorant this young peddler trudging down Ariapita is just a fat boy, sweating to the tip of a well-developed nose. But to himself as he picks his way among the huge sewerage pipes lying in the road he is a pioneer in the vanguard of a new commercial invasion. In twenty years, he dreams, established with a wife and educated family, he will be giving the orders which he now cajoles from Negro maidservants and their mistresses.

In the police court building off Woodford Square a coal-black solicitor pleads his client's case. He is a tall man whose flow of words never ceases. Talk for him is life as well as livelihood. As he elaborates his periods its humour catches him and a snorting laughter fighting to silence him shakes his body.

He is defending a plain girl, dark as he is. He calls her 'this fair damsel'. The fair damsel has lived with a boy for nearly a year. But recently he left her and returned to his mother. The mother is suing the girl for insulting language, saying that when the girl met her and her son on the street she said; "You — in Sangre Grande, you — in San Fernando; you — in Rio Claro, and now you want to — your own son."

The old lady tells this to the court without the blanks. She is dressed in black, and looks as if she has just come from church. The words issue strangely from her lips. She has nothing against the girl, she says, but having spent a lot of money on her son's education she resented the fact that he went to live with her as soon as he got a job and didn't pay his mother a cent.

The fair damsel cannot listen to this account in silence. "Oh! Oh! Oh!" she says. "That's a lie," she says, until the magistrate has to stop her.

"Your time will come," he says.

And when her time comes she tells the court that not a word that they have heard ever passed her lips. The real truth was that the boy's mother had accused her of giving him a peanut.[1] To which she retorted that as the old woman had got her son back it was she who'd probably given him the peanut.

Both statements are made with convincing sincerity. The magistrate then calls on the boy and asks which account is true.

The boy looks at his mother. Then at his late mistress. Then at his mother again. "Mother is right," he says.

The tall white resident with horny eyebrows approaches the stranger waiting for a bus. "A sailor?" says the resident, seeing that the stranger is in his shirtsleeves.

"Tourist," says the stranger. "Stopping here. Looking around."

"Well," says horny eyebrows. "Well." He props himself on his unrolled umbrella. "And what do you make of the place?"

The stranger looks anxiously for his bus. "Very interesting."

"Of course, it must be," says horny brows. "We in Trinidad don't notice the enormous changes gain' on in the island. But to an outsider it must be staggerin'."

---

1. *When you give your beloved grated nutmeg, he will fall in love with you. But f you want to be really certain, you swallow a peanut whole, and when it has passed through your body, you take and grate it and administer in his food.*

"The way I see it," says the stranger, "you'll have to make a lot more changes before you're through."

Horny brows looks at the stranger curiously. They are not alone now. Three Negroes are waiting for the bus. "The trouble," says horny brows, "is these dam niggers. They're the people that make all the mischief."

"Maybe they feel the pinch most," says the stranger.

"They should have shot more down last June. A lot more. If I had my way…"

The bus drives up and the three Negroes get into the bus before the old man. The old man can only find a seat above the rear wheel. No room for his feet. He has to sit with buckled legs, his brolly striking at his face when the bus goes over bumps.

The curling horns of hair above his eyes twitch as he thinks what he would do with niggers if he had his way. And the holy anger sweeping through his body destroys the memory of that grandmother whose only legacy to him was negroid lips.

The buses and the trams have brought the workers back from lunch. It is two o'clock. The banks are closing, except for Savings Accounts. The sweepstake ticket sellers are moving off to other beats. An Indian in native dress is waiting for his goat to decide to move. The men and women, resting, move round with the shade. Wet heat makes every movement an act of will.

There is a break at Nelson Street School. The children are playing in the yard and street. A master is looking after them.

The, headmaster is sitting at his desk, talking to one of the parents. His manner is calm and reassuring.

Into the classroom bursts an Indian bus-driver, dragging a boy by the arm. He shatters the quiet of the interview. "Dis boy bad boy," he says. "Get in de bus, play 'roun' wid de engin', play wid de brakes. Five, six other boys, too. But they run 'way, and he de worse make monkey face at me. I catch him. You punish him."

"I'm very sorry," says the headmaster, "and I'm very glad you've brought it to my notice."

"Very dangerous, them boys fiddlin' with de bus. Hundred times I tell them, 'Play 'roun' de bus but doan go inside, doan fiddle wid de engine.'"

"I can assure you," says the headmaster, "that the matter will be taken up and be suitably dealt with. It shan't happen again."

The bus-driver looks at the boy by his side. He has a bright face which he is trying hard to pull to penitence. "Look at he," says the bus-driver, "he de ringleader. I say, 'Get out of dat car presently,' and he just laugh and make monkey face."

Now many white women are sleeping off the effect of morning bridge, rum cocktails and breakfast, mostly alone.

They must appear bright for the returning husband, treasure carefully what little beauty life in the tropics has left them. For here, where flowers grow tall as bushes, the fears of the Saturday Evening Post Girl, B.O., seborrhea, enlarged pores, are nightmares.

They lie on their beds, their faces covered with cream, and as they wait for sleep they wonder.

Witness Mrs. Carmody as she stretches her hot body on the bed. She wears the regulation pink petticoat. Her legs are slightly knotted with varicose veins. She stares at her remote feet, seen over the crest of her belly, wondering about Charley.

She and Charley have been getting on worse than ever these last months. They are both in their forties, but Charley does not show his age. Mentally he is a child. Violet Carmody knows his stories, every word he will say, as well as she knows his habit of cleaning wax out of his ears in public with matchsticks. She does not love him. In fact she loathes him, and he loathes her. For the last fortnight they have communicated by the exchange of written notes left on each other's bedside table.

Violet and Charley cannot separate. Economics tie them more firmly than any bond of love. Her livelihood depends on him: his upon the avoidance of scandal, because he is a Government servant.

Mrs. Carmody thinks of the young black girls walking round the savannah, their laughter, their shamelessness. She has heard tales of other white men. But Charley? Is it possible? Are women laughing at her behind her back? She looks at her feet, so curiously distorted by forty odd years of shoes. "It's unjust," she says with passion, "it's so unjust."

She does not know exactly what is unjust, the body ageing, love dying or economic dependence. But the mere saying brings some comfort to her muddled spirit. She turns on her side and soon begins to snore.

When Cita, the maid, looks in to nab some of Mrs. Carmody's scent her mistress's breathing sounds as if she had bad dreams. But in fact that stout little woman's unconscious is whirling her round the dance-floor of the Country Club with the rich and handsome Mr. Dewsbody with an abandon that bachelor would blush to have.

On the other hand, Mrs. Stangelheimer has not retired to bed. She has got out the car and is taking her girl friend Doddie Markham for a bathe at Maqueripe. Each in their thirties, they have in common a Kensington – very much opposed to a West Kensington – background.

As they whirl out towards the sea they roar with laughter. They are engaged in exchanging the confidences dropped by Mrs. Carmody. "How extraordinary some people are. They really are."

And then they pass to Mrs. Steumer, who it is rumoured is having an affair with a black doctor. "A very educated man, my dear. But not coloured; Indian Ink."

Meanwhile, old Sarah, who has been walking down Charlotte Street with a wooden platter on her head, stops and puts down the platter on the pavement. The platter is filled with chickens tied by the legs. Old Sarah is tired and angry. She has sold nothing all day. She sits down in the gutter, gets a bit of old rag out of her bosom and binds her feet. The soles are coming off her shoes.

Two women in white dresses and sun-glasses stop by her. "If that isn't the darndest thing," one says.

Old Sarah looks up. There is the click of a camera, and the two women laugh and turn away.

The old woman curses them in patois. But they've already moved off, searching for another cute snap.

They find it outside Canning's grocery. A pukka Hindu with white native dress scooped up under the crutch, white paint down the forehead, a string of black beads and an umbrella.

"Ooh, we must get him," says the first.

"Hold it," says the second. And the gallant Hindu, entering into the spirit of the thing, poses for them, smiling. They are so touched that they give him sixpence? No, a penny is enough.

The old man thanks them with oriental courtesy. But when they leave he shakes his head. 'Hell,' he thinks, 'the model racket's not what it was. Like every other profession, it's getting overcrowded.'

A Negro, whose cheekbones protrude like knuckles, goes up to a white man in Frederick Street. "You remember me, sir?" he says.

The white man is an oil-driller from Fyzabad. "Yes," he says, "I remember you. And I don't want to go fishing."

"As you say, sir, as you say. But do you want some cigarettes, sir?"

"I've got cigarettes."

"I get you cheap. Any sort you like. Off de boats."

"All right," says the driller, "bring me two hundred Gold Flake round to the 'Paris'."

"That'll be a dollar, sir," says the man, holding out his hand.

"I'll pay you after."

"But I've got no money."

The driller pauses. He knows he'll never see his money again if he gives it now. Drumsticks says: "For a dollar, sir. I wouldn't cheat anyone for that. A hundred dollars maybe."

"Oh, well, take it," says the driller, "and see you bring it round to the 'Paris'"

"Sure, sir. Sure," says Drumsticks, snatching the bill. He is off down the street, smiling to himself. That's the second sucker in one day. That's worth a drink.

He goes into a rum shop and orders a nip, which is a quarter bottle costing twenty-four cents.

There are six different rooms in this shop, all with the same prices. He sits in Room 3, where there are two tables with rough wood benches either side. On the walls are half a dozen pictures. One is the remainder of a calendar, a cheap Japanese bamboo roll with The Complements of the Season written on it. There is a lithograph of Gomez, the late dictator of Venezuela, on a horse; an engraving of Waterloo; two German oleographs, one of Adam and Eve, the other of Susannah and the Elders; a colour-plate of Baden-Powell at the age of forty, and another of a half-nude girl whose nipples are covered by the heads of two flamingos.

Drumsticks drinks his rum neat in a small glass and follows it with a chaser of water. At the other table four men are talking.

They are discussing local politics. Two of them are secret members of the Negro Cultural and Social Welfare Society, one is an orthodox member of the Trinidad Labour Party, and the fourth belongs to the Clerks' Union, which is contemplating breaking away from the Labour Party.

Cipriani, says the Labourite, is a white man: a real European from Corsica. And white men are the true leaders, you can't get away from that.

White men, say the Negro Culturists, are leaders for white men. That's why his policy has betrayed the workers, the coloured people. That's why Cipriani keeps having to say: "On this issue, I'm at one with the Capitalists." Look at his stand on the Shop Hours Bill.

As Drumsticks listens to the conversation and drinks his rum, an idea comes to him. When he is caught smuggling contraband next time, he can get a light sentence if he offers to collaborate with the force, give them information about this sort of thing. "It's worth trying," he thinks as he finishes off his rum. "But, of course, dey've got so many people workin' for dem already."

Miriam Stephens is a girl behind the counter in a Frederick Street Store. She sells haberdashery for two dollars fifty a week. She is the mistress of Abel Kingston, a waterfront worker who averages around twelve dollars fifty. He is six foot, a dark god.

Abel buys her clothes and pays her rent. He is crazy about her.

Miriam is half-white, small and light-skinned. If you didn't notice the thick hair on her arms and legs, the way it grows low by her ears, you'd say she was European. Or anyway, you'd say she was a Spanish type, if she was your mistress.

The time is half-past three. Abel comes into the store and asks for Miriam.

A girl tells him, and as he goes off she titters and winks to other girls.

Abel goes over to the haberdashery counter. He waves to Miriam.

At first it seems she doesn't notice him. She is serving a customer. Abel wants to tell her that he has finished work early and wants her to come to a show with him right after the shop closes. He calls out to her.

As soon as she has finished with the customer, she comes across to him. "What you mean comin' in here, front of everybody," she says, "makin' me shame? D'you want me to lose my job?"

His mouth had been open to invite her. It closes. He looks at her in astonishment. This is a person he has never met before.

An octaroon shop-walker comes up, a midget, but a member of the volunteers. "I want," says Abel, "I want... I want."

The midget goes away.

" Well, what do you want ? " asks Miriam.

"I want to murder you, you little rat," he says and walks away.

The time is five o'clock. The clock in the Chinese delicatessen says half-past nine. Strips of cold roast pork hang in a glass case, smeared with fat. There is half a chicken and a bowl of gherkins in vinegar.

An Indian woman comes in and orders twelve cents souse.

The Chinaman, who contributes ten dollars a month to the Chinese fighting fund, puts three pieces of knuckle on some paper. He begins to wrap it.

"That's not twelve cents," says the Indian woman, "that's nine."

The Chinaman takes away a piece. "That nine."

The two burst into sudden flames of anger. For a moment they shout and curse. Then the woman snatches up her money, goes from the shop and turns to toss a final oath.

As she goes towards the market, she mutters to herself. But no one pays attention. Everybody in Trinidad talks to himself.

In the market they are selling off cheap the day's meat, which has now turned black with clotted blood. The flies have laid their eggs on it, and by tomorrow it will be too foul to eat. It is cut in chunks, which deforms the best parts, but disguises the worst.

As she comes to the stall, the keeper raises a banana leaf and waves the flies away. A baby girl is asleep in a box by her side, curled like an embryo in the womb.

The Indian woman picks out a number of black lumps. "Dix cents," she says.

"Vingt," says the keeper, flipping at the flies. She lets the banana leaf fall and the flies descend like flakes of soot.

"Douze," says the Indian woman, putting down her sixpence.

The stall-keeper wraps up the meat, adroitly abstracting one piece, and hands it to her.

The Indian woman goes rejoicing home. The meat is bad; but there is plenty. Disguised in curry and smothered with pepper-sauce, no one will tell the difference. At least it is meat, the luxury that makes rice palatable.

At four o'clock the shops close in Frederick Street. Shutters are pulled down, folding gates are drawn and junior assistants leave.

Chinese girls go hurrying down the streets. Stocky Venezuelans with hairy arms wait for the buses. Negresses are walking back to Belmont in the slanting sun. Mulattoes change their trams at the Four Roads.

Behind closed shutters, heads of departments give their labour free for thirty minutes, so that they can feel superior. To bolster the same feeling, the midget shopwalker and thirty others run to parade as volunteers. Be loyal to the flag, and colour doesn't matter. Take a rifle and you've made the first step to social acceptance, nigger boy.

So the sun goes down, and out come the solar topee and the khaki shorts, revealing loyal knees. And off troop the bank clerks and the shop assistants to learn how to defend the interests of the class they hope to enter against the class they hope they have left.

The professional men have shut up shop as well. Some go to drill, some to lie down, others to bathe, hit tennis or cricket balls about. The rest start drinking right away.

Of these, those that put drinking first go to a respectable rum shop like the 'Barrels': and those that put business first go to the 'Queen's Park' or the 'Paris'. The most sensible go home.

The day shift is still working on the harbour scheme. The road gangs are still laying sewerage pipes in Woodbrook. The lightermen are not ashore yet. Busmen are setting out on their second journey to San Fernando, their thirteenth to Cocorite. The coconut seller has thirty-eight still on his stall. The beggar needs seven cents more for food and lodging. The priest has Vespers to say. The Shore Patrol has another pair of drunks to send back to the ship. The prostitute has had no food all day.

The Government official is still hard at work. He has left the office, but he has to take cocktails with his boss. He has to take his boss and wife to dinner and the cinema. He doesn't like his boss, but he knows his boss holds his future in his hands. His boss doesn't like him, but you've got to get on with subordinates. They are tied by the same bond as Violet and Charley Carmody, except that they never had any love to lose.

A knot of boys and girls is standing at a corner of Tragarete Road. All but two are on skates, and as they talk, they twist and turn, unable to keep still for the joy of movement. Three of the eldest are having an argument as to who is the best skater. They have been doing tricks, crossing their legs, skating backwards, making figures.

Somebody suggests a race to decide, the course three blocks down and back. Each of them puts a penny in the pool, winner take all.

The three boys hand the stake money to Iris, a shy mulatto girl with braided hair in ribbons, to hold for the winner.

The sinking sun is behind them when they start and their long shadows leap ahead, gorilla arms swinging. Their skates clatter on the road and the crowd cheers when Johnson, a compact Negro, gets ahead. But Tournelle doesn't let him get away. He hugs close, leaving the third, Thomas, well behind. Their bodies are bent forward, arms, hands, legs linked for speed. Johnson is a quarter of a second ahead at the turn. He swings around in a wide curve and comes into the sun. Tournelle, trying to cut time, turns abruptly, falls.

He is up again immediately, but he has twelve yards to catch up. He stops caring about the surface of the road. He swings out recklessly, knowing he can't win without taking risks and getting away with them.

A bus hoots, coming round a corner. Johnson swerves and passes in front of it. But Tournelle, head down to hide his eyes from sun, sees danger too late. He cries out, raising his arms to ward the crash off.

His arms touch nothing. His body strikes the side door of the bus. There is a crack. His body swings and, falling, his head smashes against the step.

The bus stops.

The boy is lying on the steps. Blood, flowing through his short, curly hair, trickles on the floor of the bus. Blood is dripping from his shins on to the tarmac.

Everybody in the bus stands up, shouting, talking, and screaming.

"De dam fool," bawls the driver. "His own dam fault, he deserve kill himself."

The little conductor leaps down and takes hold of the boy. He shakes him by the arm, lifts up his chin. A crowd of children on roller skates comes round.

Two cars stop. A dozen watchers run from nowhere. A woman in the back of the bus begins to scream in hysterics. The conductor looks up.

"He deserve to kill himself," says the driver again to the crowd.

"That's what he done, Joe," says the conductor.

"Call me a bastard, pal," says the red-faced Cockney in the bar of Charley's Place, "but, Jesus Christ, don't call me a 'limey'."

He is gripping the old Irishman from the oilfields by the arm and a tough American driller from the South is standing beside them. He isn't interrupting yet awhile, just smiling.

The bar-boy passes the Cockney the last chit. "Mr. Hicks," he says, handing him a pencil.

The Cockney scribbles on the chit and says: "My credit's good around 'ere. 'Icks, the engineer: the nime is known all over Port o' Spine. Bloody little town, too. Too many darn' niggers."

The Irishman is very tight. He leans on the bar, swaying. "You're right," he says. "Clear out," he says. "Go Venezuela, go Mexico, go any dam place, get out o' this stinkhole." He looks at the Cockney with dawning recognition. "That's the first true word you said tonight, you goddam limey."

The Cockney flings off his arm, leaps back a dozen yards, strips off his coat.

"Easy on there," says the driller. "Easy on."

But the Cockney takes it hard. He has his sleeves rolled up, a snake and anchor, Eva and a naked woman on his forearms. Step by slow step he advances, his underlip thrust out.

"Pal," he says, "pal. Call me a bastard, please, call me what you goddam like. But don't use that word."

"My dear good fellow," answers the Irishman, "there still remains the fact that you are a limey."

The Cockney darts forward, grabs the old man by the shoulder. His glass falls and smashes on the floor. No notice taken. Bar-boy and driller watch the tense Cockney shake a red fist in the old man's face. "Yer an old man, pal," he says. "And I respeck them grey 'airs. By Christ, if you'd been younger, I'd a knocked you for a fourpenny one."

The old man seems to have gone to sleep.

But the Cockney shakes him till he opens his eyes. His voice mounts. "Grey 'airs or no grey 'airs," he bellows, "if yer calls me... calls me by that there nime again... I was welterweight champion of the R.E. I was, and I'll knock you over that bleedin' bar. I'll take you to them stairs and knock you round the corner till you roll into the gutter. Grey 'airs or no grey 'airs." He lets the old man go and steps back. "Now doan say I didn't warn yer, pal."

"Of course, my dear fellow," says the old man, "with fists you could do anything you liked with me." He turns to the bar-boy. "You got a revolver?" he asks. "Got a six-shooter here?"

The bar-boy laughs.

"Or a machete," says the old man. "When I was in Nicaragua, I remember." He makes passes in the air. "Snick, snack, snick. Fini."

Tension relaxes. The Cockney comes back smiling. "All I want is to be pals, pal," he explains. "It's just that word. Let's 'ave another round and call it a day, eh?"

The driller pays for this round. "Say," he says, "I been wonderin'. That word you don't like, we used to call the British sailors 'lime-juicers', or for short..."

"Not that word, pal. Not you."

"Or that other word," says the driller, "because they gave 'em lime-juice so they wouldn't get a hard on."

"No, pal," says the Cockney. "Know what that word means? Call me a bastard first. It means the lowest scum of the bleedin' earth."

"An' what's that?" asks the driller.

"What's that?" asks the Cockney. He lowers his voice to a whisper. "It's someone born in the colonies."

"Well, cheerioh!" breaks in the Irishman's voice. He is on the way to the lavatory. "Cheerioh, Yankee. And cheerioh, limey."

Five hundred arms are lifted. Five hundred shakers shaken. Beads of moisture gather on the shakers' brows and sides. The red tongues of many coloured men and women watching lick black, pink and scarlet lips.

Screened by ferns, they sit in rocking-chairs on galleries or like waxworks round the walls of living-rooms.

Here the bright ball of conversation is lightly lobbed from mouth to mouth. "We're going back to England for the summer." "Let me see, last year it was a Thursday, wasn't it?" "Oh! Mr. Parker."

There, the dark rum running in flood, they turn the radio on or put dance records on the gramophone. One starts to sing: two, four, a dozen to dance.

Now the day's heat is over and the day's work done, the sun's fiery setting is quenched in cloud. Cocktails are shaken. Music blares down twilit streets. The lights are up and a crowd gathers on the pavement to watch the dancers through the gaps in ferns.

Outside the front gate, at the back gate and where the hibiscus hedge was cut back yesterday, groups gather to watch. Two start dancing in the street. Neighbours open jalousies, fling back the shutters, spy from galleries: noting who have drunk too much, watching who will dance with whom, asking who'd you say was rowdiest.

Thick clouds mass overhead, painting the sunset's orange out. Then, forming monstrous drops, they pierce the dense air and burst impartially on pavements, rubbernecks and galvanised iron. Like lizards into crannies, the spectators vanish.

Rain gives the parties privacy. A gust sweeps the galleries wet. A window slams, bangs, slams. Everybody runs into the living-room. Damp steam floats through open doors and windows, but the thermometer does not drop.

Now the dancers dance on the inner floor, cocktails are shaken in the kitchen. But music from the gramophone is louder and the rum stronger than the rain, drumming on the roof and pouring from the eaves. Voices are raised. The titter of an hour ago becomes a gust of laughter, the whispered confidence a bellow, the delicate pressure of hand on hand a grip.

In the centre of the city 'The Sly Mongoose' blares forth one calypso after another. Between records, a voice calls bargains through a loud speaker. A blaze of light illuminates the shoddy hanging from the roof and walls. The pavements are crowded and the attendants wait like challenging wrestlers ready to take on all corners.

But few are buying. Most stand enjoying the music, the hospitality of an awning, until the rain stops.

The rain comes racing from the hills. It trickles down from every seam and gully. It gathers in converging valleys, finding force and speed in mass. A hundred thousand trickles make each torrent, tearing towards the city.

On the east side, draining the valleys of St. Aims and Belmont, Laventille Hill, runs the Dry River, which twenty minutes' rain will turn from trickle to flood, a muddy spate dashing past Piccadilly to the sea.

But in the city centre and to the west, there are only drains, four feet in depth and two in width, to carry flood water from St. Clair, Maraval and Woodbrook.

A few minutes and the closed drains choke, the open drains overflow. The streets are rivers. St. Vincent, Abercromby, Richmond streets run five inches deep in places. With canvas blinds drawn, buses splash through ponds at intersections. London Road is impassable, Wrightson a risk. A taxi has stalled at the corner. It has no side curtains, and the marooned passenger is cursing as he dodges the rain driving in at the sides and dripping from the roof.

Men and women, gently sweating in the heat, stand under galleries or in the shelter of jutting roofs, waiting until the rain stops, watching the steam rise from the hot pavements.

Ten minutes to seven. Rum shops close at seven. At least the doors are barred. No more drink is sold and ten minutes' grace is given to finish up what is left.

In Fereira's rum shop, Roderigo Gonzalves is sitting over half a bottle of White Star with two volunteers. The one with fat knees, Bertie Hewitson, distinguished himself in the June strike. Pollinger, the other, in his sun helmet, is a little candle with a giant snuffer.

Gonzalves is trying to sell life insurance to Hewitson. "Bertie," he says, "Bertie man, what provision you made for the future? What you done for security of wife and children?"

Bertie pours a stiff one, adds ice and soda. "Shan't die, man. Not this boy. Not yet awhile."

Roderigo, made solemn by rum and thought of a commission, leans forward and says gravely: "S'posin'. S'posin' you get up from this table, man, an' drop down dead. Where your wife be, where the kids, what they do without you?"

"Woulden have a brass cent," Bertie agrees. "Woulden have a nickel to buy… to buy five brass cents with." He laughs.

"There," says Roderigo, "that's what I mean. That's what I'm telling you, man."

"But," says Bertie, "when I get up from this table, I'm not going to fall dead. Not even for you, man. Not even for my pal, Roderigo, I woulden' do that. No, sir. No, sirree."

Fereira comes up. "Long past time, Mr. Gonzalves. Police. Big fine. Lose my licence."

"We're comin', man," says Roderigo. "We're comin', man. Gosh, give us time." He pours the rest of the bottle into their glasses and turns on Hewitson again. "You pay ten dollars down," he says. "Four bucks a month. All the time you're saving. Then you die next week and the missis gets three thousand."

Hewitson shakes his head. "I'm a business man," he says. "You try someone else. But not me, man. No flies on Bertie. You try Pollinger."

"If you don't die, you get three thousand plus interest when you're sixty," Roderigo says.

"Ha! Ha!" says Hewitson. "Ha! Ha! Ha! You try Pollinger."

Roderigo looks at the snuffed candle. He has taken off his solar topee and is looking down at it, like a beggar at a begging bowl. "Come on, man," says Roderigo, shaking him. "Vamos, mis chicos."

Little Pollinger staggers up. The Negroes have been turned out already.

"Quarter-past seven," says Fereira, clearing away bottle and glasses.

'Quarter-past seven," mutters Pollinger. "The missis! Christ!"

"Pull yourself together, man," says Hewitson. "She's gone to England."

A smile comes over Pollinger's tiny face. "She has? By God, and so she has. Come on, boys. Let's go to the 'Paris.' Let's make a night of it." He sees the open door, runs towards it, trips on a spittoon and sprawls headlong, his topee bowling down the floor as if it was a skittle alley.

At this moment, three thousand seven hundred and eighteen hot bodies rock on galleries throughout the town. Twenty-three hundred women, leaning on windowsills, watch the world go by and chat with neighbours. In a thousand barrack-rooms, they talk beneath the yellow pitch-oil light, one ear acock for strange noises in the yard. Up fifty passages young girls await the custom that their sweet men bring them. And at the corner of Woodford Square and Abercromby Street an old man is shouting: "Woe! Woe! Woe unto ye! For ye is a sinful and perfiduous generation and I shall come wid scorpions and vipers, aye, I shall come wid de whole panoply of heaben to cast ye out into de uttermose darkness." While round him stand a small crowd laughing, shouting: "Crazy man, shut yo' mout', or they shut you in de crazy house where you belong."

Daytime is ended. Daytime is the white man's time. Then coloured folks work for the white bosses: and the white boss has the whip-wages hand. Then white lady steps out of her limousine, walks along the street with her pompous head in the air, looks at coloured folks like dirt.

After sundown comes darkness and white folk go to their houses in rich suburbs. If they come down town to the cinema or the Chinese restaurants then they take cars. They do not walk in the street after sundown.

White folk in their houses tell one another stories. They say last week old Mistress de Sante was coming back from Vespers with her Prayer Book in her hand when a coloured man came out of the darkness and showed his manhood to her.

White folk are afraid to walk under the tall trees in the darkness with only fireflies for light. When they hear foot-steps of coloured folk going home they think the footsteps follow them. They fear the coloured man, who's had a nice high-brown for a tumble, will spring out and show his manhood.

Night has come, the twelve hours when the white man abdicates his dynasty and the coloured man walks the streets as *his* streets. Standing at the street-corners joking, sipping soda in a parlour, walking down Frederick Street, round the savannah, he is alone with his colour, except for prowlers.

This is not part of pride or consciousness. It is a fact. Except in Laventille, where they dance the shango, where the shouters hold their meetings and Mother Holy Ghost saves souls. There on the hill that hatred of the white man, which is dormant in the city, springs into the open. Sight of a white face in the dark lanes brings curses. The Negro at the water-tap stops drawing water. "What the – hell you doin' here?" he asks. And he stands watching till he sees the stranger walk back to the city.[1]

From half-past six to eight those who have food eat. After supper they play games: bridge or poker if they are white; romey, whappy, all fours, fantan or dice if they are poor. Or they go to the second house of the cinema. A colour bar is invidious, so the whites go to the best cinemas in the most expensive seats, to which no one in shirtsleeves is allowed to go. Octoroons are, of course, even more punctilious than whites to sit in the best seats.

There are cheaper cinemas in St. James and Belmont, Woodbrook and Piccadilly. But the whites do not go there.

If people do not play games or go to the cinema or country club they sit on their galleries watching the fireflies flit through darkness, talking occasionally. Or they walk arm in arm across the savannah, down lanes

---

1. *The strong colour hatred which exists in Laventille, I was told, existed because the only white people to go up there at night were detectives. But this explanation was given me by Negro workers, who had come to distinguish between class and colour. I don't think this distinction is general in the Laventille district. The bosses are white, so all whites are bosses.*

high-arched with trees, where frogs croak and cicadas call to one another. They sit on benches in dark squares, kissing. They tumble in the grass. From dark alleyways comes the high sound of laughter.

The 'rats' are in their runs; down Frederick Street, along Marine, up Charlotte and back by Queen's. But business is bad, too many on the job and too few on the grind. Some work in with taxi-men, coast around, and call "Hello, darlin' " at intersections. Others stay home and wait for business to come.

But tonight, because the American boys are in, most are at the 'Cambridge'.

The American boys have left the New Harbour. A few have been sent aboard by the Shore Patrol. But most, miraculously keeping to their feet, have driven round to the 'Cambridge.'

The 'Oxford' and the 'Cambridge' are next door to one another. At the 'Oxford' a pianist is hammering out jazz for a black girl and her sailor boy. The black girl has brought him here because she has seen him earlier with Phenia, and she is afraid Phenia will be in the 'Cambridge', next door. She doesn't want a fight: just wants to get the business over quickly because the sailor boy is getting restive.

She has danced with him, making it hot. Drunk as he is, he dances pretty well and holds her tight: She has felt his interest rise.

The pianist stops playing, and they go back to their table on the gallery. A blare of music and the blaze of lights come from next door. "Whoopee," bellows a voice.

The sailor stands up, puts his hands to his mouth and bellows "Whoopee" in return.

A head pokes round the partition which separates the two galleries. "Christ, it's Sam. What the hell you doin' in that dump?" the head says.

"Whoopee," shouts Sam. "I'll be right over."

The girl catches him by the wrist. "Don't go," she says. "Come wid me, darlin'."

"I gotta be wi' my pals," Sam says. "So they can look after me when I pass out. Come on over to the Cambridge'."

"I doan like dat place," says the girl. "I doan like de class of people go there."

"Oh, come on, sister," says the sailor. "They got a crowd there."

"All right," she says. As she gets up she belches.

"Sumpen you eat?" asks the sailor.

"What?" she asks, belching louder.

"I said..." then he realises that to her belching is like breathing, only more so. "Aw, ferget it."

When they get out into the street two S.P. men are there. They look at Sam and the girl. "Mebbe you'll interdooce us to the girl friend," one says, grinning.

"No, sir," Sam says, "she's kinda nice, the company she keeps,"

As they walk towards the 'Cambridge' the girl sees that Phenia is standing at a stall with two other girls buying peanuts. She slips past quickly and Phenia doesn't see Sam or her.

As they go up the stairs at the back the girl puts Sam's cap on her head. She has had nothing to eat all day and feels rather tight. But she knows that her best chance of keeping Sam is to have his hat.

At the head of the stairs the bouncer stands like a ring-master watching the bar, the dance-floor and the bedrooms round the courtyard. There is never trouble at the 'Cambridge.' His eye anticipates, his tactful arm averts. Beside him, leaning over the banisters, a line of touts silently watch the stairs, the men and girls who come, the couples who depart.

The dance-floor is packed. The King and Queen regard the couples from the walls with Imperial benignity. Above the yellow-keyed piano Susannah is being hard pressed by the elders. The Negro, whose dusty fingers leap from note to note, lifts up his eyes. His mouth widens, lips part and gold teeth gleam. By his side, beating time with his foot, the guitarist bends over his instrument like a mother over her baby. A red-headed sailor is taking his girl through the crowd like a tank through brushwood.

There are too many girls. Some sit around the walls talking, watching, smoking. Others are on the gallery drinking beer with the sailors. The men shout, lurch across the room elbowing dancers aside, call to one another. One catches hold of a girl, whirls her around, slaps her bottom. She laughs. The sailor is boisterous, half-amorous, half-insolent. There is the recognition of this in her laughter, a brittle element of fear and resentment. He puts his arm round her and leads her to the gallery.

This is a big night. Uncle Sam pays his boys well. They spend free and easy. If they lose five bucks, well they lose it. Maybe it fell out of their pockets. Not like the German and Brazilian cadets. They made port the same night with hardly a dollar between them. They stood around all the evening, the little dark Brasileños waltzing very softly, very smoothly, while the tall Aryans leaned against the walls, wanting the girls and expecting them, for nothing.

But the American boys have dough and something more. They take the girls laughing down the galleries. All paid. No rows.

The girls who come to the 'Cambridge' live all over town, out in the suburbs, down the barrack rows which exist in the centre of the city blocks. They are the product of the slums, where from infancy no phase of sex has been hidden from them. Children have been born and been begotten in the beds beside them. Their desires are quick and strong. Jobs are scarce and underpaid. Usually they have lived with one man before and only take to the trade when they cannot find a keeper. They hate their trade, look forward to the chance once more of becoming a respectable concubine.[1] But they lack both will and opportunity to earn their living any other way.

The Shore Patrol comes up the stairs and stands looking at the dancers. By sixth sense the sailors know the Shore Patrol is here. Reeling drunks straighten up, smile and sit down sedately. "Christ," they say as the S.P. goes away. "Oh, Jesu, lover of my soul!"

The music goes round and around. Piano, saxophone, drums, guitar. A woman in a brown cloche hat walks from table to table selling peanuts in paper bags. Her skin is bistre colour, and the flesh drawn across broad cheekbones in to the mouth. The fingers, holding out the bags of peanuts, are shrunken between the joints. In her eyes there is a look of uncomprehending sadness, that deep sadness that comes not from sorrow but starvation.

She comes silently up to sailors, with girls sitting on their knees, famine in a brown cloche hat. She holds out a bag of peanuts and the sailor, looking from the girl, whom drink has made more lovely in his eyes, to the woman, whom drink has made more repulsive, shakes his head. He cannot bear to see the taut sinews of her neck, the gouged channel in between. He lifts his glass and toasts his girl.

Some of the girls will take a bag from her basket. "Give her six cents," they say. But there is another peanut seller, a dark woman, near Negress. Her face is a circle, with sunken nose for centre. She wears a wide straw hat and walks as silently as the starved conscience-figure. She draws a cloth back from her basket showing nuts; and then she smiles. Her white teeth, set apart, show in a black face. Placid, she demands nothing. You buy or not as you wish. And, wanting nuts, the sailors buy. The girls give her cigarettes. A drunk man stands her drinks. She takes all – coppers, cigarettes, alcohol, always smiling, never laughing – and then she moves away. She is like a shadow the sun casts beside the other woman's night.

Up the stairs comes François. We met him in a parlour with Netti early this morning. He's looking dandy in a boater and white trousers striped with black. He looks as if he was acting in a film, as a bouncer on the Barbary coast. He struts around, nodding this way and that. He leans up against the wall, looking at the dancers. He winks at Netti, who is dancing with a sailor. He waves his hand to the pianist, the drummer, the saxophonist.

His left hand is in his pocket, fingering his possessions: a blunt knife, a piece of rag for handkerchief and three cents.

The dance ends, and Netti goes back to a table with the sailor. She speaks

---

1. *Marriage is not regarded in Trinidad as an essential for respectability by the poorer classes. A very large number of women live with men and bear them children outside marriage. They are grandiloquently described as 'paramours' or 'concubines,' very seldom as 'mistresses'.*

to him, pressing her leg against his. They argue for a time, and then they get up and go out. He turns towards the gallery.

Three sailors are sitting round a table. He goes up to them. There are two bottles of beer on the table. "Boss," he says, "I thank you for a drink."

One of the sailors shakes his head to focus on this figure. "Hell," he says. "We're just three bums. What you standin' us, patron?"

It is ten o'clock. Most people have turned out their lights and shut their shutters. They lie in utter darkness, cut off from air and mosquitoes.

In a twelve by ten room, with twelve by ten rooms on three sides, a man and woman and four children are trying to sleep. The air is foetid, the only ventilation what drifts through the lattice work beneath the roof.

One of the children starts crying again. She has toothache and cannot sleep. The mother goes over to her and sits on the bed.

There is no mattress. The sagging springs are covered with sacking. As she hushes the child she listens fearfully for her man moving the other side of the screen. He has no work. He hasn't had regular work since the strike of last June, when he came out strong for the union. Rent is two months overdue, and the collector was round for it again today. He gave them till tomorrow.

The man is lying on the bed with his eyes open, staring at the moon through the lattice work. His hands are clenched, his nerves raw. He listens to the child whimpering. He takes every sound in, pricking his tender nerves with every irritation.

His life passes before him in a minute: a careless childhood in Arima, the job on the water scheme, marriage and hopes of a new life, lay-off, three months for stealing a tin of condensed milk when Anita was nursing. Barrack-life, children, failure, penalisation for union activity, unemployment.

Anita is singing a creole lullaby in a soft, tender voice. He has known that lullaby since his mother sang it to him. He listens tense with envy for his child, wanting to exchange responsibility for toothache.

He closes his eyes and sinks his head upon his hands. For a verse he is a child again, Anita's voice his mother's coaxing sleep.

Then the child's voice rises, breaks through and drowns the lullaby. A fist drums on the wall. And he stands up, taut and quivering. He looks around. He wants to smash something, to break what binds his life intangibly. "Christ!" he says. "Christ!"

His wife stops singing. She is the other side of the screen, but he knows how she looks listening for what he'll do. There, he knows, is his one power in a world of weakness. She depends on him. She binds him with her children and dependence. He shoves his head round the screen. "I can't stand dis," he says. "I goin' out, Chrise, where there ain't no bebies squawlin'."

He runs to the door and opens it. The moonlight falls into the room. He sees Nita's face. He has hurt her, the only person in the world he can hurt. He slams the door. He is sorry, but not as sorry as he's glad to hand her on the pain the world is handing him.

He steps into the yard. His feet sink into mud. He has forgotten to put on shoes. Should he go back?

A group of neighbours watch him from a doorway. They have heard every word, but they say nothing. To go back would be ridiculous. "Good night," he says, walking across the yard to the passage leading to the street.

"Eh, eh," comes a voice. "Since when you go barefoot in de bright moonlight, Mistah O'Rourke?"

There is a burst of laughter.

He turns, blazing with rage. "Since long before folks kep' deir nose out of what doan concern dem," he says. As he strides off he wonders if that was half as crushing as he meant it to be.

The Council's plan for a bigger and better Wrightson Road includes a line of flower-beds down the centre. Today the public works men have unloaded twenty waggonloads of special soil and manure and filled their flower-beds.

Now, the moon being hidden behind clouds, a black figure issues from a garden gate. It is Mistress Fournier armed with spade and pail. She looks cautiously to the left and then to the right. The road is empty. She trips softly to the nearest flower-beds and with a dozen thrusts the pail is full.

Another cautious survey. Then back she slips, empties the soil in the front garden where her son is digging up the heavy clay. And off on a second journey.

A third, fourth, fifth. A twenty-fifth. And by the end the flower-bed in the road is looking just the same as before, but two inches lower. But Mistress Fournier's garden – she loves flowers – holds a new promise when at last she and her son straighten their backs and view their handiwork.

The Country Club has honoured the tourists from the S.S. *Antigua* by making them members for an evening and throwing a dance for their amusement. The band is larger than the 'Cambridge's', and what it lacks in rhythm it makes up in decorum.

The floor is spacious, so spacious that at the far end the band is inaudible. There are no walls – just a floor, a roof on pillars and the great outside.

The lights shine a distance across the garden. Beyond that are tall dark trees from whose bewitching shade come moths and fireflies, gnats, bats and the sportive mosquito.

A brilliant array of dancers circles the floor. A dog runs barking from couple to couple, till he fixes attention on the band. The tourists are rubbing shoulders with the high tone of Trinidad. Lawyers and bank clerks, grocers and doctors, schoolmasters, business men, professors from the Imperial College, a Government official, planters and lads from the oilfields. Scotsmen and creoles, Latin Americans, Englishwomen, French, Germans, Spaniards, Greeks, Americans, Jews.

The tourists keep to themselves. They are ashore for a good time. Tomorrow they make another port. All is romance, on a 135 dollar round-trip. Bats swerving away from the lights, flies in the highball, bites on the legs: these are small things compared with the glamour of the tropic night: the tree-frogs croaking in the trees, the nagging cicadas and the fitful beacons of the fireflies.

But the residents are different. They have been here dozens of times. Though they affect to despise it, they come over and over again. Some come because it is the only place they can dance without losing caste. Others because it is the only place they can gain it. With their small salaries they cannot entertain at their cheap homes. But here they pass an evening in society, with a few carefully spaced drinks, for which they can sign chits. They are living, moving in the right circle. Others again come to add to their store of gossip, to observe all probable scandals and invent all possible ones. To a few – and these are very young – it is a place of gaiety, to dance, to flirt, to realise new powers of attraction.

On drones the band. The couples sidle round. The dog, chased off the floor, returns with his mate. Mr. and Mrs. Carmody are sitting in stolid silence by the floor. And the desirable young Mr. Dewsbody is favouring Miss Lomas with a waltz.

The market women are already sitting on the pavement with their baskets round them, babies in their arms. The bright moon casts heavy shadows across doorways. Shoes echo down silent roadways. Shadows follow stealthily. Ducking, they run abreast; then dart ahead, with each step growing more gigantic.

Already there are human bundles piled in doorways. The destitute of daytime are falling into crime again. They twitch and shudder on the damp grass.

Ten joints further on, the nightshift is working on the pipeline, shovelling up to the thighs in welling water. Lightermen are working under arc lights on the aluminium boat, reloading bauxite for New. Orleans.

A group of Negroes is standing round the sweet drinks stand on St. Vincent Jetty waiting for the last batch of sailors. The *Trinidad* left for Tobago two hours back. But it is always worth staying on when the Americans are in port. Sometimes it is better than the movies, always cheaper.

A car drives up and three sailors get out. The middle one is berserk drunk. He has been ordered back by the S.P., but he resents it. He feels he could go on for another couple of hours.

His buddies calm him in an infuriating way. "That's all right, Schnozzle," they say, binding his arms tight. "That's O.K."

"What's O.K.? Leggo my arms and tell me what's O.K." He suddenly wrenches himself free and staggers back from them. "You gotta drink?" he says. "Hey, gimme a drink."

"You had enough, Schnozzle," one buddy says. "You had a skinful."

"Whadda pal," Schnozzle says. "Whadda pal." His eyes catch sight of the sweet-drinks stand and he reels over. "Hey," he says, "hey, you nigger. I wanna Scotch."

The stall-keeper shakes his head. "Lemonade. Orangeade. Coca cola. What you want?"

"You heard what I want, nigger," says Schnozzle. "Double Scotch, an' make it snappy."

The Negroes standing by the stall come closer. They stand silent, waiting, some with a smile.

"You want a soft drink?" says the stall-keeper.

"Soft drink to hell," says Schnozzle, throwing his buddies aside. "Get away all of you. What the hell all you riggers wanna come around here for?"

"We just standin'," says one.

Another says: "We just watchin'."

"We just laffin'," says a third voice from behind.

One of the buddies takes Schnozzle's arm: "Come on," he says, "let's beat it." The other runs over to two more sailors who are coming up.

"Lea' me alone," Schnozzle bawls. "Lemme deal with these coons." He shoves forward and catches one by the arm. "You know what we do wi' you niggers back home? We keep you black bastards in your place."

"But," says the same voice from the back, "you not back home. You in Trinidad."

"God damn!" says Schnozzle. He picks a glass from the stand and tries to crash it on the nearest head. It smashes in his own hand, blood streams from his palm.

In an instant the stall is overturned. Bottles and glasses crash. Negroes and sailors come running up. They form in two lines, hurling glasses, bottlenecks, stones at one another. Between them, in no-man's-land, the stall-keeper pokes his head above the stall pleading for his stock. A man, caught by jagged glass, falls crying, his hand pressed to his cheek.

There is a whistle, more whistles. Two policemen run up, followed by the Shore Patrol. Bang, whack, thump. Three sailors are lying on their backs. One is out like a light, another cut from eye to mouth. The third writhes on the ground, holding his belly with his hands as he vomits.

The policemen look round. There is not a Negro in sight, bar the stall-keeper.

"What's the hell's goin' on around here?" pants the Shore Patrol.

No one answers.

"You're for it," says the S.P. "Here, get these guys aboard. Take 'em straight across to the hospital. Send another launch back."

The wounded sailors are helped aboard the launch. The rest follow very soberly. The prospect of a hundred and twenty-five dollar fine is like a cold douche.

The stall-keeper rises from the wreckage like a phoenix. "Eh, eh," he says, "see what they do to my stall."

"You hurt?" asks the S.P.

The stall-keeper feels himself all over slowly. "I think so," he says doubtfully.

"Hell," says the S.P., "this is the best break you had in years. Sold out completely. Send the check in in the mornin'." He turns to the policemen: "O.K.," he says. "Uncle Sam's payin' for this."

The clocks begin to strike twelve and from the Police Station the relief squad marches forth, clicking its heavy boots on the pavement: a row of black buzzards stalking in step down St. Vincent Street.

PART II

I. THE TOURIST'S TRINIDAD

TRINIDAD is the southernmost of the West Indian islands, whose arc separates the Atlantic from the Caribbean and the Gulf of Mexico. It lies close to the coast of Venezuela, stretching its arms out south and north to the mainland. Slightly to the south the great delta of the Orinoco flows into the sea, one half of its muddy current washing the southern shore of Trinidad, the other coursing northwards up the channel made by mainland and island. This channel is treacherous, shallow and inconstant. Though Columbus approached the island from the south, when he discovered it and named it Trinidad, punning geography and religion, today all steamers sailing to Port of Spain use the northern channel, even though they are coming from the south.

The approach to Trinidad is made through the Bocas, those deep but narrow channels between the islands stringing the northern arm of Trinidad to the shore. These islands rise steep from the sea, hummocks of rock as closely grown with shrubs and trees as the hair on a dog's coat: gigantic bouquets of greenery floating on the sea.

From the steamer you can see in coves, on headlands, the weekend houses of the rich, their launches anchored near the pier-heads, gardens like patches of baldness in the thick undergrowth.

You pass from the long waves of the Atlantic into the calm of the great bay formed by the western coastline. On the left is Trinidad, thickly wooded, rising up in jagged lines of mountains. There is a small island, whose white Spanish style buildings glisten in the sun. "Whose house is that?" you ask. That is the prison island of Carrera, where longterm prisoners serve their sentences. You wonder if it is half as lovely within as it is from without.

Further down the coast there is a cluster of even smaller islands, lying low in the water. They look like plates of trees and houses. They are the Government quarantine islands, which are let cheaply to holidaymakers on condition that they are evacuated immediately they are needed for isolation purposes. People round you murmur that they remind them of Japan.

The mountains recede and in the shovel-shaped plain you catch the first sight of Port of Spain, rows of white houses set among palms. In the distance, someone points out the quay and the customs house.

If you have never been to the tropics before, there exists in your mind a concept of a tropical island, based on photographs, on films, on Seabrook, Somerset Maugham and the Mutiny on the Bounty. It is a queer hotchpotch of tropical derelicts and native girls with gardenias in their hair, a pendulum swinging from cliches like 'island paradise' and 'tropic night' to fears of scorpions, syphilis and snakes, a *collage* of rosy daydreams and black nightmare.

As the boat drops anchor half a mile from shore, bags packed, passport in pocket, you lean over the rail, wondering with fear and anticipation how far the reality will correspond with your imaginings. Launches race out from the quay. The immigration officers board. You show your return ticket, without which you must make a deposit of fifty pounds before you land. You are rather surprised, because you had imagined that a citizen of the British Empire was allowed to travel through the Empire without let and hindrance. But it does not worry you much, because you are a tourist and you have the money if necessary to make the deposit. You go back to the rail and see the company's tender come up. It is towing a barge, steered by a Negro stripped to the waist. The sweat on his back glistens in the sun and he looks up and shouts to someone aboard. His white teeth burst from the split in his black face.

You go down the gangway and get into the launch. The first person you notice is the Negress who came aboard at Barbados and slept deck passage. When she was on deck she lay in her deckchair wearing blue mules. She was surrounded by her own colour and she was like a queen, as gracious and as certain of her position. Now she is sitting opposite you, between two men in white ducks. She is dressed in electric blue sateen and has a floppy summer hat on her head. She has rubbed some white liquid on her face, which makes the cheeks look mauve. Her lips are painted, her nails lacquered scarlet. She is dressed to kill.

Yet the whole effect has failed. She is the only coloured passenger in a tender full of whites. The two men in ducks have moved as far from her as they can. Despite the war paint, she looks shy and embarrassed.

The man sitting next the Negress takes off his hat and wipes his forehead. His hair is black and curly. You would not have noticed it in England or in the States, but here you suddenly realise that he is not pure white, but half-caste. His own colour-consciousness towards the Negress gives this fact special importance in your mind. You look at him more closely. His lips are slightly everted and darkish. His complexion is very red, a network of tiny veins is spread just below the skin. His pores are enlarged and deep, like a doll's face made of stockinet.

He is a type whom you will meet very frequently on the island. And the man on the other side of the Negress is also a common type. His complexion is sheer white. There is no touch of colour on the cheeks, no sign of sunburn. He is whiter than any European living in the tropics. He has the same curly hair as the red-faced man.

You will notice many men and women of this sort among the middle class during your stay in Trinidad, great numbers of tall, slender girls with small heads, pale complexions, and black curly hair. As a physical type, they are pleasing, until you realise that there is little fire in their fine eyes, their delicate features are almost immobile and their small heads empty. The white blood in them seems to have run thin and lassitude has usurped the place of breeding.

But at the moment experience does not carry you this far. You are intent on landing, passing through the customs with the aid of one instead of four porters, getting yourself and your hand luggage into the same taxi.

The taxi takes you rapidly through the city to your hotel. Your eyes, keen to absorb new impressions, are strained by the ugliness of the houses. You have travelled elsewhere. You have seen the filth and squalor of tenement life in the great cities of America and Europe, seen but avoided it for the grandeur of civic centres. But here in Port of Spain the civic centre is so small that you cannot ignore the shabbiness that surrounds it. The impression that the entrance through the Bocas wrought in you is shattered by this first sight of the city.

The town, heavy with moisture, is like a hot-house. Your shirt sticks first to your armpits, then your shoulder-blades and finally your breast. The corrugated iron with which almost every house is roofed absorbs and gives out the beating rays of the sun. Pedestrians creep down the narrow corridors of shadow made by walls.

I have met no one whose first feeling on landing in Port of Spain was not one of repulsion. It is not prepossessing. "I don't know what it is," said an American lady to me, who had only spent one evening in Port of Spain. "There was something I didn't like about the place at all, something evil, something corrupt."

It is obvious that the first impressions of everybody are governed chiefly by the occasion of their arrival. Port of Spain seen for an evening, any evening in the year, would give the impression of evil and corruption. To me, arriving at dawn, this feeling was not so strong. It was just that in everything I encountered, there was something wrong. The service I met with at the hotel, the streets, the houses, the people, all seemed inefficient, shabby, second-rate. Then, in the afternoon, it rained in torrents for three hours, while I sat drinking rum with a British mercantile marine. During the rain it grew if anything hotter, and afterwards the streets steamed under the evening sun.

This first impression of evil and corruption is partial, but not untrue. It is recognised by the natives, who talk of their island as 'Trickydad.' "I have never met so evil a place," said a Government official after two years' residence. "I never believed that a place could be completely and utterly evil. I don't want to believe it, but I'm afraid it's true of this place." The portrait of the city which precedes this chapter shows what forms this corruption takes. As my job was to investigate whatever I found in the island, I pursued the analysis of this corruption further and found elements and movements which I believe will finally eradicate the evil from the life of the island.

But in this chapter I wish to give the impression that any observant tourist gets of the life of the island. The desires, with which he may have started, of getting to know and understand the life of the Negroes quickly disappear. The Tahitian visions of sliding down waterfalls with flowery native girls give way to the reality of the Englishman's life in the tropics. He spends his time with people of his colour at the more expensive hotels and the Country Club. He learns that it is not done to ride in buses or drink in rum shops. The Negroes he meets are servants, whose natural independence has been corrupted by low wages and big tips. He dislikes them and generalises his dislike to include all Negroes and East Indians in the island.

The middle-class white people whom he meets receive him with open arms. In a small closed community any stranger is interesting and the West Indians are naturally generous. Parties are given for him. He is driven round the island to bathe at different beaches.[1] He is taken shooting in the marshes round Caroni. He spends weekends fishing, bathing, boating out at the islands. He visits the Siegerts distillery, where Angostura bitters and bouquet rum are made; he is given a free drink in their excellent bar, a small bottle of bitters and a swizzle-stick. He has tea at the monastery of St. Benedict. He is shown round the oil refineries and the fields. He goes over a sugar refinery, stops a weekend with a planter and learns how lazy the workers are, the extent of praedial larceny. He visits the pitch lake, where Raleigh caulked his ships. He is told how suddenly whole trees appear from the pitch, rise feet into the air, and in a few days sink again from sight. He looks at the mud volcanoes, little coffee-coloured wells bubbling up into cones, like giant ant-heaps, and sees where suddenly a few years ago the road was shifted twenty feet from its path by subterranean action. In the south he is shown the relics of the hurricane that struck the island three years back, the fallen palms and uncleared desolation. He sees the Black Virgin of Siparia, the wooden image that they say was found in the jungle and has powers of healing. Calypso players are hired so that he may hear the local music and they sing songs decorously expurgated for his delight. He

---

1. *The bathing on the southern and western coasts is bad, because of the dirt discharged by the Orinoco. To the north and east there are good beaches. But to reach them a car takes anything from half an hour to three hours. Bathing is much better in Tobago.*

goes to the races at Arima, plays golf and tennis, rides, plays bridge and poker, dances.

In the cars of friends he will visit all places of beauty, La Blanchisseuse, the Blue Basin, Maracas Falls. They will picnic under the palm trees, swim by moonlight. They will drive through the forest reserves, pick pineapples by the roadside, look down from the hills on the broad grapefruit groves.

Three weeks or more can be spent in this way with the greatest pleasure. In Trinidad, among the middle class, there are as many cultured, charming and individual people as anywhere in Europe or elsewhere. The opportunities for sport are enormous for those who have money and leisure to enjoy them. The first impression of evil and corruption fades before enjoyment. The enemy becomes the coloured man. There is a diversity of opinion among the people you meet at lunch and dinner, at cocktail parties, bathing. Some are sympathetic to the coloured people, some openly pronounce their hatred. Some say they 'love' the Negroes: others that they are a lazy, good-for-nothing people, who have got above themselves and ought to be controlled with the knout. Some say that the East Indians are the backbone of the island, thrifty, industrious and well deserving. Others that the Negroes are like children, good-hearted, swift to anger, quick to forget: whereas the East Indians never forget a good deed or a bad, nourishing it in their hearts.

But whatever the opinions, sympathetic or antagonistic, foolish or critical, they all agree in regarding the coloured people as different or inferior. The choice lies between benevolent patronage and aggressive tyranny.

The tourist can see almost every activity of the island from on top. But if he tries to vary the angle from which he views the island, he immediately encounters suspicion, discouragement and prejudice. None of those things need prevent him from making further discoveries. He is not bound, as every white man who earns his living in the island is bound, by economic blackmail. He has no job to lose.

But there exists in each of us a nucleus of prejudice and conventionalism, formed in our childhood and governing a great deal of our conduct. The tourist usually succumbs to the kind warnings of his *bourgeois* friends. He resigns all efforts to penetrate beyond the middle class. The men and women passing in the street are just Negroes, Chinese, East Indians, an unknown rabble.

After his holiday, his memory filled with the recollection of a dozen warm and generous friends, his album crowded with indifferent snapshots, half a dozen bottles of rum and a cocoa pod in his suitcase, the traveller returns to his native land. The pod breaks. He finishes the rum the evening before making port. He shows the photographs to boring visitors. And the memory of a very pleasant holiday matures with time.

The chapters which follow this are devoted to what any tourist would find, leaving that small group of delightful middle-class people, and meeting those who form the majority of the islanders, the petty *bourgeois* and the working class.

In the following chapters the reader must not forget the tourists' reality, the bridge, the drinks at sundown, the pleasant weekends for those who can afford them. He must not forget the Government functions, such as the prize-givings, select concerts at Government House. Nor the frolics of the younger *bourgeois* rips, trips in the moonlight, love in a Ford V8, The dimity curtains, imaginative Victorian vases, bamboo whatnots, ormolu clocks and German oleographs that comprise the furniture of most respectable middle-class families. And most importantly, he must not forget the enormous riches amassed by a dozen or more families whose enterprise may have exceeded scruples; a generation of commercial pioneers, unhindered by education or tradition: men who came to the island to make fortunes and have stayed to double them. This aristocracy, who may proudly boast that they began as nobodies, and have made their way by their own efforts, have now political and economic dominion of the island. The reader should bear this in mind, as he follows the progress that has been made in social services and other spheres.

2. WHERE'S MR. GANGES?

"In no aspect of our inquiry have we been more impressed by the evidence placed before us and by our own investigations than as regards the conditions in which large numbers of the working population, both urban and rural, are housed. Here, as in other directions to which reference will be made hereafter, the policy of those responsible appears to have been influenced by bad traditions, and a system of what are termed 'barrack' dwellings, which dates back to the early days of indentured labour, is prevalent. Under the terms of indenture it was provided that 'suitable dwellings will be assigned to immigrants free of rent and such dwellings will be kept by the employer in good repair.' These 'dwellings' for the most part consisted of a long wooden building roofed with galvanized iron, divided from end to end by a partition and sub-divided on both sides into a series of single rooms, each of which would be occupied by an indentured immigrant and his wife and family. These are designated as 'back-to-back' dwellings as distinct from those which comprise one range only of single rooms. . . . We visited barrack dwellings in Port-of-Spain which are indescribable in their lack of elementary needs of decency and for which, we learned, monthly rents varying from twelve to fifteen shillings a room are paid."

(*Report of Commission on Trinidad and Tobago Disturbances*, 1937, p. 5)

IT is impossible for anybody visiting Trinidad not to see the sort of houses in which the majority of the population is forced to live. And the reason why it is impossible is that there has been no control of building development, at any rate since the island has been in the hands of the British. Where there is a road, houses have been built. Roads have not been built to connect one house with another and both with the main street. There has been no planning of villages, no centre of village life in squares.

Roads have been constructed from one place to another. Along these roads for miles on miles of ribbon development, the hovels hug the roadway. Port of Spain becomes San Juan; San Juan, St. Joseph, Tunapuna, Tacarigua, Arouca, Arima with scarcely a break. Two straggling lines of wood shacks roofed with galvanised iron, an arbitrary boundary between each name. You cannot see when you leave one village and enter the next. Driving down the East Road, you think what a big place Port of Spain is, and you find that you're five villages away.

There has been no planning of towns or villages and the most primitive planning of houses. I have seen houses as bad in Southern and Central America: but the only places I have seen as ugly are the native quarter in Casablanca and some hick towns in the United States. Driving round the island, wandering through the poor districts of Laventille and John John, I was struck over and over again by the appalling ugliness of these houses.

In certain of the country districts, houses are built from wooden poles with a mixture of mud and grass for walls and trash for roofs. They are poorer houses than these horrors of galvanised iron and packing-cases. They are more dangerous to live in, because the trash harbours tarantulas and sometimes snakes. But the way they are made, with the wall of the gallery slightly irregular, and blue lines washed on the mud, distinguishes them from the wooden shacks, whose walls are botched with hammered-out tins. They become part of the landscape in which they are set: whereas the lines of wooden boxes look like the litter of a city dump, a car wreck by the roadside with seats uptilted, tyres rotted from rims.

At first I felt great embarrassment on entering a barrack yard. I did not know how people would regard me. I felt so implicated in the white man's shame at letting people live in such conditions that I was too guilty to intrude.

For help and courage I went to Dr. Marcano, the officer for Public Health in Port of Spain. I asked him if he would show me round the city, indicating fair samples of the good, bad and medium houses in which the workers lived. I had been told of 'East Indian Hotels', where Indians slept on spaces marked on the floor. I said I wanted to see these.

The doctor, a middle-aged man of charm and education, who had studied and practised medicine in England, gave me every assistance in his power. We arranged to meet next morning at half-past eight and begin the tour.

I found that he had misunderstood me, when I asked to see an East Indian hotel. He had thought that I meant a hotel kept by an East Indian. But I wasn't sorry, because we blundered lucky. The doctor took me to a block in the centre of the town. We turned down a passage, which said Ganges Restaurant. This passage divided at the end, Ganges to the left, and boarding-house to the right. Here the doctor made his second mistake and charged up the stairs of the boarding-house, shouting: "The doctor. Good morning. The doctor from the Town Hall. The doctor."

A Negro was shaving in the hall and he jerked his head and out of a little scullery emerged a large lady in cream, wiping her hands on her skirt. "Oh, doctor," she said. "Good morning, doctor."

"Good morning, Madame," said the doctor, "come to look round." He turned abruptly and strode across the room. It was about thirty feet square and, from the tables set about, was obviously a dining-room. But one side of the room was partitioned off into sleeping cubicles with walls about seven feet' high.

The doctor grunted. "This isn't the 'Ganges'," he said severely.

"No, doctor," said the large lady in cream. "This is a boarding-house."

"You haven't been here long," said the doctor.

"Seven years," said the large lady. "Don't you remember me from the last time you came?"

The doctor turned and made for the stairs. "Might as well look it over," he said, striding up.

But he stopped before he reached the top. Water was dripping from a skylight onto the stairs. "Water," said the doctor. "Water. What's all this? What's all this water mean?"

"Oh, doctor," said the large lady in cream, "it's the landlord, doctor. I tell him. I tell him. I tell him. And he does nothing, doctor, nothing."

The doctor grunted again. "Can't keep a place like this. Scandal. Against all the rules."

"With my own money, doctor," said the large lady, shaking with self-pity. "How can I repair this? I'm a poor woman, doctor."

The top floor was a garret covering the whole storey. But it had been divided up into a dozen or more closets, just large enough to take a bed. Most had no direct lighting and the partitions were made of cardboard about a quarter of an inch thick.

The doctor burst. "What's all this? It's irregular. It's most irregular, woman. Can't have it. Can't have it at all."

"Irregular," protested the lady in cream. "No, doctor, no. I have only bachelors. Only single gentlemen. No, doctor, not irregular."

I looked into one of the interior bedrooms and in the gloom I saw a large double bed.

"You'll have to change all this," said the doctor. "It's most unhygienic. Most unhygienic."

"Come and see the bathroom," said the large lady. "Please, doctor, come and look at my bath."

We went downstairs again, this time to street level. There was an old mattress lying behind the front door. The doctor kicked it. "What's this, woman?"

The large lady has rushed ahead to what looked like a closet under the stairs. "That's mine, doctor. It's going away. But here's the bathroom."

The doctor wasn't going to be rattled. "What's that?" he asked, pointing to a wardrobe lying on its back under the stairs. "That's going away, too, doctor," said the landlady, snapping on the light in the bath-closet. The walls were of rough cement. As is usual, there was no bath: just a drain in the floor and a douche with a battered shower which leaked in a steady stream. "There, doctor," she said triumphantly. "And the landlord does nothin'. Time and again. Time and again, I've asked him."

"You're a rich woman," said the doctor. "You must be making a lot of money here. Dividing your rooms up like that. Give it a wash over. And see you get this trash cleared away."

"A rich woman! Would I be here, doctor, if I was? You can be sure, no. Dollar a week I get for the rooms. Dollar fifty, two dollars a day for full board. No, doctor, I'm a poor, poor woman."

"Well, see you get this place into decent shape before I get back," said the doctor, "or you'll be getting a summons,"

As we went out he said: "Trouble is we haven't got any decent bye-laws yet. We can't do anything till they come into force. Got to bully them."

We went across the passage to the 'Ganges,' and as we climbed the stairs, the doctor called: "The doctor. Doctor. Doctor. Doctor from the Town Hall."

We burst on a harassed group of East Indians, huddled in the entrance of a kitchen off the hall. They looked up with hopeless resignation. "Mr. Ganges?" said the doctor. "Where's Mr. Ganges?"

A man with a grey beard stepped forward, muttering a long Indian name. "The doctor," said the doctor. "Come to look around."

We walked through four eating-rooms. Two men and many flies were having breakfast. Then, like a pointing hound, the doctor made for a corner and pulled back a door. "Filthy," he said. "Filthy."

"Yes, doctor," said the man, shutting the door.

The doctor had already opened the next door. This was a bathroom, partly tiled. The shower did not drip enough to splash the eight chickens cowering in a crate against the wall. From the smell of the crate, it seemed as if they ought to have been in the room next door.

"What's that, man?" asked the doctor, pointing to a tub next to the chicken crate.

The Indian said nothing.

"An icebox, man," said the doctor. "Food. You keep your food next to this crate. In a bathroom, man."

The Indian made a noise, the unrepentant admission of guilt.

"You can't do that, man," said the doctor.

The Indian was getting ready to make another noise, but the doctor was already off on another scent, He was grubbing under the stairs like a spaniel down a rabbit hole. The women in the kitchen looked on with defensive contempt.

"Cabbages," came the doctor's voice from the glory-hole. "A bed. Wood."

They gathered round in curiosity. I don't think they knew what he was going to find next.

"Yams," bellowed the doctor's voice. "A pair of ladies' knickers."

2. WHERE'S MR. GANGES?

He turned around. "Whose cabbages are these?"

The Indians looked at one another. Then they retired to the kitchen. Finally the man with the grey beard came back. "None of them," he explained, "had ever seen those cabbages before. They could only suppose that somebody had come in, deposited the cabbages among the yams, the bed and ladies' knickers and gone away again."

"Clear the rubbish away," said the doctor, and went into the kitchen.

"Yes, doctor," said Mr. Ganges. "Yes, doctor."

In the kitchen there was a dish of meat on a bench. The doctor waved his hand over it and some of the flies rose. The rest were too busy. "Look at that, man," said the doctor. "What you call that?"

The Indian nodded gravely. "Meat," he said.

We went to several other restaurants and in each case the attitude to the doctor was the same. Here were poor people trying to make a living in the best way they could: and the doctor came along from the Town Hall to harass them with a lot of silly nonsense about watercress carrying typhoid or the danger of having a water-closet in the kitchen. Their life was already complex. They had grown used to dealing with customers or with the pressure of landlords. But the doctor was difficult to place in their scheme of things. He had no profit motive. And so he appeared merely as a paid nuisance, a man who was hired to be nasty about a lot of trivial matters. Even when I gained the impression that the doctor was going to be obeyed, which was not often, I felt that he was going to be obeyed, not because what he said was wise, good or in their own interest, but because that was the easiest way of ridding oneself of a nuisance. I could tell that by the sceptical way they looked at the doctor when he was complaining of the drain from an upstairs lavatory passing over the loaves in a bakery. 'Health-fiend,' they were thinking, 'germ-crank. Haven't we had this drain here for years? Who's complained about being ill?'

I think that the doctor was giving me an exhibition of high efficiency. In his non-conducted tours he was probably more persuasive and less brusque. But it was quite obvious that the majority of the people with whom he was dealing had not accepted the most elementary ideas of hygiene on which his orders were based. The reason for this I shall explain in the next chapter.

In each case the Chinese were much cleaner than the Indians in their kitchens. For anybody to cook in kitchens which are little better than open sheds is very difficult. Gas and electric stoves are unknown in these kitchens. The fuel is charcoal and the food is cooked usually in open iron pots. Flies abound. Water-closets are seldom far away, and more often than not they are choked and stinking. There are few electric refrigerators. The icebox is usual. And it is difficult to store all perishable food in these boxes, which are not provided with trays and which open from on top.

Even when these difficulties are overcome there is the problem of the open drain. Numbers of sculleries have no closed drains, And if they do, the foul water often is taken off to an open ditch, where it flows sluggishly towards the sea.[1]

Education in hygiene for children and adults could do a certain amount. But the most useful effect that it could have would be to mobilise public opinion to demand the wholesale destruction of properties in which elementary hygiene is impossible.

After we had visited these restaurants we went to different slum dwellings in the city. Certain of these slums are built in barrack form. In the middle of the town they are in the centre of a block, approached down an alley or passage under a house. They are either built in single rows or set back to back. The prices charged usually do not vary from singles to back-to-backs. The single rows are ventilated from the front and from a high long window in the back. Back-to-backs have the same high long window in the back, but as there is another room the other side it means really that the stale air of one room is transmitted to the next. The measurement of each of these rooms is about twelve feet by twelve. The average population per room is 2.5 persons. But this estimate omitted to count in children under twelve. Since many of these rooms are occupied by single persons, a large number of others have five or six occupants at least.

In each of these rooms one family eats, lives and sleeps. Because few have mosquito nets they usually sleep with the shutters closed. Cooking is done sometimes in the open: sometimes in an adjoining shed about twice the size of a rural water-closet, and sometimes under the shelter of the jutting roof.

In Illustration A there are twelve single barrack-rooms on the right and on the left twenty-four back-to-backs. The galvanised iron set on end in front of each room hides from the central alleyway a small space which is used as kitchen, scullery and larder. The slop-water is carried away in the narrow gulleyways seen either side of the alley. The rent of these rooms is three dollars fifty a month, which means that the whole property brings in $1632,[2] or £380 a year. The doctor told me that he estimated that a property like this

---

1. *A good idea of the level of public hygiene can be gathered from a remark of one of the San Fernando borough councillors. During an inter-view, he was telling me about the drainage scheme for the town. "Is that going to take just the sewerage, or the slop- and bath-water?" I asked. "In closed drains?" he asked. "Man, there's not a city in the world with closed drains for bath-water."*
2. *The Trinidad currency is based on the pound. One cent equals one halfpenny, one dollar four shillings .and twopence,*

would cost around four thousand dollars to erect. Estimating the cost at five thousand, a landlord would get over thirty per cent per annum on his outlay on building. Adding in the cost of land in a poor part of the town, the profit would lie about midway between twenty and thirty per cent.

The lavatories in this barracks were set on the far side of the back-to-backs. There was no covered way to them, and a resident in the near rooms on the right has to walk nearly two hundred feet to use them. There were a dozen closets to the whole barracks and two showers, which can be seen at the end of the range in the photograph.

"One must aim at an ideal," said Dr. Marcano. "But one must often be content with very much less." In this case, he wanted to have every third room demolished so that each roam had ventilation on three sides. But the owner, realising that he might be urged to do that, was assiduously painting the corrugated iron, so that the barracks always had an air of comparative smartness.

While we were at these barracks – where by the way we caused uproarious laughter by asking out of curiosity where the lavatories were – a conversation took place between the doctor and one of the tenants that seemed to me to illuminate the attitude both of the doctor and the tenant.

I had said to the doctor, just by way of conversation, that I didn't see how people could stand living in such conditions. It was a silly remark, because I knew exactly why they stood it. But the doctor stopped an East Indian and said to him: "You've seen the nice houses they are building. Which would you prefer, to live here or to live in one of them?"

"What do you mean?" asked the man.

"To live in one of the new houses or to live here. Which would you prefer?" In Trinidad *bourgeois* circles, as elsewhere in the world, the conscience-saving argument is popular that the working-class really likes to live in squalor.

The man didn't answer.

"You needn't be afraid of me," said the doctor. "I'm the doctor from the Town Hall. I just want to know."

If anything, this would have made the man afraid, because landlords hold the threat of eviction over the heads of anyone who is behind with his rent, laying complaints.

"You mean..." said the man. "I've got a wife and family. How I pay more rent?"

"But supposing, man, the rent was the same. Then which you prefer?"

The man shook his head. He knew that the rent wasn't the same. His imagination was incapable of conceiving the new houses at the rent of the barrack-rooms. "I was rich once," he said. "I had money. I understand you perfectly. But there are children."

The doctor shook his head and we walked away. We went round to a barracks owned by an English company. The first barracks had been owned by a local man, Only a court conviction could force him to do anything about his property. The coats of paint safeguarded him. The doctor had no hope of getting a conviction. The English property made no pretence at being in repair. They felt powerful enough without that. "At first I thought they were free lodging for their workers," said the doctor. "But they aren't They charge the same rents as the rest."

There was no semblance of order in this barracks. Rain and slop-water stood in pools. Cooking was done in little sheds, papered with old newspapers and movie magazines.

"The trouble is that at the moment we can only get the landlord on the Nuisance Act," said the doctor. "If we can prove a nuisance, then we can get the place... But a landlord will drag out and drag out proceedings. Says he's going away for two months. This excuse; that excuse. And then finally he makes some change, and all that time and money's lost."

He pointed to some barracks across the way. "That's one of the worst. We've been after the chap for months. We write and tell him to put his property in order within thirty days. Two days before the time is up he writes and says he's been down to the place and can't see anything wrong with it. We give him specifications. He lets more weeks go by and then challenges our specifications. So it goes on month after month, and every month he collects his rent."

I thought of the Commissioners' report. "Our inquiries lead us to the conclusion that, despite Slum Clearance and Housing Ordinances applicable to Port of Spain, the housing conditions in the city area are not likely to be dealt with in the near future in any prompt and satisfactory manner. It is in our view that powers of slum clearance vested in a City Corporation *composed in sufficient part of persons who are owners of or who have interests in insanitary property to create opposition to schemes for its abolition,*[1] will not be effectively carried out, and that in such circumstances slum clearance is doomed to failure and the public interest must suffer."

We visited Slum Clearance Area No. 1. Illustration B is a view of part of it. In this case the council has provided alternative dwellings at what is called Gonzalez Place. The rentals at these new shacks are little more than in the old slum clearance area. But accommodation is not sufficient even for those in the area. The shacks are already full, and though most of the dwellings in the slum clearance area have been abandoned, some people go on living there, as can be seen from the photograph.

What usually happens with condemned barracks is that when the owners are compelled to pull them down, they put in their place dwellings such as Illustration C, which conform to the building regulations. For example, if six villas rise where twenty-four barrack-rooms stood before, for those six villas

---

1. My *italics*.

the owner demands a rental equivalent to that of twenty-four barrack-rooms plus perhaps a little for the expenditure of fresh capital.

In consequence, workers' hovels are being pulled down and replaced by homes for families on a higher salary level. The evicted workers are forced into other barracks or into houses such as Illustration D. This particular house is an old house in Port of Spain. The house has very little furniture in it because the residents are so impoverished. It is divided up into separate rooms, which are even worse equipped than barracks, because they have not been planned as separate dwelling-places. The upper floor is a garret under bare corrugated iron. This gets so hot during the day that you burn your hand if you touch the roof. It is scarcely possible to stay in the room for more than a couple of minutes. The roof-beams divide the garret naturally into four or five sections, each of which is let off to two people at night for a few cents. Two of the sections showed signs of permanent occupation.

I asked the doctor to whom this property belonged. He told me that it had belonged to a high dignitary of the Church. He had intended to prosecute this cleric for allowing people to live in such surroundings. But it was pointed out to him that it was impossible for him as a good churchman to do this. He had found a way out by deciding to prosecute the tenants for living in such a building, when the property was disposed of to an old lady.

Later, not in the company of Doctor Marcano, I saw another effect of the destruction of workers' houses and the erection of expensive villas. I visited a house in a very respectable square, not two minutes' walk from the savannah and the fashionable Queen's Park Hotel. This house had been built for a middle-class family of medium size. It had had a large living-room and three bedrooms of decent size. The house had been rented by a family with several children. The bedrooms had been divided up with partitions of paper. Twenty people were sleeping in the house, their cooking being done in the single kitchen.

More slums are caused by the overcrowding of people into buildings that would be hygienic for a few than by buildings that are unhygienic for anyone. The effect of housing regulations which condemn privately owned houses without making any provision for the people evicted from these houses is to drive them either into similar barracks or to create slums from property which *was* formerly perfectly good. The solution of the housing problem in Port of Spain is the acquisition of land-sites by the council and the public building of workers' dwellings at prices which they can pay. Such a course of action, as the Commissioners say, is impossible to envisage coming from a council many of whom own, or are the representatives of owners of, slum property.

When I put this solution to the doctor he rejected it hopelessly. Why, he said, should a private owner be expected to rebuild his property and then

When barracks like these

or hovels like these are destroyed

2. WHERE'S MR. GANGES?

they are replaced by model dwellings at three times the rental

and the workers are driven to live in houses like this.

receive only a fraction of the rental which he had formerly received? (In the light of the exorbitant rents charged there is a moral reason why he should do so; but it is certain that with things as they are no legal authority could be gained for this.) When I suggested an impartial board to assess the land at its site value his answer was: "But think of the litigation. Every case would be fought..." And, of course, there would be a union between all the property-owning classes, the local business man, foreign-vested interests and the ecclesiastical landlords.

The two forces in Port of Spain with the interest and the desire to act in this matter for the public interest are power-less. The British Government, according to the Charter granted to the city, has no authority to act in this case. The workers, in whose interest such legislation would be, are debarred from voting for their representatives because they have no financial qualifications as burgesses; and if they had they would find it hard to get the representatives with the property qualifications for office.

The middle class of Port of Spain is therefore comfortably entrenched against attack by a Government which, in this case, might be prepared to act in the interest of public health, or by the workers, whose health is being sapped by the greed of property owners represented on the city council.

An example of the way schemes initiated in the public good are sidetracked can be seen from the city drainage scheme. Most districts in Port of Spain have nothing but cesspit drainage. The Piccadilly and St. James's district is most in need of proper sewers. Yet the first place to get sewers is Woodbrook, a middle-class section of the city, recently built and equipped throughout by sanitary septic tanks. Piccadilly and St. James, though most in need, will probably have to wait till last.

Dr. Marcano offered a solution of the housing problem by two means. Firstly, Port of Spain must be expanded. At the present time houses are concentrated in the valleys running from the town up into the hills. This has been due, firstly, to the fact that houses have been built along main roads – a fact that the doctor hopes will be remedied by the recommendations of the town-planner at present working on the city – and, secondly, to the difficulty of obtaining water, a difficulty that has already been overcome by the new water scheme. Sewerage must be laid down in the hills (but will it be, in the light of Woodbrook?). Rentals cannot help being higher. But they must be met by an increase in wages.

This scheme seems to ignore certain facts. Dr. Marcano is an employee of the Port of Spain City Council. If the doctor advocated municipal housing, he would meet with strong opposition from the council, whose vested interests he was threatening. As it is, the increase in wages is already being demanded by the Port of Spain workers. This demand, if successful, will operate against a rather different group of capitalists than a municipal housing scheme. It absolves the doctor of any need to extend his job beyond the immediate duties of a public health officer into the sphere of politics. But it does not solve the housing problem.

The present demand for a wage increase is being made because of the increase in the cost' of living. Its objective is not for the worker to live in houses with a higher rental, but to live in his present house on a slightly better diet, able to buy those things of which increased costs have deprived him.

As I said above, there are two forces potentially capable of dealing with the housing question, the Government and the common people. As the Charter stands at present, neither can exert pressure on the council. Therefore, either the Government must curtail the Charter, taking away from the Trinidadians rights which have been vested in them, or those rights must be extended to a wider circle of Trinidadians. The first step would be retrogressive, an entire reversal of colonial policy, such as was taken in Cyprus. The second is a logical development of colonial policy, a step that should be tried fully before any retrogressive measures are taken.

Furthermore, if the British Government was instrumental in extending the democratic liberties of the Trinidadians, it would win over to its side the support of the working class, an ample compensation for the alienation of local property-holders. On the other hand, the infringement of the recognised rights of the council would unite the workers with the middle class and present the Government with a solid opposition.

These recommendations and arguments are based on the assumption that the Government of Trinidad intends to take serious steps to improve housing conditions in Port of Spain. There is no evidence, however, that they do. The Commissioners are more outspoken on the question of housing than on any other, since the vested interests are less powerful in this field than in the sugar and oilfield industries. But, as they point out, the Royal Commission of 1897 and the Olivier Commission of 1930 both condemned housing conditions in the West Indies, without anything being done. Their specific recommendation, despite their admission that the basic trouble lies in the constitution of the City Council, is that the import duties on building materials should be remitted in the case of workmen's dwellings. The effect of this provision, without any other clauses limiting rentals, will merely be to increase the profits of local builders and property-owners without substantially reducing rents.

In the sugar industry housing conditions vary from estate to estate. Employers of labour come from many different environments and in consequence approach their labour with different standards. One type of man, from small beginnings, becomes a large employer. All his life he has scraped and saved, sparing neither himself nor others in the accumulation of a wealth which he does not spend. He acknowledges no responsibility of employer towards labourer. His own struggle has been hard and he cannot conceive it possible that the struggle should be made easier for others. Representations may be made to him to improve the living conditions of his workers. Government officials may visit him and give him little talks about the new employer-employee relationship: how, by improving the conditions of work on the plantation, he will improve its quality. But these talks get nowhere. "I see nothing wrong with their conditions," he says, "and I think that stuff about pampering workers is nonsense."

Such a situation is usually due to the avarice and hardness of an individual. In other cases, the pressure is due more to economic causes and to the tradition of the plantations. The Olivier Commission said vaguely that bad housing was "traceable to historical conditions". The Commission of 1937 amplifies this by adding: "Equally it may be said that to the same conditions may be traced the absence, amongst a large section of the population, of a due sense of the value of home and family life, the importance of which in the creation of a stable, contented and self-respecting community, cannot be gainsaid."

Seen in historical perspective, the present state of affairs is easy to understand. From the earliest occupation of the colony, the most savage means were used for the recruiting of plantation labour. On the other hand, under the conditions of chattel slavery, that labour was bought body and soul and the plantation owner had an economic interest in the health of his workers. He had paid money for them and they were as valuable as cattle. The better their condition, the better the work they would give him and the healthier their children would be. The plantation owner was not interested in the family unit: he was interested in the growth of his slave population as a whole. Certain Negroes of remarkable physique were fed up, were laid off work and given special indulgence with the women of the plantation. They were the stallions of the slave stud.[1]

The transition from slavery to indentured labour caused a modification in the attitude of the plantation owner. He was only interested in what he could get out of his labourer during the period of the indenture. As his children were free, it did not matter whether they were healthy or not. It

---

1. *The 'sweet man' of today is probably a survival of the slave-stallion. The 'sweet man' is kept by his woman in return for his favours. But he has almost none of the stigma of the European gigolo. He is envied, and his supposed sexual superiority is a matter of admiration. Maintenance of 'sweet men' is not confined to prostitutes and Society women, as in more civilised communities. Peasant women have them, too: and all they demand is fidelity. I have seen a peasant woman beat her 'sweet man' in the street, with a whole crowd standing by laughing: and by the time she had got through with him, he was lucky to have his trousers on.*

did not matter if a man's health was ruined by the end of his service as an indentured labourer.

The further transition to wage-slavery meant a further decline in moral responsibility. By this time the population of the island was increasing faster than the demand for labour. The value of the individual worker correspondingly decreased, because he could easily be replaced. The barrack system was the cheapest way of housing the workers. It had persisted from the time of slavery and no economic argument presented itself for its abolition. It is true that visiting Commissions, notorious in the eyes of local employers for sentimental humanitarianism, expressed horror at the conditions under which workers were living. But, with the exception of a few plantations, up to this present time, nothing has been done to remedy the situation.

The human conscience needs constantly to be satisfied that what a man does for his own interest is at the least not morally wrong. For one group of human beings to exploit and oppress another group, to treat them as animals or worse than animals, it is necessary to evolve some conscience-salve. This is the origin of the belief, widely held and almost as widely expressed, that the coloured workers are animals or worse than animals. The very condition in which they have been forced to live is made the reason why they should continue to live in that way. When the coloured worker rebels against this treatment, demanding the right to a greater share of the profits of his labour so that he, too, may live as a human being should, the animal becomes either 'a wild beast' or a 'maniac'. He cannot be treated as other people are. Anyone who says that he can is told that he does not know the temperament of the Negro or the East Indian. Violent measures are invoked, the white man using rifles, shotguns and machine-guns against the raving madmen with sticks and stones and bottle-ends.

The picture of the Negro with sticks and stones, however, is not sufficiently bloodthirsty. Even to the West Indian, the idea of men with bottlenecks menacing an armed force is ridiculous. The concept of the berserk Negro brandishing a cutlass is, therefore, introduced. Practically every worker in the island has a cutlass. It is the tool with which he cuts cane, coconuts, bananas. He uses the reverse side for breaking the backs of snakes. Cutlasses were carried in the last strike. They were even brandished. But there's no evidence of anyone being wounded by one, and the casualty list does not read like the work of a mob bent on killing. Of police and volunteers, two were killed and nine wounded. Of civilians, fourteen were killed and fifty-nine wounded, forty-three with gunshot wounds.

This philosophy of the coloured man as an animal when he accepts the conditions of his life and as a maniac when he rejects them has been evolved over a century and a half. Economic though its basis is, it has become ingrained in the psychology of the Trinidadian employer. Arising as a means of justifying exploitation, it is now an irrational barrier to the discussion of better conditions. The processes of conciliation, which were only evolved in Europe after a long struggle by the workers, are resisted in the West Indies by this philosophy of colour superiority. It seems likely, therefore, that the struggle will be even longer and fiercer in these islands. For the present generation of employers, any modification of this belief will imply the acceptance of a monstrous burden of retrospective guilt.

In the oilfields, however, four factors make for the improvement of housing conditions.

Firstly, the oil industry is comparatively young. It took over from the plantations their attitude to labour and their method of housing. But it is not bound to them by a long tradition. The employers are men whose attitude in most cases is not insular. They have come from abroad and they have knowledge of better conditions in other fields.

Secondly, the oil industry is much more prosperous than agriculture. Out of their enormous profits they can easily afford to improve housing conditions, once they are convinced of the need.

Thirdly, the concentration of labour in the fields has made possible an organisation of the workers more efficient and more militant than in any of the other industries of the island. While the employers are fighting this union tooth and nail, they realise that the improvement of living conditions on the field, undertaken without pressure from the union, may be a tactically useful step.

Fourthly, if this housing is used, as it is being used, to make distinctions between one group of workers and another, the employers think they will be able to bring disunity into the ranks of the workers. Houses are distributed according to rank and not need, the size of a worker's house depending on his grade and not on the size of his family.

But though housing is of a higher standard on many of the fields, even on these it is an essential part of the system that there should be more workers than houses. A company house is the first reward of good behaviour, the sign that the worker may regard himself as a regular, unless he does something silly like becoming prominent in the union.

On other fields housing is as primitive or more primitive even than on the plantations. Outlying fields recruit their labour from copra workers, used to a very low standard of living. The workers are given plots on the field on which to erect their houses. The houses become company property when the worker leaves the field. No union meetings are allowed on the field and the company will place most of the workers' plots several miles from the village: so that a premium of enthusiasm is put on union attendance.

2. WHERE'S MR. GANGES?

The houses that the workers build themselves in such parts are crude shacks, some constructed from planks, others from trash. The nature of such a housing scheme does not encourage elaborate or permanent building. The sanitation is negligible.

Here, as elsewhere in the island where houses are provided by employers, the same rule applies. Housing conditions are as bad as employers can get away with, unless it serves a useful purpose to cause distinctions among the workers. Within that framework, however, there are degrees of enlightenment. 'A' believes that he will make the greatest profit by housing his men in smoke-blackened back-to-backs, with closets that no creature except the dung beetle would use. 'B' considers that a coat of paint would cheer things up. 'C' makes a serious effort to stamp out the hookworm, which is sapping half the energy of his men, is careful of the sanitary conditions, gives instruction in hygiene. 'D' doesn't think about things much: spasmodically he does repairs or lets his property fall into neglect.

The improvement of housing conditions throughout the island, however, will come not through the enlightenment of the men at the top, but from the active and persistent demand of those below that these conditions be improved. At the moment there are other questions which are more important in the workers' minds. The horror that the Commissioners feel, making a tour of the island, is in many cases a horror which is not shared by the occupants of the houses themselves.

In the hot, steamy climate of Trinidad a house is not a protection from the cold, but a shelter from the intermittent downpours. Fuel, the major problem of the poor in other climates, is needed only for cooking. To the Trinidadian, the first questions that must be answered are how shall he get the food to be cooked, the clothes for himself and his family, security of employment? When these are answered, he may turn to the housing problem with greater enthusiasm.

3. MEDICINE AND MAGIC

"They place a greater amount of confidence in all these healers and more enthusiastically support them than they do the regular members of the medical profession. Why? Are they more skilful? Not at all! But they give the patient some kind of explanation or reason or working hypothesis for the results they attempt to attain or claim to secure. In other words, they educate the people in their theories, beliefs or sophistries, and that is what the public wants – in fact, what it demands."
(Dr. J. B. Murphy, Inaugural Address to the American Medical Association, 1911.)

THE task of the Medical Service is broad. It is responsible not only for the treatment of disease, but its prevention: and for the improvement of sanitary conditions in districts not specifically delegated to other bodies, such as the Port of Spain and San Fernando city councils.

Malaria, hookworm, tuberculosis, deficiency and venereal diseases are the main causes of death and illness in the colony.

Malaria cannot be thoroughly eradicated in a colony producing copra. Coconuts thrive in damp, brackish country, and whatever care is taken, rain collects in empty husks and in the cups formed by the joint of the leaf with the main trunk of the palm. The anophelis mosquito, therefore, can never be completely stamped out. But it can be reduced in number by land-drainage, oiling and reclamation.

The malarial mosquito is not a producer, but a carrier of the disease. Infection is carried by the mosquito which has already sucked the blood of a malarial subject. Treatment, therefore, is very important for the reduction of infection. All malarial cases ought to be registered immediately and treatment undertaken. The absence of sick benefit makes this impossible in Trinidad. Despite this, however, 18,902 cases were reported in the year 1936 and there were 473 deaths (as compared with 606 in the previous year).

The Government scheme for land drainage and oiling is not as extensive as it might be. Only those areas under cultivation in the proximity of dwelling-places are considered necessary to be treated in this manner. Complaints are made by the Assistant Director of Medical Services that the friends and relations of subordinates in the service are always trying to get their own land drained and oiled, so that they may reap the profit of its increased value. This is a problem arising from the Government's setting

3. MEDICINE AND MAGIC

itself a limited objective. If it proposed to drain and oil all malarial districts, it could apply a common rate to all land, whether under cultivation or not: either all land, treated by the Government corps, should be liable to a tax which would pay all or part of the cost, or all should be done at the public expense. As it is, no long-term plan has been made along these lines.

Recently it was discovered that a mysterious disease which caused the patient to die in fourteen days through slow paralysis was transmitted by a small vampire bat, called *desmodus rufus:* 5.7 per cent of *desmodus rufus* were infected with the germs of paralytic rabies. This bat, entering a house at night, makes an incision in some part of the body, usually the toe, and gently fanning the sleeper with its wings, laps the flow of blood. This is done with such delicacy that the sleeper does not awake, knows nothing till he sees the blood upon the sheet next morning.

The Medical Service conducted a propaganda campaign against paralytic rabies, which succeeded in eliminating deaths from the disease. Encouraged by this, they intend to launch, what is far more ambitious, an attack on hookworm, using the same methods.

Though hookworm does not produce sensational deaths in the way that malaria does, it is probably even more destructive of human life and energy. In its first stage the hookworm larva lives in excrement. It survives there for forty-eight hours in dry places, but in wet its life is three weeks. It is found, therefore, chiefly in and around dirty closets. It enters the human body through the pores of the feet, especially the ankles. Once in the bloodstream it changes its larval form and circulates in the blood until it passes through the walls of the lungs. Thence it travels up the air-passages to the mouth, where it is swallowed and enters the stomach. Now a white adult worm, a centimetre in length, it adheres to the walls of the upper intestine and lives on blood. Here it lays its eggs, which are evacuated in excrement, and grow into larvae seeking another hospitable ankle.

The effect of hookworm is to produce a generalised anaemia, to sap the normal store of energy, and in the case of women to render them in childbirth peculiarly susceptible to septic complications and heart failure. In young adult cases, infestation with hookworms is accompanied by a generalised oedema and pallor with fatty degeneration of the heart.

From 1914-1924 the Rockefeller Institute carried on a special campaign against hookworm in the colony. They did not receive the co-operation which is essential for the eradication of the disease. It is useless to cure a person of hookworm unless the danger of reinfection is removed. Finally, after ten years of almost useless work, the Rockefeller Institute withdrew its assistance in disgust. The Government then appointed two hookworm units, each consisting of two men, one unit for the Northern and one for the Southern Division of the colony. Their work consists generally "of census-taking, examination of specimens, treatment of positive cases, improvement of latrines, educational measures and propaganda", quite a job for four men in a population of four hundred and forty thousand.

In the year 1936 the Northern Unit found that 78.97 per cent of the population of the Cunupia district was infected, while in Caparo and Todds Road the percentage was 80.3 per cent. The Southern Unit had good news. In the Guaracara district the percentage had been reduced from 98.04 to 79.46.

It is clearly high time that the hookworm campaign was undertaken. But it must be realised that it is not so simple as the paralytic rabies campaign. The only two factors in that campaign were the biter, *desmodus rufus*, and the bitten. Any hookworm campaign demands not only extensive propaganda by film, lecture and poster, but also the co-operation of employers, who shall demand, as they already do in certain oilfields, that no worker should suffer from the disease, and of landlords, who shall see to it that the sanitary conditions of their properties do not lead to reinfection.

A complaint is usually made that in many cases East Indians refuse to use closets, even if they have them. The stench of these closets does not make this surprising. In some cases this is not due to the inefficiency of the closet but to a lack of imagination which has placed the closet seats so high that small children cannot use them and consequently use the floor around.

If the Medical Service has to depend, as the Commission seems to think it must, merely on the goodwill and collaboration of the public, and especially employers and landlords, it will find its task insuperable. While certain employers and landlords are farsighted and public-minded, others are so retrograde that they will only respond to force, and then unwillingly.

The view of the Medical Service is that the present deficiency diseases will be found to disappear once hookworm is eradicated from the colony. There is, however, another view, expressed by Sir Murchison Fletcher in a speech, which the Commission has condemned as "inopportune". He said:

"When I arrived in Trinidad I was somewhat painfully struck by the poverty here, and more particularly by the physical appearance of the East Indian population. I had come from the South Seas, Fiji, where the East Indians were introduced in exactly similar circumstances (they were brought in for the sugar estates), and the men there are definitely of a finer physique. I have with me a report written in 1935. It refers to a visit of a Dutch doctor from the Dutch East Indies, who during some weeks went through the country in association with one of our Medical Officers, and he was obviously shocked by the evidence of malnutrition which he observed. He stated that, although he had twenty years' experience of the Dutch East Indies, and although he had personal knowledge of conditions resulting from vitamin deficiencies, he had never seen such distressing conditions as existed here among the East Indian labouring population, where, apparently, men and women suffered from an absence of all known vitamins.

At the hospital the Medical Officer took cases at random and showed the ravages which were being caused by deficiency diseases among the East Indian labouring population. There follows a list of these diseases, all due to this condition of malnutrition. The Medical Officer stated that every adult above the age of twenty years was affected, and that the working life of the population was reduced by at least fifty per cent.

The main argument used by the Medical Service in support of its decision to deal with hookworm before tackling the question of deficiency diseases and malnutrition is that it would be unscientific to examine the two questions at once. The effects of hookworm might be ascribed to malnutrition and vice versa. This argument, however, is merely an excuse. Riddled though the East Indian population is with hookworm, there are considerable sections, especially among the Negro workers, where it does not exist. If the Medical Service honestly wished to tackle the question of malnutrition and deficiency diseases it could conduct its investigations in those sections.

The true explanation, in my view, is that the Medical Service considers that it has its hands full in the hookworm campaign. Here the sphere of medicine already touches other spheres. There is liable to be a conflict with local vested interests. This department, as other departments of the Colonial Service in the island, cannot depend on the support that it will receive from the Colonial Office. The disgrace of Sir Murchison Fletcher and Mr. Howard Nankivell, both of whom have been censured for taking an independent line in the affairs of the island and coming into conflict with local vested interests, has taught anew the lesson that caution and not enthusiasm is the highest virtue of a colonial servant and that the policy of the Colonial Office is not progress but quiet.

If the hookworm campaign is gunpowder, an investigation of malnutrition would be dynamite. The findings of a Commission would be liable to imply the necessity for that increase in wages and the establishment of unemployment benefit which are already demanded by the progressive leaders. If even half of what the Dutch doctor said is borne out by an investigation, the demands which are at present resisted as extravagant would receive scientific ratification. There might be the danger of what are known in Parliament as 'disturbances', and the medical officers responsible for the investigation would get a black mark against their names.

Hookworm is the lesser evil now that the romantically sinister *desmodus rufus* has been routed. To postpone all other campaigns until the eradication of hookworm is not a realistic and scientific course of action, but an adjournment of action *sine die.*

Tuberculosis, according to the Annual Medical and Sanitary Report of 1936, has among its contributing causes bad housing, overcrowding, hookworm, malaria and malnutrition. In 1936, 447 cases of pulmonary and 31 cases of non-pulmonary tuberculosis were recorded. This first figure was sixty-five in excess of the preceding year, though over a period of years the figures show a decline.

Subscriptions were made towards the construction of a sanatorium as a memorial to the Silver Jubilee of George V. No move has yet been made, however, because the site has not yet been agreed upon. The climate of Trinidad is particularly unhealthy for tuberculous cases. "Nothing to do about them," said Dr. Cook when showing me round the Port of Spain Colonial Hospital Tuberculosis Ward, "we just have to keep them here until they die." Dr. Cook's suggestion, made I don't know how seriously, was that the new sanatorium should be built in Tobago, where the climate, is more favourable. The ideal site, of course, if the only consideration was the health of the patients, would be in the mountains of Venezuela. But it is unlikely that the Trinidadians would part with good money for that purpose.

There are no figures in existence as to the prevalence of venereal diseases. In 1935 and 1936, 1142 and 1007 cases were treated. But that is admittedly absolutely no indication of the prevalence of these diseases. There is great reluctance to come for treatment until the disease is in its advanced stages. The facilities of treatment, both as regards opportunity and secrecy,[1] leave much to be desired. Instruction is seldom given in schools, the attitude of the Catholic Church, which controls many of these schools, being opposed to this. Ignorance of sexual hygiene is responsible for a great deal of unnecessary cases. In the child-welfare clinics expectant mothers are encouraged to take anti-syphilis injections, even though these can be of little use at this stage: and they are given no direct instruction as to the nature of venereal diseases. The injections are given 'just to make baby healthy.'

Just as the preventive measures of the Medical Services have been lamentable in the past and are full of promises for the future, so the hospitals admit to past and present incapacity, but point to a rosy future.

I visited the Port of Spain Colonial Hospital and was shown round by Dr. Cook. This is the prize hospital of the colony, the finest example of the Medical Services. The main building was originally a barracks. When it became too antiquated to house the militia it was turned into a hospital. This building is constructed of stone on two floors. Each floor has been gutted and divided by low wooden partitions into separate wards some thirty feet square.

For many years now this building has been condemned. The result is that the paint, which was put on the walls and partitions a long, long while

---

1. *The new V.D. clinic at the Port of Spain Colonial Hospital is a great advance in privacy.*

3. MEDICINE AND MAGIC   103

ago, has not been renewed. The partitions are stained, spotted and filthy. The walls are flaking. But in two or three years time this building will either be demolished or redesigned, and until that time nothing will be done about redecoration.

Dr. Cook's office, the waiting-room and the kitchens are in a long bungalow, dating from the same period. The kitchen serves all wards. Meals are carried sometimes two hundred yards. There are no continuous covered shelters against rain.

The kitchen is open to the outside air. Dust from the square is sterilised in the cooking. The chimney of the kitchen is held upright by joists. The ovens are primitive, and insufficient for the service of four hundred patients and a hundred and eighty nurses.

For several years all suggestions that new ovens should be installed have been rejected on the ground that new kitchens were being built. Work will start, it is hoped, this year. Meanwhile the patients and the nurses suffer: even though the new ovens, when they had fulfilled their use at the hospital, could be handed over to another institution in the Medical Service. The chief cook looks hopefully at the crack which runs through the central arch and says: "Well, anyway, when this falls down they'll have to build a new one." "It can't be long now," says the second cook hopefully.

The washing of hospital laundry is done under a corrugated iron shed, and the atmosphere is so damp, the rain so frequent, that clothes and sheets are never properly dried. But when the kitchens are built a new laundry will be built as well.

Meanwhile building is going ahead with new wards, designed finally to accommodate 420 patients. The present capacity of the hospital is 380 beds. There are 400 in-patients, however, the remaining 20 sleeping on chairs and benches. "Do you know," said Dr. Cook indignantly, "when I first came here they were sleeping on the floor. Things are different now."

The conditions in San Fernando Hospital are worse than in Port of Spain. They are still in the stage of sleeping on the floor. But pressure from Rienzi, Legislative Council member for San Fernando and President of the Oilfield Workers' Union, has resulted finally in the starting of work on new buildings

In addition to three colonial hospitals, six district and two emergency hospitals, there is a Leper Settlement on the island of Chacachacare and a mental hospital at St. Ann's.

I went to see Dr. Rankine, the Director of Medical Services, for permission to see over these two institutions.

He listened while I explained what I wanted. Then he shook his head and said: "If you were going as a visitor I'd raise no objection; but to write about these places... that would never do."

"I fully understand," I said, "that you have only been here for a couple of years. I don't expect to find things perfect. I know that you're doing your best to put things right."

He shook his head again.

"But what is wrong, then?" I asked. "Are you ashamed of what you're doing? Why should you think any account of these institutions must be unsympathetic?"

"It's not that," said this softhearted Scotsman. "I've got to think of the feelings of these poor people. I mean, having you write them up…"

"Do you really mean to say that you think that anything that I write about them will be smuggled in and studied by the lunatics? Can you see the lepers poring over my articles on that island?"

"Well," said the doctor, "perhaps Sir Robert Archibald might give you permission to visit the Leper Colony. But the Mental Hospital, certainly not."

"Well, will you ask Sir Robert next time he comes over for a weekend?"

"Yes," said Dr. Rankine. "I'll do that."

Whether he did or not I can't say; at any rate I never obtained the permission I wanted, but I intended to follow up this line by insinuating myself into the asylum one morning with a gaggle of American tourists and seeing what Dr. Rankine was so anxious I shouldn't see; things began humming too soon and I had other work to do.

I read *Franklin's Year Book* which said that the Mental Hospital "is located in an extensive block of buildings in the St. Ann's Valley, and here some 756 cases of nervous and mental disorder are treated on modern lines." I made inquiries about these modern lines, but the only authoritative information I could gather was that there was not a single trained alienist on the staff. "It is said," added Franklin, "to be one of the best institutions of the kind in the West Indies."

Chacachacare, the leper island, is close to the Venezuelan coast. It is rocky, mountainous and the bush is impenetrable. All communication has to be made by boat. The colony is not centralised. In one cove are the lepers, in another the Catholic nurses, and in a third Sir Robert Archibald. Sir Robert is picked up by the morning launch and taken home by the evening one. He has no launch of his own, and in an emergency it takes three-quarters of an hour to fetch him. That is provided that the launch doesn't break down, which it often does. Then, of course, it may take any time. In 'the future' Sir Robert is going to be given a launch of his own. But though he is a very distinguished medical scientist it is not certain that he is going to be allowed a properly equipped research laboratory.

The great merit of Chacachacare as a leper colony is that it is a long way from Trinidad. That in fact is its only merit. Since leprosy is less contagious than tuberculosis that merit is small.

The nature of the island is such that it is almost impossible for the lepers to perform any of those light tasks which keep them psychologically in contact with the healthy world. An attempt is being made to establish in the old leper colony at Cocorite on the main island a convalescent settlement for lepers who will soon be ready to go into the outside world again. But, through ignorance, public opinion is strongly against this.

Despite recommendations to the contrary, District Medical Officers, who are engaged as civil servants for their lifetime, are allowed to conduct private practices. I heard from all sides complaints against this custom. Public patients were neglected for private ones. It is possible that in certain cases these accusations were unjust. But in a place such as Trinidad it is important that such accusations should not be able to be made at all.

Furthermore, both from social workers and public patients, I heard the complaints that doctors did not turn up at their clinics at specified hours, and that when they did they took those patients who could afford to pay the charge for public aid before they took those who had only a pauper's card. I asked the Director of Medical Services whether this was true and he said it was not, adding that whenever a case was brought to his notice the doctor was severely reprimanded. I also asked the Deputy-Director and he said: "Hang it all, do they expect to be taken first?" I gathered that the conduct which was expected of a District Medical Officer was to take people in the order of their appearance, except in urgent cases.

There seem, however, to be many exceptions. Many doctors take all their paying patients first, and the fact that the Director of Medical Services does not hear of it more often is due to the fear of the patient that he will be penalised by the doctor if he makes a complaint.

In certain cases I was told that by the end of the day the 'pauper' patients were sent home, still unattended. In others, indignant complaints were made that the doctor, who was being paid by the Government to attend to them, was brusque, unsympathetic and gave his services as if it was a privilege.

The important point about these complaints, which were supported in many cases by voluntary social workers whose only emotion seemed to be indignation, is not whether they are true, but the indication they give of the popular attitude to medicine.

It was the possession of this background of knowledge that gave special interest to the following incident.

One Sunday evening Tony de Boissière and I set out to try and hear some Shouters. The Shouters belong to a Negro religious cult, rather like the Holy Rollers, and I was interested to hear them shouting.

We knew that we would find them somewhere up Laventille Hill but we didn't know quite where. So we went to call on Françoise, who lives in a street at the bottom of the hill in the Piccadilly district.

Most of the houses in this part are bungalows, but Françoise lived on the upper floor of a two-storey house. It was a very poor district. Since she had taken up political work she had been almost starving.

The street ran with an open drain and the stench was appalling. We went up the staircase at the back and here the smell of burnt oil diluted the stench of drains.

Every room in the house was let off separately, and the cooking was done in charcoal burners on the gallery. At the far end of the gallery there was a weak light, and under the light was an old woman in a white shift working at a tub. We went along and asked her if Françoise was in.

"No," said the old woman. "She gone out." She looked very suspicious.

Tony went and sat down on a box.

"Excuse me *deshabille*," said the old woman, clipping her shift between her knees.

"Where she gone?" asked Tony.

"She gone Seamen's Union," said the old lady. She wanted to get us away.

We got up and asked her where we could hear some Shouters, and she pointed vaguely up Laventille Hill.

We went out and asked two other people. They said they didn't know. The Shouters are for black people. They distrusted two strange whites coming in. They might be detectives.

We started to climb towards Laventille but it came on to rain. We took shelter under a jutting roof and sat on a door-step waiting for the rain to stop. Figures ran past with handkerchiefs on their heads.[1]

As we started to smoke, a black man in brown came into the shelter of the roof. I offered him a cigarette, and Tony asked him if he knew where the Shouters were.

"Down de street," said the man: "Right here in de next street at de corner, dere's a woman cures de sick."

"But they don't shout," said Tony. "Not down here, they don't shout."

"They don't shout," agreed the man, drawing at his cigarette. "But she do cure de sick. I been there all the evening. Just come from dat place to smoke a cigarette."

Our cigarettes made three red points in darkness.

---

1. *It is a custom among Trinidadians to shelter the head in rain. The leaf of a banana is a common umbrella. When a woman is wearing a thin dress which will spoil in the rain, but no hat, she shelters her head, not her shoulders. Even when the covering for the head is quite inadequate, the same formality is observed. I have seen a man bicycling along in a shower, holding an ordinary envelope over his head. I asked a lot of people if they could explain this custom, but no one could.*

"I see de lame walk," said the black man in brown. "The blind do see, the deaf do hear and dumb men do speak."

"Let's take her in before we go shouting," I said.

"If I have de clap," Tony asked, "if I have de clap, she cure me too?"

"Aw," the man was shocked. "Aw, aw. Aw, aw."

"We creole folk," Tony went on. "We so many run wid de clap. She cure us?"

"I never seen dat," the man said, laughing. "But the lame do walk like whole."

The rain had stopped and we walked with him round the corner. The noise of singing filled the street. The doors and windows of the last house were wide open. Men and women were standing on the pavement, staring in. We found it hard to see anything. But the black man in brown took us round to the side and we could see everything.

It was a room some twenty feet by eighteen. It was packed with people, sitting on benches and leaning against the walls. Most of the women were dressed in white and the men in their Sunday suits. There was no altar, just an oleograph of the Virgin and Child hanging on the wall. At an invisible altar rail were kneeling five women and one man.

Bending behind them were two girls, dressed in white as nurses, and two men with stewards' badges (the star of David and a coloured ribbon) in the coat lapels. Before the oleograph stood a stout Negress of middle age. She was dressed in white, with a scarlet cape across her shoulders. The hood of this cape covered her hair, and in the centre of the forehead was embroidered a cross of gold. She wore spectacles and her hands were pressed palm to palm between her large breasts.

She opened her mouth and in a full voice told the kneeling penitents to repeat a *confiteor* after her. It was no orthodox confession, but a mixture of religious tags joined by improvisations of her own. She said the words sentence by sentence. Then the nurses and stewards leaning forward swelled the inaudible repetitions of the penitents into a hearty murmur.

The force of the service was derived from repetition. There were two slogans. "I t'ank you, dear Jesus," and "In Jesus mighty name." The second was pronounced, "In Jesus my tename." On 'my' the voices rose, heads were thrown back and eyes closed even tighter than before. On 'tename,' the voices dropped, heads came forward, chins on breasts.

"I t'ank you, dear Jesus," chanted the Scarlet Sister.

"I t'ank you, dear Jesus," echoed penitents and prompters.

"I t'ank you, dear Jesus." "I t'ank you, dear Jesus." "I t'ank you, dear Jesus."

Meanwhile the congregation craned slightly forward, muttering every now and again, sometimes with the Scarlet Sister, sometimes with the penitents and sometimes in the rare silence, "I t'ank you, dear Jesus."

When they had paid full thanks to Jesus, the Scarlet Sister told them to repeat after her the words, "In Jesus my tename." Three times they were to say it and on the third time they were to relax and let Satan pass from them.

Napkins were placed on the heads of the penitents. There was not a murmur from the congregation. The Scarlet Sister approached the first penitent and stood with her arm out-raised, her body quivering.

Her hand began to jerk at the end of her arm like a writhing snake. She seemed to be trying to control it. She brought it slowly, still quivering with its own life, on the head of the penitent. "In Jesus my tename," she said, and bending forward muttered, "Say it with me."

"In Jesus my tename," they both repeated. "In Jesus my tename." As they said this, the Sister moved the penitent's head backwards and forwards under her tense fingers. Then, at the second repetition, she raised her other hand, waved it above her head and brought it down touching one of the lowest vertebras in the small of the penitent's back.

"In Jesus my tename, In Jesus my tename." The tempo quickened. The congregation half rose from their seats. The Sister gave a tiny push and the penitent fell back limp into the arms of the two waiting nurses, who stretched her out along the floor, her white feet facing the oleograph of the Virgin and Child.

In the Sister's movements there was power and decision. The shaking hand at the end of the quivering arm, the sure placing of the finger on the vertebra, the gathering excitement of her full voice, 'In Jesus my tename,' led to that strange climax in a way that was at least theatrically inevitable.

She went from penitent to penitent, repeating the process until all six were stretched along the floor, like six corpses laid out for burial. But though her ritual was the same in each case, it seemed to me, watching carefully, that when the penitents relaxed to let Satan come forth, they passed out in different ways. I could see their faces very clearly during this time. They all looked Negroes of a low mental type.

They showed no sign of ecstasy. But while some appeared to be in a state of semiconsciousness, as if hypnotised, others were in a hypersensitive state, with a latent hysteria which music might have caused to burst out.

The Scarlet Sister looked down at her handiwork, then, trembling no longer, she turned away and burst into song. The nurses and the stewards took it up and finally the congregation joined in.

The penitents lay motionless upon the floor.

After the hymn; the Scarlet Sister turned again to the penitents. "In Jesus my tename," muttered the congregation, "In Jesus my tename."

She bent down over the first penitent and touched her eyes, her mouth, her breast, her navel and the caps of her knees. While she did this the penitent muttered softly "In Jesus my tename."

Finally the Scarlet Sister put one hand between the clasped hands of the penitent and raised her to a kneeling position. One or two of the penitents tried to stand up during this process, but the nurses had them quickly down on their knees. "I t'ank you, dear Jesus," murmured the congregation. "I t'ank you, dear Jesus."

Back in the altar rail position, the penitents were given water to drink, with the command 'Drink' as the cup was handed to them. Each drank from the same spot in the glass with eyes tightly closed. "I t'ank you, dear Jesus. I t'ank you, dear Jesus."

In the last stage of the ceremony the penitents rose to their feet and the Sister went over them with a vigorous mime of massage. Her hands passed over head, over back, down arms and hips. But in each case, she devoted most attention to the knees. As she twisted at the kneecaps, legs bent and opened, the whole body shivering.

From the side they looked as if someone had put a cold penny down their backs and they were trying to shake it out. But from behind, where the congregation sat, I have no doubt that this shaking presented the very appearance of the devil leaving his human habitation. "Satan, come forth," said the Scarlet Sister as she tickled the knees of the only man among the penitents, who by the way had gone into his trance quicker than any of the women.

"I t'ank you, dear Jesus," the man murmured, as she passed on to the next.

After driving forth the devil, came the benediction: "Relieved of sin, go ye out into de street, rejoicin'," said the Scarlet Sister.

Deftly the napkins were removed. The penitents opened their eyes. The women groped for and found their fawn straw hats. The look of blank stupidity went from their faces. They were six people, dazzled by the sudden light, and they stumbled as they made their way towards the darkness and the door.

"Want to go po-po," piped a child, wriggling on his mother's knee.

The Scarlet Sister and her acolytes burst into song. There was no time for pause. Sinners were waiting for forgiveness. The old napkins were laid on new heads. Different voices began to repeat the same *confiteor*.

We turned away. The black man in brown was immediately behind us. He moved into the gap that we had left. He could not leave. He had seen the sick healed. Blind men do see, deaf men do hear. The dumb do speak.

The Scarlet Sister is not unique. A little farther up the hill, in a two-story building off the road, is Mother Holy Ghost. In every barrack, every third house, is a woman with the gift of 'obeah'. She knows how to bring the beloved to the lover. She can turn the lawsuit in the favour of her client. She can throw a spell upon an enemy. She can cast out devils from the body, cure the sick of fevers. She is the woman with a magic gift. She has books which no one else can read.

Her magic is acknowledged. This man died of a spell she cast and that recovered from a dire illness. This girl won her lover through her, that man had a successful lawsuit.

No one understands the ways of her magic. They are mysterious like the ways of a doctor. Her decoctions are secret, like the medicine which the doctor gives in his bottles. There is need of faith.

The doctors in Trinidad have been abroad to study at great hospitals. When they return with their degrees, they have forgotten the superstitions of the land they left as boys. They believe that the people of the island have grown up with them, accept the science of the white doctor as solemnly as they do themselves.

The medicine of the white man may cure. Or it may not cure. The people of Trinidad do not accept it on faith as the only way of treating illness. It is one of several ways. The doctor as well as his medicine is on trial. They judge by manners, courtesy, kindness and the desire to help, as much as by cures.

The doctor is on trial and the evidence is that when a man is trained in white magic, medicine, he is proud. He talks high language like the obeah woman, but he is not close to the sick, he is not a friend with the power to help. He keeps far from the people, is difficult to approach. He puts on airs, makes style. He harries people with absurd regulations, which no one understands. He works eagerly for the rich, because they pay him money. The poor he treats because he has to.

People like the Scarlet Sister to perform miracles. For that reason she is hated by the police and persecuted. The doctors, trained in white hospitals abroad, want to be the only ones to perform miracles. That is why they forbid the Scarlet Sister to perform miracles.

She is kindly. She calls to the sick and they come to her. She sends them away rejoicing. But when the sick come to doctors trained in white magic, they wait all day and then are turned away without treatment. Police and ex-police guard their doors.

Medicine and magic are still fighting one another. Medicine has the stamp of official approval. It has the wealth and power of big hospitals. The Government is behind it.

But the doctors do not realise that they are fighting against magic as well as disease: that their medicine is no stronger in the eyes of the people than the power of the obeah woman, no more scientific. They do not realise that when they are thoughtless, inhuman or unsympathetic, they are driving the sick into the arms of the obeah woman.

The way of science is in competition with the way of magic. The men of science think the power is all on their side. But they are wrong. Their mystery is a hard, proud mystery, which turns the sick away. Then magic steps in, offering instead a flummery which warms the heart, restores the confidence.

4. CULTURAL EVENINGS

IN the previous chapter I referred to Tony de Boissière. Cruel as it is to bring him under the heading of this chapter, it is time that he was brought forward and introduced.

Before I went to Trinidad, I was told by a friend who had recently returned from Jamaica, "You'll probably find some journalist there who'll be a sort of social outcast and know the place backwards. Anyway, that's what we found in Jamaica. He was a nice chap, but because he mixed with the natives everybody cut him dead."

A fortnight after I landed I met Tony, who was then working for the *Port of Spain Gazette*. "Here," I said to myself, "is the man my friend was talking about."

We liked one another from the start. And the very first evening we had a tremendous argument, which was resumed in different forms over and over again during the next six weeks. Tony is descended from an old French creole family. He was educated in New York. Returned to Trinidad. Inherited a small legacy, and instead of playing safe, invested in a trip to Europe. He went to Oxford and Cambridge. ("A week in each of the universities, going to parties, and you learn all they've got to teach you. Or all they teach most people.") He travelled in France, Italy, Germany, bummed his way across North Africa. He worked on boats and for the Hearst organisation in New York. As a de Boissière he was entertained by the society of Barbados and two months later as a beachcomber got work on the water-front. He bought a jitney bus in Trinidad to make his fortune. He drove down Marine Square and South Quay, calling: "San Fernando! San Fernando!" "The bus was full in a moment," he said, "but when we got to San Fernando everybody got out and said, 'Thank you,' because they couldn't believe a white man'd drive a bus for profit. After that I used to drive 'em straight into the police station and let 'em out one by one."

Though most of his family had made terms with the British Government, Tony hated the very guts of British officialdom, to which he ascribed the ruin of his family fortunes. Late in the evening, when the rum was getting low, he would sit opposite me, his lips curling with contempt and curse me as an Englishman, while I cursed him back for insularity and petty-mindedness. The next morning, however, this basic racial antagonism would be forgotten again.

As soon as I met Tony I realised that he had invaluable contacts and information. He mixed without embarrassment with people of any class or colour. His judgment of character was quick, intuitive and nearly always correct. He had a humour that was usually malicious but always witty. He proved excellent company, a person I should enjoy being with in any part of the world. He had evolved a philosophy which was often erratic, but always stimulating. His jokes were the better because they had an edge to them.

Tony had called the bluff of Trinidad society. He did what he wanted, said what he wanted and got away with it. In consequence, his name stank with the *bourgeoisie*. They are never over-careful of slander. But when it came to talking of Tony, they took their coats off and let themselves go. Person after person drew me aside and warned me against associating with such a man; they told me of the damage that my reputation would receive and the personal injuries I would sustain.

I recognised Tony's faults, which were as many as mine or another's. But his faults weren't dull faults. His vices were gay. He was not a coward. He used his brain. And he got from life a greater enjoyment than any man I have known. To go out with him was a joy, because he responded so quickly and accurately to the spirit and humour of the life around him. He couldn't walk along the street without a crack at every other person, whether he knew them or not. And his jokes went home with an accuracy that would have been unforgivably rude, if his tone had not been so correct.

His gaiety and enthusiasm were his major faults in the eyes of the *bourgeoisie*. A tropical derelict they could understand. They could tolerate a hangdog sinner. But a man, who did everything that their code forbade, who despised their conventions and made open fun of them in the street, was inexcusable. The good-humoured said he was crazy and confessed that they admired him as the happiest man they knew. The strait-laced sharpened their tongues and cut him to little bits.

Despite warnings, I continued to associate with Tony. And, unfortunately, the prophecies of my counsellors did not come true. Tony was a known danger, a thorn without whose familiar prick Trinidad society might almost have felt uneasy. But before I had left I had become an unknown danger to the security of the community. It was obvious that I was not a writer, as my letters of introduction said, because I was not stopping at the Queen's Park Hotel. The first theory evolved was that I was a spy in the employ of the Trinidad Leaseholds Company. But this lost favour as soon as it became clear that I was a Moscow agent, with my pockets bulging with Soviet gold.

This had the most unfortunate repercussions on Tony. His reputation from being scandalous became sinister. And, as I shall describe later, that large but pathetic body, the police, began to move

4. CULTURAL EVENINGS

It was through Tony that I originally came into contact with the cultural leaders who exist on the outer orbit of the labour movement. But there was an intermediary, since Tony had too good a sense of humour to be popular with the intellectual vanguard.

The intermediary was a young man who had been one of the original organisers of the waterfront. He had worked as a sailor on the Furness Withy Line and so come in contact with the C.I.O. National Maritime Union. He had been one of the founding members of the Trinidad Seamen's Union, had taken an active part in the strike of June 1937, but had made the mistake of overestimating the militancy of the workers. His union activity got him in wrong with the authorities. He complained of being penalised, of being unable to get work for nine months. But, at the same time, the union had repudiated him for 'over-zealousness'. 'Over-zealousness' is a local term for leftism.

This separation from the movement, combined with unemployment, had sent him back into a contemplation of the events of nine months before. In his imagination and in his conversation, he relived that period of his career, justifying himself and vilifying the executive which had succeeded him.

He was not very stimulating company. The man who has a grudge never is. But, as he was very anxious to introduce me to the friend from whom his ideas seemed to stem, I agreed to go along and meet Rupert Gittens, the President of the L'Ouverture Club.

Rupert Gittens had also been to sea, had also helped organise the waterfront workers, and had also been flung out for over-zealousness. But his background was petty *bourgeois* and not working-class. His mind and education were far superior to his friend's. He was a poet in the Langston Hughes tradition, and a firm believer in the existence of a West Indian culture and the possibility of its development.

Gittens had made several attempts to work in with the trade union movement, but in each case he had been ejected. He was heartily hated by the militant workers, some of whom accused him of being a police spy. He had now decided to work in the cultural field, educating along broad lines.

I never had any evidence that would prove the accusations made against him. But, on the other hand, I never felt at home with him. This was partly because he was an intellectual type. He remained in what appeared to be a single mood, talking in a soft, level voice, with a reserve of pride and patronage. I never heard him laugh or make a joke. Though we always arrived at agreement on policy, I never felt that there had been an exchange of more than ideas. He kept his emotions well hidden, and the only positive feeling I developed of his character was that he had a great love of power. I suspected that his failure in unions had been due to an inability to work on an equality with other men, to fight for his ideas in an open forum and accept defeat loyally if they were rejected. His L'Ouverture Club was better suited to his temperament because it was a one-man organisation.

I attended in all three functions under the auspices of the club. At the first I gave a lecture on the development of modern literature. Having never published a play I was rather astonished to be introduced as the 'famed novelist and playwright'. I had not then discovered that no artist, writer or musician has ever visited the island without being 'famed'. And as no one has ever read anything you've written, imagination supplies you with extraordinary versatility. At different meetings I was introduced as famed essayist, poet, scenario-writer, trade unionist and feature writer.

The audience of the L'Ouverture was large and sympathetic. I outlined briefly the increasing preoccupation of the arts with politics in their broader sense. I oversimplified issues to make my meaning clear. I tried to describe the way literature springs from the relation of the author, with his gifts, to the society of his time, and the variations thus entailed between literatures of different countries and ages. I pointed to Alfred Mendes as a Trinidadian novelist who represented the native qualities of the island. I deplored the local verse as derivative from the Victorian and Edwardian traditions of English literature and having no relation to the life of the island.

The house was thrown open to questions and there immediately leapt to his feet a burly white man, who had been sitting in the front row listening impatiently. He and three others were the only pure whites there.

He was sitting towards the end of the front row, but he did not speak from his seat. He advanced menacingly towards me, wagging his index finger. "I protest," he said. "I protest against this lecture as a malicious travesty of the truth. I protest against the use of a literary society for the purposes of Marxist propaganda. I protest against this utter distortion of the principles of art and literature to political purposes." Every moment he got closer and closer towards me. His resonant Trinidadian voice filled the hall. He was bellowing, first at me, and then turning a broad back on me and facing the audience.

"Who," I shouted to Gittens through the storm, "is this?"

"Bertie Gomes," he said. "He comes to every lecture. Try to take no notice."

It was impossible not to. As well ignore a hurricane. I asked him to confine himself to questions, and these it was possible to deal with as they came up. "How dare I say that poets were interested in politics. What about the sublime Yeats?" "What about Auden and Spender?" "What about Eliot, Swinburne, Oscar Wilde?" "Had I read Dostoievski, Turgenev, de Maupassant?" "Had I heard of Shakespeare?"[1]

---

1. *I don't pretend to represent the exact words of Mr. Games, but I think his general position is not misrepresented.*

4. CULTURAL EVENINGS

Cosmic questions were flung at my head one after the other: were flung in most cases right above the heads of the audience. But it was a dog-fight, and everybody enjoys dog-fights. It made up for the dullness of the lecture itself.

The general position of Mr. Gomes was the familiar Art for Art's Sake attitude. But it had a particular application, to Trinidad 'culture'. Great art is universal. It rises above its time and place. Dostoievski is not for Russia but for the whole world. Therefore the accusation that the verse written by the Trinidad poets is derivative and divorced from West Indian life, springs from an entire misunderstanding of the nature of art. I tried to explain the misunderstanding of the 'universality' of art: that the type figures of literature, Hamlet, Don Quixote, Falstaff, Faustus exist as exaggerations, extreme particularisations of universal tendencies. That universality is only achieved by particular definition of character. I tried to make plain that a great work of art could be enjoyed by a wide audience, but that it would only be a great work of art if it had its roots in the life and thought of a particular time and place.

But no. Mr. Gomes held firm. He published open letters in the press about me and about Bert Birtles, the Australian journalist who appeared in Trinidad about this time. He accused us of corrupting the islanders. He published articles in the *Trinidad Guardian,* inveighing against the wave of Marxists that had inundated the island. Whenever we lectured to a literary society he pursued us and continued the argument from the meeting before, whether it had relevance to the lecture of that night or not. I always looked for his heavy, eager face. If it was there, I knew, however badly I spoke, the meeting would be a success. He succeeded in putting with enormous enthusiasm questions which other people in the audience wanted to ask but were too shy. He was the ideal lecture stooge. One could be as devastating as one wanted and he still came up for more.

At the conclusion of this first lecture in Trinidad I was apprehensive how it had gone. I knew the discussion had been a success, but I wasn't at all certain how the lecture had got across. Gittens told me in his address of thanks. "We are very grateful to the lecturer for speaking to us this evening," he said, "and I am sure that we have all heard a great many words we have never heard before, and we will go back and look them up in our dictionaries."[1]

---

1. *I couldn't imagine anything more crushing than this. But I do not believe that it was meant to be crushing and I heard from several sources that the lecture was considered a success. In the West Indies, as in India, there is a confusion between words, thought and knowledge. West Indians are fascinated by long words. They always use them in preference to short words. Very often they use the wrong long word, but the impression given is still more weighty than the*

My second appearance at the L'Ouverture Club was as guest of honour at its first anniversary banquet. The time on the invitation card was 8 o'clock, and as I was late I took a taxi. I arrived at the hall at five minutes past eight. All the lights were on in the hall and I went in.

The hall was divided into two main rooms. In the front room there was no one, but there was a girl in the back room laying the tables for the banquet.

I went in and helped her spread the tablecloths, and we laid out the forks and spoons. But there were no knives. The knives, said the girl, were coming later.

So we went into the back and unpacked the food and set it out ready.

By the time that was finished it was eight-thirty. "Will people be coming soon?" I asked, looking at the empty hall. "Oh, they won't be here till nine," she said.

I decided that it might be embarrassing for them to arrive and find the guest of honour had already been there an hour, so I went across the road to a little parlour. I ordered a bottle of soda-water and talked to the parlour-keeper, who was Chinese, about the war. He said he could only afford to contribute two dollars a month to the fighting chest.

I could see the hall across the way, and gradually people began to go in and others hung about the gallery waiting for things to start. At five to nine I thought that it was possible that they were waiting for me. So I went across and found about three rows of people sitting down patiently waiting for something to happen. But as there was nobody official to welcome me I went back to the parlour and had another soda.

At a quarter past nine people on the gallery started hallooing and so I went back to the hall again. There was still no one to welcome me. But I decided that I couldn't drink any more soda. So I sat down on a bench and waited. There wasn't any sign of the banquet going forward. But they told me there was going to be a concert first.

By half-past nine the hall was very full, and I realised suddenly that I was the only person who wasn't wearing evening dress, or a pretence at it. All

---

accurate use of short words. The underlying idea is that the word itself contains a residuum of knowledge. A wise man is therefore one with a large vocabulary, just as a rich man is one with a large bank account. The only thing that beats a long word is a quotation. The sentiment of the quotation and its applicability to the rest of a speech are of secondary importance.

Both these tendencies are due to uncertainty, a desire to impress on a plane below clear, simple thought. Though it appears to an outsider, often, to be the negation of sincerity, it is not so in fact. Exactly the same tendency is found in English schoolboys from the age of sixteen to about twenty, and in a large number of adults, especially politicians and Government officials.

these boys, who I knew worked as clerks, labourers, builders' assistants, were togged out in tuxedoes and vests. The girls wore long dresses for dancing, and some had put a white lotion on their faces which gave their skins a mauve look. Its advantage was that they could sweat without it coming off, as powder would; its disadvantage that it did not improve their looks.

Gittens arrived about twenty to ten. He sat down at the chairman's desk and, looking round, beckoned me to come and sit with him. I refused. As guest of honour I was going to enjoy myself and I thought it was about time the fun started.

Gittens stood up and announced that before the banquet began there would be a concert, an expression of Negro and specifically West Indian culture. The first item would be a pianoforte solo.

The pianist was a girl in evening dress. She was a fine looking girl, but wearing that white liquid on her face which makes the complexion mauve. She sat down at the piano and began to play. She was by no means an experienced pianist. Her sense of time was far from perfect. The notes she struck were not always those on the score. But she differed from performers I have heard at village concerts in one important thing. Where others might be embarrassed, stumbling and pathetic, she was bold and unselfconscious. She never faltered at a slip. She went bravely on with such energy and rapidity that by the end I wondered whether indeed there had been a piece of music to listen to.

But there she was, standing bowing to the applause that swept the audience. Everybody was clapping and I joined in, hoping to hear a second piece.

But no. The show had to go on. One turn after another was presented with startling speed. Gittens stood up and recited a poem by Langston Hughes in that soft, level voice of his. A duet followed, a sentimental American song. A girl recited a poem by Gittens on Toussaint L'Ouverture, the club's eponym. It was a revolutionary poem, and it sounded strange coming out of the mouth of that slender mulatto girl whose beau was in the volunteers and who might be called on to shoot strikers. She herself was conventional, a product of the Belmont petty *bourgeoisie,* whose dimsy furniture and queer Victorian provincialism she accepted. Yet when she spoke this poem about the Negro leader, not a very good poem but effective for recital, there was a conviction in her voice which surprised me.

This surprise was one I had constantly in Trinidad, because though it is an island so riddled with class and colour distinctions that one expects never to see unity emerge, even at this time, that feeling of unity will suddenly show itself and merge the most conflicting elements against a common enemy.

The poems recited had been by Negro authors. The music was European, at least in intention, until Gittens announced the great event of the evening, the singing of a Negro spiritual.

The singer came up to the piano. Then he said: "I'm sorry, but I don't know any Negro spirituals. But I'll sing a sentimental song." So without an accompaniment he sang 'Lonesome', or 'Twilight', or something. And then there was a quartet, and then everything broke up for a time and Gittens came over to speak to me.

We went out on the gallery and he said: "Well, how do you like it?"

"Fine," I said. "It's a great success." And so it was. "But when are we going to eat?" It was a quarter to eleven by then, and with just a couple of sodas in me I was feeling more like food than culture.

"Of course, you're going to speak," said Gittens.

"No," I said firmly. "I'm sure everybody is just as hungry as I am, and any speech from me would be most inopportune."

"Nonsense," said Gittens, "they like hearing you speak."

"All the same," I said, "I'll have to ask you to excuse me."

The quartet had been filling in the interval and everybody was sitting in the concert-room, without so much as a glance at the banquet hall. The quartet stopped, and Gittens got up and said: "And now Mr. Arthur Calder-Marshall of *John o' London's* fame will say a few words."

I was on strike. I wanted my supper and I wasn't going to sing for it. And anyway, since when had I been of *John o' London's* fame?

"I don't know about you," I said, getting up, "but I'm just itching to get my hands on that food. And all I want to say is to propose that we adjourn into the next room just as soon as possible. Those in favour needn't say 'Aye'. They just have to follow me."

I made straight for the banquet hall. But no one followed me. I had committed a breach of manners in not praising the concert and in not realising that though it was a quarter to eleven the meal wasn't ready yet.

There was no going back, so I went forward into the kitchen. In the kitchen things were at a standstill. The Homeric task of preparing sixty plates of food was too much. There were the plates, there were the chickens, there was a carving-knife, fork and spoon. I set about repairing my blunder: carved up the chickens, helped sixty people to stuffing, lettuce and whatnots.

At last the meal was ready.

Gittens came up to me. "Will you go and tell them it's ready?" he said.

'What marvellous discipline,' I thought as I went into the front room and found everybody waiting. 'What incredible restraint that they haven't mobbed the kitchen!' If there'd been sixty of me and no meal before eleven I would have done. "Ladies and gentlemen," I said, "the banquet is now ready."

It was a very hot night and the hall was hotter. I wiped the sweat from my face with a sopping handkerchief. And behold the concert room was empty.

I went through to the banquet hall. Every seat was taken and several people were standing up. 'Thank God I'm the guest of honour,' I thought.

I looked round for the guest of honour's seat and there wasn't one. So I went into the kitchen. I saw someone eating. "Where did you get that from?" I asked.

He pointed to a pile of sandwiches in paper. I made for them straight away and got three. There was a crowd of people in the kitchen and the sandwiches soon went.

Gittens came into the kitchen. "You oughtn't to be here," he said, "there ought to be a seat for you."

"That's all right," I said, "I'm doing fine here."

"Well," he said, "come and help us broach the L'Ouverture wine."

We went over to a packing-case, but it was nailed down. I looked around and found a screwdriver or something and we prised open the lid, revealing half a dozen tubby glass bottles. Gittens bent down, picked up one, and held it to the light. The wine was the colour of glyco-thymoline, and on the label was PORT. "The L'Ouverture wine!" said Gittens.

There was a crowd of us standing round and a murmur of appreciation and wonder ran round the group.

Gittens unscrewed the bottle, glasses were brought and the wine was poured out. Gittens lifted up the first glass. The port was sparkling and bubbling like a vintage cider. "Good!" he said.

Somebody handed me a glass. The mere sight of the wine sent an irrepressible feeling of gaiety through us all. I said: "I always believe in drinking the wine of the country. Is there any rum?"

"Sure," said someone; taking my glass and handing me a small dark bottle. I looked at the label. It was a brand I had not seen before. It said LIGHTNING.

There was no corkscrew, so I got the cork out, beating the base of the bottle with the palm of my hand. Then I went over for a glass.

"There aren't any more glasses," said one of the girls. "You'd better have one of these." She handed me one of those paper cups you get in offices and on trains.

I poured out half a cup of Lightning and gulped it down neat. It was well named: It streaked down my gullet and landed like a thunderbolt in my belly. A man came up and took the bottle out of my hand. "Good stuff," he said.

"It's got a kick," I answered, and I looked down at the paper cup. It had passed out.

The banquet was over around twelve, and then the dancing started. We danced for two and a half hours, until the band packed up and went home to bed. It wasn't a large room for forty couples and it was a very hot night. But we kept at it. After the first dance I was so hot I took my coat off and hung it up. Then I went up and asked a girl for a 'set'.[1] "O.K.," she said. "Put your coat on."

It is a convention to dance with your coat on, at this sort of dance, where they're 'making style'. And after dancing for two and a half hours I came to the view that it was a good idea. The theory is that whatever clothes you wear you will sweat like a pig. So that the more clothes you wear, the more absorbent material you have between yourself and your partner. Even as it was the smell of sweat was so strong that I felt I had only to put my hand out and squeeze the air and drops would fall on the floor.

The L'Ouverture dance was a good dance. The only place I went to where the dancing was dull was the Country Club. Because the L'Ouverture was slightly pretentious, the club members conscious that they were a cut above the people staring in from outside, it wasn't as good as the 'brams' and 'whams' I went to, where you pay twenty-four cents to go in and eat pickled souse and dance your head off. Those are the places for dancing, in an old school hall with the floor-boards rough and the band piled up on a dais, so thick it's a wonder they can all stand on it, much less play. And they can play, with the intuitive rhythm of the Negro people, giving themselves right out in the music because they love the music and not because of what they're being paid for the evening. It is not sophisticated music; there is little subtlety in it; to listen to it would be monotonous. But it is music for dancing. You have got to dance. Even the old women behind the scrubbed wood table dishing out chicken *pilau* can't keep still. They are jogging from foot to foot. They are waving their spoons in the air. There is no show, no formalism of manners, no coquetry. The girls have come in their best clothes in order to look their best. But before that they have come to dance, to enjoy themselves. And they can do both. Fat and thin, short and tall, almost without exception they can dance, men and women.

They start at nine and they dance till three or four, on and on, set after set, sweating and laughing and dancing and having a swig of rum now and again.

Outside on the gallery are the rest of the people in the village, without the wish or the money to come in. They stand watching, the light from the dance room falling on their faces and casting great shadows across the ground outside. And the noise of the band goes out through the great open windows, through the darkness under the coconut palms, calling everybody to dance.

---

1. *One does not dance dances, but 'sets' in Trinidad. And that is not just another name for a dance. A set goes on for anything from twenty minutes to half an hour with a couple of thirty-second intervals in which to clap the hand for encouragement.*

And when the dance is over they go under the trees or back to their houses to finish what they began in the dance. This is the natural, uncomplicated climax of the evening. They take it without qualm of conscience, and they finish the business there and then.

Melita showed this point of view, though it is unfair to quote what she says as typical, because she is not a typical woman. In any part of the world she would stand out as exceptional.

Tony and I went to see her, after bathing at Manzanilla with Sam Bagaloo. Sam had a theory of economical driving. He drove with the accelerator down till he reached seventy miles an hour. Then he turned the engine off and coasted till he was doing twenty. Then he started up the engine again. No amount of argument would convince him that the harm he was doing the clutch cost more than any gas he saved.

We went to see Melita with half a bottle of rum. Tony had lived in a cottage up the street from her and when Melita saw him she ran out and they both started 'eh-eh-ing' like a couple of twitting birds. We got out of the car and Sam came in and we made a West Indian punch with eggs and nutmeg and milk and the remains of the rum.

While she was making it and beating the punch up with a swizzle-stick, and selling sweet bread to children who came into the parlour, she told us about the dance. The dance had been at the Prince's Buildings in Port of Spain the night before. And there had been a girl with rouge on her cheeks, a coloured girl. And she had all the men running after her. She looked so pretty.

"And what about you?" said Tony. "You didn't get a man?"

Melita is thirty-five, a mulatto without her first looks, but with an effervescence of humour and gaiety that will last her another twenty years. "Me?" she said. "Yes, I got one. A fine one with a car. And when we came away from the Buildin', he asks me, 'Woulden you like any-thin', a present?' And then I remembered I hadn't bought any bread for the parlour today. So I said, 'Four loaves', and out he got and bought four loaves. So I had me bread and I had me man and a ride home in a car for nothin'."

The white people have invented a myth that the presence of whites at these dances is resented by the coloured people. It is another aspect of the white colour excuse, which forbids the whites to ride in buses or go into rum shops. It disguises itself under sensitivity. 'They would resent it.'

The coloured people do resent the presence of white people who go 'slumming.' But what they resent is not the colour of a skin, but a patronising attitude of mind. I have seen this operating against white people who cannot mix without self-consciousness. But even when I went to places where my sympathies with the coloured people weren't known, I never found this attitude shown to me.

The colour excuse operates even more strongly with women. "Of course, you're a man," people said to me. "But a white woman couldn't go to places like that."

Three weeks before I left, my wife came out to join me in Trinidad. The second evening she was there we went down to San Fernando, where I was speaking to a meeting of the Oilfield Workers' Union. Very few coloured women attend these meetings and she was the first white woman to do so. But she sat in the audience with Tony, and when I had finished speaking, they thanked her for coming and asked her to say a few words. Their attitude was scrupulously polite and at the same time friendly. They did not resent her presence, but the artificially erected barrier which prevented people of any colour mixing freely.

Again, when we were in Tobago, we went to a dance at Mason Hall, which has the reputation of being a tough village. We had asked an American and his sister to come with us. The American handed us the line about resentment at intrusion. The girl wanted to come, but she couldn't make up her mind. She wavered and shallied, said yes and then no, unable to accept the thing just as a dance. A New Yorker, she had been to dance-clubs in Harlem, but this was different, because Mason Hall is a tiny village about twelve miles from Scarborough and there's no chromium plating. In the end, we went without her and danced till four in the morning. And again there was not the slightest resentment, just delight that a beautiful white girl, who was a good dancer, had come to the dance.

The only place where we went and found the atmosphere unpleasant was a dance at the Prince's Building during a race meeting. The atmosphere was unpleasant, because the riff-raff of Port of Spain was there. Our table was surrounded by spongers and coloured people who had been corrupted through contact with the tourist trade in the capital. These people differ from the majority of the inhabitants of the island, in that they have accepted from the whites their doctrine of colour inferiority and within those limits are trying to get their own back by any form of trickery. As in other parts of the world, they form an unimportant minority.

If the word culture means anything, it is a way of life rather than the artistic expressions which may be the flower of that life. But it also has a moral quality. It implies that there are admirable qualities in that way of life, that it is productive of fuller and more generous life. It is in that sense that one talks of Germany or Italy today as being countries without culture, meaning not merely that they have persecuted their artists and killed the arts, but that they have made a way of life in which it is impossible for the arts to flourish.

In this sense the West Indians have a culture. It is different from the culture of which Gittens talks. Or rather Gittens, when talking of it, intellectualises and distorts it into something it is not. He makes it a conscious growth among the petty *bourgeoisie* of Belmont, when it springs naturally from the temperament of the Negroes and to a lesser extent the East Indian people, living and working in the villages, on the waterfront, in the oilfields.

Its most popular and vigorous form of artistic expression is in the calypso. The calypsos are composed and rehearsed for Carnival, which takes place early in March, just before the beginning of Lent. For weeks beforehand these songs are rehearsed, in tents, where formerly you could enter for nothing and now you pay an entrance fee. Today there are three kinds of calypso, the first and truest form is the formalised ballad about events which have interested the islanders. This may be based upon a local event, such as the dance on the pier when the pier collapsed and everybody fell into the sea, or on Mussolini de Bully, or Mrs. Simpson. The second type is pure virtuosity. A simple ballad is made up around someone sitting at a table with his friends. It is a delicate form of flattery and designed chiefly to get money. And finally there is the decadent commercialised form, the advertisement.

The calypso is musically uninteresting. The tune is monotonous and the words are built around some half a dozen different tunes. The words are the important thing. They are either Rabelaisian, political or topical. In every case there is the delight of the long word, to which I referred above.

Here are the texts of three different types:

If you want misery, give an ugly woman matrimony.
   Refrain:
Dere's an argument goin' aroun' de worl'
About de pretty and de ugly girl.
Dere's an argument goin' aroun' de worl'
About de pretty and de ugly girl.
De pretty girl might make you shame.
Because she got de looks, she can't be blame.
But if you want misery,
Give an ugly woman matrimony.

1.
If yo're a gambler with plenty pluck
Wit' a pretty woman she will keep yo' luck.
If you like to play rummy, whappy or dice,
Before you leave de house she will treat you nice.
But wit' an ugly woman, you will be a crooked man
An' you'll be always safe in de poliss han'.
So if you want misery,
Give an ugly woman matrimony.

2.
Wit' an ugly woman you wouldcn have a friend,
And your prosperous days boun' to meet an end.

If you an' her are invited out to a dance
You'll only be takin' a sportin' chance.
For while happy couples are dancin' aroun'
She will be the laughingstock and clown.
So if, etc.

3.
If you're lookin' for a sweetheart to make you glad,
Don't take an ugly woman to make you sad.
For at night when you go to bed you're bound to frown
To see de beast, how she's lined up in her long nightgown.
Den to make a little fun you woulden' have de taste,
You'll have to take de pillow and 'bash yo' face.
So if, etc.

4.
A pretty girl goin' to be de pride of yo' heart,
In her silk gown she'll be nice and smart.
Pretty dresses goin' to fill her heart wit' joy,
And she boun' to call you 'Pappa Toy Loy.'
Especially if she's a nice high brown,
She will adore you as a king that wears a crown.
So if you want misery,
Give an ugly woman matrimony.

There are any number of these discussions of erotic questions. For example, the lamentation on the depravity of the older generation, called 'You can't tell de Old from de Young,' which ends:

To go to a dance is somethin' provokin'
To see how de old queens are shakin'.
They even give her de tango
An' now they are dancin' de rumba.
When you dance them nice, dey will chat you down,
An' you'll go home jus' like a clown.
You'll wake up in de mornin' and den you'll feel blue,
To see an old lady shake she bumper on you.

One of the better local calypsos of last year was made around the June disturbances. But it must be remembered of this, as of all the calypsos, whether sexual or otherwise, that they undergo a rigorous censorship from the police. The censorship was originally tightened owing to a particularly successful calypso on the behaviour of the gallant Colonel Mavrogordato, late commissioner of police, at a dance. But, after the June strike of 1937, Government felt itself so insecure that it tightened censorship all round. This accounts for a certain namby-pambiness in the words:

4. CULTURAL EVENINGS

MURDER AT FYZABAD[1]
   Refrain to be repeated after each verse.
Murder at Fyzabad!
It's the worse riot we ever had.
The oilfield workers of every grade
stopped working and said: "More money we must be paid."

1.
This was brewing for months ago
and the constabulary then got to know
and sent Major Power immediately
to protect the great South Vicinity.

---

1. *The 'disturbances' of June 1937 started at Fyzabad, the nearest village to the Apex Oilfields and Trinidad Leaseholds Forest Reserve. Uriah Butler, president of the Empire Home Rule Party, called a strike of oil-workers. During a meeting which he was holding in Fyzabad, Inspector Power arrived with a detachment of police to arrest him on a warrant. Power, instead of approaching Butler and presenting him with the warrant either before or after the meeting, decided to make a show of police omnipotence and interrupted the meeting, an excellent example of police psychology. Butler demanded that the warrant should be read. Lance-Corporal Price then produced the warrant, but literacy not being the first qualification for the force, he was unable to proceed. He handed the warrant to Superintendent-Sergeant Belfon. But before that officer could prove his superior education, Butler shouted: "Are you going to let them take me?" and the crowd cried: "No, they can't take you." Belfon had caught hold of Butler, but he found himself being carried into the crowd. Inspector Power and Detective-Inspector Liddelow then drew their revolvers and the party beat a discreet retreat.*

   During this time, however, Corporal King had been in the crowd in plain clothes, acting as a police spy. King, a fat Negro, was probably the most hated member of the police force. Stories were told of his habit of jailing the lovers of women he wanted, of going into bars and drinking with criminals till their money was exhausted and then arresting them. He had, however, a superstitious belief in his inviolability. "I am King," he would say. "I am the King."

   When King saw Butler escaping from the police, he followed him and caught him by the arm, trying to arrest him. He was recognised by the crowd, who suddenly realized that now was the time to effect a revenge that had been long waiting for him. The crowd turned on him. He took to flight and ran into a house, which was about six feet above street-level. He ran through the house to the back, and was either thrown or more likely jumped out of the back. It was a drop of about eighteen feet on to grass. But he was a heavy man and the fall broke his leg. Some women, whose husbands he had jailed, it is said, poured oil over him and set him alight. He burned to death and the smell of his fat hung around that place for hours.

   Power, who was as popular as a police officer can be, died later in the year: but not as a result of the strike.

2.
Then it occurred on the nineteenth of June,
– it was a Saturday in the afternoon –
the workers from de fields form a sit-down strike
and send deir leader Butler to seek deir right.

3.
He said de company didn't give him satisfaction.
Therefore he gave them his opinion.
Then dey telephone immediately
to San Fernando Constabularee.

4.
Up came Sergeant Belfon, Hunt and Power
with a warrant to arrest de great Butler.
Den he turned back to his crowd and asked: "Must I go?"
Everybody shouted out: "NO!"

5.
Den the constabulary men pointed a gun
wit' an understanding that the people supposed to run.
Dere and den dey started to leave for deir home,
an' what were they doin'? peltin' bottle an' stone.

6.
Charlie King landed like Mussolini.
Po' fellow, he was defeated quite easily.
Dey beat him to de groun', den burn him to death.
Inspector Bradburn receive a shot to his neck.

7.
Den they telephone down to Port o' Spain,
sayin' that we needed mo' help again.
Send 'em by buses. Don't wait on de train.
So not a police in de station remain.

8.
De strikin' fever went all aroun'
an' every business had to close down.
You must believe me, friends, it is true,
de fever even attacked Barbados, too.

9.
Po' Major Power, he is dead an' gone,
leavin' de whole island loud to mourn.
So let us extend our sympathy,
now he has gone to eternity.

Now that the censorship has closed down on candid local comment, calypsos are being made about foreign affairs. The Japanese, Mussolini and

4. CULTURAL EVENINGS

Hitler, the figures of war and oppression have taken the place of the local oppressors, the British Government and their warships. Both *Mussolini de Bully* and *De whole World in Confusion* throw a valuable light on the humour, the interest and sometimes the lack of realism with which the creole sees foreign affairs.

MUSSOLINI DE BULLY
Refrain repeated after each verse.
Oh what a bully is Mussolini!
Dat dictator of Italy!
Oh what a bully is Mussolini!
Dat dictator of Italy!
He did everything to violate the League
and that is why he is so fatigue.
But Selassie said: "'Tis best to die free,
than to live in de world without libertee."

1.
Mussolini's only playin' de fool.
We know that Ethiopia will bring him cool.
It's the very country that give them licks,
it was in the year 1896.
You know they altered them and they was so sore!
And look at hell, they goin' back for more.
But this time what they'll have to do
Is to hold Mussolini and alter him too.

2.
The greatest bandit the worl' can possess
is an Italian, I must confess.
Look at de behaviour of their delegate.
It was at Geneva, I must relate.
He broke de meetin' not once, not twice.
An' Mussolini found dat was nice.
He insulted de League and give it a blow
with the drinks in de glass he said 'Cheerio.'

3.
De smallest infant will realise
That man Mussolini's uncivilise'.
I must say he's jus' a big tramp.
In other words, I'll call him a scamp.
Napoleon and de Kaiser, both tried de same.
And after all, dey could play de game.
For twenty years has passed quietly
And de Kaiser is still absent from Germany.

4.
Dere is no difference in any way
Wit' Judas and Mussolini, I'll say.

Judas betrayed Christ and was fatigue
Jus' as Mussolini betrayed de League.
But de Bible made us to understan'
dat Ethiopia will stretch its han'.
But I only hope when it's stretching out
dat it will grip Mussolini's mout'.

5.
On Judgment morning when de Holy Master
Should call on Mussolini to stand and deliver.
He shall be perished and cast to hell
wid de devil and the imps he will have to dwell.
For those horrible crimes and disasters
that he have permitted in Africa.
And in Paradise will be Selassie
smilin' down at barbarous Mussolini.

6.
Have you ever heard of de ass in de lion's skin?
Dat's de position dat Italy's in.
In Addis Ababa they're not at ease.
For dey are surrounded by great armies.
Dey have to watch Hitler move on de Rhine.
And many other things that brewin' behin'.
Now dey've gone and joined the revolt in Spain.
So Selassie bound to start up again.

7.
Those Roman people really fool our folks
Some of you boys may take dese for jokes.
First dey came around wit' all their bad deeds.
Wit' de little medal and the shapely beads.
Dey made our young ladies stand to attention
To talk dere privacies and call it confession.
If it's so, dey gets de wine, de whiskey and rum
Dey wouldn't catch me wit' de Bobby's num cum.

This calypso was written at the beginning of the year 1938, when the majority of European papers had relegated Ethiopian news to the wastepaper basket. The Abyssinian war is still being followed in Trinidad with fervent interest, and the average creole can give one a very much better account of what is happening in that country than the average Englishman. *The People,* a creole newssheet, published weekly, devotes considerable space to the war.

De Whole World in Confusion dates from the same period. Because it is dealing with much wider problems, it is not so acute as *Mussolini de Bully:* but it gives a good commentary on the state of Europe as seen by the creole.

DE WHOLE WORLD IN CONFUSION
Refrain:
Trials and tribulation put de whole world in confusion.
This I must mention.
Trials and tribulation put de whole world in confusion.
This I must mention.
We have troubles in de East, Nort', West and de Sout'.
I dunno what to say. We have troubles all about.
Even de Pope saw de things look brown.
And he had to see de whole world upside down.

1.
Since we born, we never seen things so before.
Everybody's lookin' for war.
De Japanese boastin' dat dey rulin' de East.
So Asia is not at peace.
At Nankin' an' Shanghai de people are in dread.
We don't know why Japan always want poor China head.
So de Pope saw de things look brown,
An' he had to see de whole world upside down.

2.
Dey form a League o' Nations and things are introduce'.
But we see it's no use.
Mussolini have insulted it and said he will prevail
And cause de whole League to fail.
He has broken every chapter in the covenant an' uses poison gas.
An' de po' League had to keep meetin' till de las'.
But when Selassie saw that was fun,
He had to catch up all of his treasures an' run.

3.
On de continent of Europe, it's a funny place to dwell.
For a statesman said: "It's like hell."
It seems like religion is causin' plenty row.
So they usin' all de 'isms' now.
Some want communism. Others want somethin' new.
Dey're usin' fascism and barbarism too.
Who must be blamed for dat confusion?
Hitler. Mussolini. And de Holy Vatican.

4.
Now I mus' come to de fightin' in Spain,
Where thousands were killed an' slain.
If dey fought against deirselves so ferociously,
What they goin' to do against you an' me?
Before de other nations have sympathy an' do what is right,
Dey are givin' dem arms and den dey join up in de fight.
But when dey start wit' de poison gas crime,
I know de Holy Master will be comin' dis time.

5.
In Germany Hitler have de people in a heat,
About war: an' nothin' much to eat.
He took up his troops and he threw dem on de Rhine
An' leave de gentlemen to grine (mope).
But de great Russia said: "If he dare to interfere,
Our planes like bigass[1] will be flyin' in de air.
But Uncle Sam, he said I'm neutral.
For not me again in dat festival.

6.
De presumptuous Mussolini want to do what isn't right.
Only lookin' for boys to fight.
Every man today seems to be a diplomat,
Watchin' each others like a cat or a rat.
But de Great John Bull said dat dey gone back on de track,
I don't know why dey only barkin' at de Union Jack.
Only rearm and leave dem to shout.
For we'll soon put a muzzle on top one mout'.

Carnival is the great time for calypsonians. They enter in rivalry, extemporising against one another. They march down the streets, singing and dancing the Congo Barrio with masks on their faces. From morning till night and all the night through, sustained with rum and the excitement of Carnival they run riot, into the hotels and out again, with the white people coming down to watch in motor cars and not feeling that it's very amusing after all.

But the calypsonians eke out a living during the rest of the year, singing at parties, at restaurants, making tours of the other West Indian islands. The censorship has limited them to a certain extent. But the other songs exist underground. They are sung in select circles and, as always happens, the fact that they are forbidden has added spice to their humour. Their jokes pass around, like the underground jokes against Hitler in Germany. Hitherto in allowing the licence of Carnival and freedom of speech in songs, the Government has given an outlet for the irrepressible criticism of the Negro in the form of humour. A subject race whose form of political expression is limited to a travesty of freedom must have some outlet. It is absurd that a race whose native intelligence is high despite the poverty of education, should agree with its rulers on all its measures, if on any. The calypso proved a safety valve, a means of canalizing public feeling and giving it an aesthetic outlet. The clamping down of a censorship will not have the effect that Government desires. The hidden calypso has a malice in it, which is not dissipated in laughter, because it is forbidden. And the

---

1. *Bigass is a local bird.*

emotion, the criticism that found its expression before in the public calypso, will not be overcome by forbidding it expression. If a man thinks you're a fool, you can forbid him to say so, at least in your presence, but he will think you even more of a fool for doing so.

Before I leave this chapter on cultural evenings, I want to describe my third evening with the L'Ouverture Society. On this occasion, a 'symposium' was staged, designed to bring together five conflicting points of view in a public discussion of what was vaguely called the Trend of Modern Ideas. Besides myself, the speakers were Mr. Bertie Gomes, Dr. Achong, Gittens and the Reverend Mayhew. Gomes, maliciously termed The Seer of Belmont, stood for the white petty *bourgeoisie* of Belmont, Art for Art's Sake and all that. Dr. Achong, a native Trinidadian Chinese educated at Harvard, had a certain labour following in the capital. But he had been taking a reactionary stand on the question of the immigration of refugee Jews, against whom he suggested there should be special discrimination. I had written a letter in one of the local newspapers attacking him on this point, in the hope that the symposium might be the more antagonistic. The Rev. Mayhew was a popular preacher.

The Rev. Mayhew was supposed to start, then Dr. Achong, Bertie Gomes and I were to follow, in that order. Finally Gittens was to sum up the discussion. The Rev. Mayhew, however, asked to speak last. So Dr. Achong began, defined the subject as the struggle between fascism on the one hand and the forces of democracy in the capitalist countries and the U.S.S.R. on the other. He spoke well and lucidly, and he finally came uncompromisingly down on the side of a popular front against fascism.

Gomes then rose, and advanced to the centre of the hall. He had apparently written his speech in the style of Burke. It began with a couple of magnificent periods in the grand manner. He appeared nervous but his great voice came out of his chest like jets of steam.

And, surprisingly, this red baiter who had lost no opportunity to expose the pernicious influence of Birtles and myself, came out fully in support of Dr. Achong's position. His speech was short. But it was filled with a vigour and sincerity which I had never suspected. It was like listening to a wind-elemental. But when he sat down after five minutes, there was no doubt of his opinions on anti-fascism.

I had expected, and rather hoped for, opposition. As it was, there was nothing for me to do but to expand the remarks of the previous speakers, raise a point or two they had missed and hand the torch to the Church.

The Rev. Mayhew was embarrassed. He had prepared a homily on the Trend of Modern Ideals, which to him meant the tendency of the younger generation to attend the cinema rather than church, to wear cosmetics and smoke cigarettes. His speech was facetious, in the tradition of Dickens, and was spiced by little stories. He seemed to me to concentrate on small questions of personal conduct with that buoyant flippancy characteristic of many clerics all over the world.

Apart from the Rev. Mayhew, the temper of this meeting was uniform. The audience came from widely divergent colour groups, each, speaker attracting a certain following. But here was the merging of colour questions, the agreement in a common attitude of people who would not ordinarily have met.

As I said above, and as I will show more fully in the next chapter, colour distinctions are still one of the most important elements in Trinidad life. But at this meeting, as I was to find at subsequent trade union meetings, the colour question is submerged as soon as men and women meet to discuss and formulate a common purpose. This is one of the reasons why Government, which thrives on the disunity of the people it rules, is trying to oppose activity of this sort.

5. STILL WAITING FOR LEFTY

SOON after my arrival in Trinidad the idea came to me of producing *Waiting for Lefty*. It is an easy play to produce and act. The cost of production need not be high, and with suitable casting amateur actors can produce a competent performance.

I approached various people connected with the trade union movement. They were all enthusiastic. It was planned that a performance should be given on Butler Day, June 19th, to a mass meeting at which Rienzi expected to get 20,000 workers. I wrote to New York for copies of the play and awaited their arrival.

They came about four weeks later. And Tony and I immediately set about collecting our cast. We had spoken to various people about the idea, and we told them to send along suitable people who wanted to act.

For our try-outs we borrowed the hall in which the Seamen's Union held their meetings. Certain of the seamen were physically the right type and we asked them to come along. At the same time I told Gittens about the play. He immediately asked me why I did not turn the play over in its entirety to the L'Ouverture and let them produce it within the Club. I answered that as time was short I wanted to have a larger group than the Club to draw on for talent. I also knew what the unions thought of Gittens, and feared that there would be a working-class boycott of the play if it appeared under the Club's auspices. If the play was a success I intended to suggest that the proceeds should be put to the credit of a new dramatic society, composed by members of the cast.

Gittens said he was sure that the L'Ouverture was capable of filling all the parts easily. He took a copy of the play and promised to send round suitable people for each part.

These people arrived at the Seamen's Hall at the same time as the seamen. The Union Executive was having a meeting in one corner of the room, and I immediately realised that a mistake had been made. Though Gittens wasn't there, his younger brother was. That was quite enough. "We won't have them in this room," said the Executive, "they're spies. We don't trust them. Take them away. Take them away."

Tony and I explained that we had to unite as many people as possible in the play in order to get wide backing for it, and that the more talent we could draw on the better the play would be. "All right," said the Executive. "But don't let that Gittens shove his nose in here."

As soon as we started trying people out we realised that we were up against a tough proposition. The play was referred to generally as 'the concert'. Only one or two had ever seen the text of a play before. None of them had acted. They read stage directions as well as speech. Some even read their own names at the beginning of the speech.

We soon found, however, that the seamen showed less ability than the L'Ouverture. The seamen found it difficult to read at all. It would have taken months and maybe years to train them to their parts. The L'Ouverture Club members were more literate. But we found that without any reference to us Gittens had already selected their parts for them. "You," he said, "will be Joe. And you will be Edna." So they came down to the hall, not for a trial, but to take over their parts.

Of the people we tried out the first day, one girl showed an aptitude for her part. About three others could be used at a pinch. The rest were impossible. Then another difficulty, the girl with talent had read her scene with her husband. The husband was no good for the part. He had little acting ability and he was the wrong type. Would the girl be prepared to act away from her husband? With perhaps too elaborate tact we told her how pleased we were with her performance. We were not quite as pleased with her husband's. Maybe we should have to get someone else for the part. And her husband could take some other part. Did she object?

She looked a bit dubious. Then she said that she didn't object. Then she said she thought personally that her husband was very good in the part. We said it would be a good idea if the husband would try and work the part up, and then maybe he would be better than anybody else we could find.

This play was something so new in their experience I thought I had better give them some idea of what we would be up against. I explained that we wanted to get the best performance we could, and that could only be done by co-operation. That the casting was very tentative at the moment, and that they must realise that not everyone would be taken in the end. I urged punctuality, and told them to give me their names and I would get in touch with them when I wanted them again. Meanwhile I asked one or two to come to a further rehearsal in a few days' time.

"I can't come," said a young man in volunteer's uniform.

I didn't want him to come. I hadn't intended to ask him as he had no acting talent. "That's too bad," I said.

"Well, I can," said the girl who had shown definite promise.

"What?" said the volunteer. "You come here?" His eyes swept the room and lighted on the Executive of the Seamen's Union. "Among these people?"

To a person like myself, who did not know Trinidad and appreciate its niceties, this remark was mysterious. The difference between the Seamen's

5. STILL WAITING FOR LEFTY

Hall in George Street and the L'Ouverture Club rooms in Belmont Circular Road seemed to me negligible. They were both bare, except for a few wooden benches. Both useful rather than beautiful. But to the volunteer there was an enormous difference. George Street was a low district. Belmont was respectable and residential. Again, the Seamen's Executive were low, working-class people. He probably thought also that he was a shade or two lighter than some of them. He himself worked in a shop or was a clerk. He was 'educated'. There was an enormous gulf fixed between him and the seamen.

Difficulties of this sort beset every meeting, the difficulties lucidly being the greater the worse the actor or actress was. From the L'Ouverture we succeeded in selecting an excellent Harry Fatt, who walked straight into the part, a good Agate to make the final speech and three or four other characters. We then had to look elsewhere for other talent. We approached one man, a Negro, who promised us the co-operation of his dramatic group. But as soon as he heard that the rehearsals were in George Street he dropped the whole business. We asked the help of Mr. Roberts, schoolmaster-playwright, who produces his own plays with the boys of his school. Mr. Roberts explained that he was very busy on his own play, but that he would give us any assistance he could, either in production or in obtaining actors.

We then approached Mr. Govia, a Portuguese shopwalker in Fogarty's drapery store. He runs a dramatic group and promised us his assistance. He had produced plays himself. He knew the difficulties and he would be prepared to take any part we chose for him. His wife also was a very good actress, and he was sure she would like to come in.

Since George Street did not seem a very popular meeting-place and the seamen were getting tired of harbouring potential spies, we had selected another hall just north of Woodford Square in the centre of the town. But when we were trying out individuals we usually did so on the gallery of my lodgings in Woodbrook.

This was resisted by the L'Ouverture group, who wished to transfer activity to Belmont. The fact that Govia and two shop-girls we had recruited lived in Woodbrook was a good argument for a compromise on a central hall.

We were very pleased with the discovery of these two girls. I do not know what nationality they were. Though sisters, one looked Chinese and the other Portuguese or Venezuelan. We rehearsed them carefully alone, taking the men's parts ourselves. They made quick progress, and they had less difficulty than most with the American dialect.[1]

---

1. *The whole method of voice production differs enormously between Trinidadian and American. For example, it was almost impossible to get anyone to give the proper value to "Mister, he's* laying *there* in a *hot per*foomed *bath." Each time it came out: "Mister, he's laying there in a hot perfume bath." The voice, naturally a sing-song, rather like a Welshman talking like a Midlander, could not give value*

When Govia came along with his wife they got along well together. Mrs. Govia, however, pleaded that she was not well and could not read through a part. Her illness, she intimated, would last as long as the play.

We were taking them through their scenes together when one of the L'Ouverture actors arrived. He had to act opposite one of the girls. Though not pure Negro he was very much darker than Mrs. Govia.

I immediately felt a *frisson* go through the others. Nothing was said except that the girl who was to act opposite him said she thought she preferred to have another part acting opposite Govia. She consented, however, to go through her old part and did it very well.

After that we arranged to meet the next evening at the hall and go right through the play. We had now assembled more or less a full cast.

The next morning Govia 'phoned me up. He had already told me that he couldn't be present because he was a volunteer and they had to parade in readiness for the reception of the new Governor. I knew we were in for trouble.

"Mr. Marshall," he said, "I hope you don't mind me 'phoning you up."

"Not a bit," I said. "Go ahead."

"Well, Mr. Marshall," said Govia, "I know Trinidad much better than you do." I waited. During the fortnight the play had been in rehearsal I had heard that phrase a dozen times. It always preceded some outrageous expression of snobbery or colour distinction. "Of course," I said.

"That man," said Govia. "Where did you get hold of him? Where did you pick him up?"

"He's a member of the L'Ouverture Club," I said. "What about him?"

"Well," said Govia, "I don't like to have to say this, but you asked me when there was any trouble to let you know."

"What is it?" I asked. "The colour question?"

"No," said Govia. "Oh, no. Not that." He paused. "Well, people wouldn't like to see a man like him on the stage. They wouldn't feel nice."

"I think that's ridiculous," I said.

"Mr. Marshall," said Govia, "you don't know Trinidad like I do."

"If this isn't a question of colour," I said, "that's all I care about. I think it's absurd. But he's not terribly good. I can get someone else."

"Thank you," said Govia. "You see, I know Trinidad. I know how people feel here."

That evening the two shop-girls didn't turn up. A certain proportion of the rest of the cast turned up, and a great contingent of people who'd already been rejected but still seemed to consider they were in the cast came. Mrs. Govia arrived with an olive-complexioned girl for the stenographer, and a Negress came from the L'Ouverture for the same part.

---

to two or three consecutive words and almost invariably sank into inaudibility on the last syllable or word.

I tried them both out. The Govia candidate had no idea of the part at all. The L'Ouverture girl was good. I went up to Mrs. Govia and said: "What can have happened to those two girls? They promised to come last night."

"I can tell you," said the olive-skinned girl. "They won't come. They're roller-skating."

"Why not?"

"You don't know Trinidad," said the girl. "You can't produce a play like this. How could you expect me to go on the stage with those people?" She pointed towards the L'Ouverture crowd. "Why, my social career would be ruined. I couldn't look my friends in the face again."

"Will you explain this a little more clearly?" I said.

"If you want to have your play," said the girl, "you can have it with a white company. Or with black people. But you couldn't expect them to appear on the stage together."

"If I want to have my play!" I said. "Thank you for that one. Because people have asked me to put on this play I've bought the copies of it, given up the last three weeks to producing it for nothing, just to be told about your social career." I got up. "I'm through with this," I said. "This cosmopolitan little town is the most provincial, petty-minded, snobbish little hole I've ever been in. You Trinidadians talk about being an oppressed people, but by God you deserve to be oppressed. You deserve to get the dirty end of the stick every time." I was angry, because of the hundred and one stupidities I'd come up against in the last three weeks, and that girl got the brunt of it.

I went over to the L'Ouverture crowd. "The play's off."

"Why?" they said.

I explained why.

"Perhaps," someone suggested, "you didn't handle the situation tactfully."

"Tactfully!" I said. "Tactfully! Do you realise that in the last three weeks I've been around licking more behinds than I've ever done in my life? And what do people do? Expect me to be grateful. As if they'd got champagne there."

Tony laughed.

"Come on, Tony," I said. "Let's get a bottle of rum. At least that isn't as rotten as the rest of the island."

And that is where the play stands. They are still waiting for Lefty. Govia intends to produce it. The L'Ouverture wants to produce it. And the Oilfield Workers' Union want to produce it. And it is they who finally will produce it, in my opinion.

All I got for my pains was an insight into the colour question, which I couldn't have got in any other way. That experience with the Amateur Boxing Bouts gives the full picture of colour division.

6. FIGHT! FIGHT! BLACK IS WHITE!

THE Amateur Boxing Bouts were due to start at eight-thirty. By eight o'clock the street was already lined with parked cars, the pavement before the Empire jammed with people, and the cinema itself, a classical structure conceived after the divorce of Construction and Ornament, was more than half-full.

We were not surprised because this was a big evening. The bouts were being staged by the *Trinidad Guardian,* the island's leading newspaper. And the climax was a contest between Alkins, the sports writer, and Assam, the people's favourite.

Alkins was the white man's favourite. He was the aristocrat of the ring. Assam, on the other hand, was unassuming: a decent fellow, half Chinese and half East Indian. His father, so they said, had wagered his shop that his son would win.

We fought our way through the foyer, bought tickets and went in. There were three prices – stalls, pit and gallery. We sat in the pit at one side, where we had two fans playing on us. No seats were reserved, and if you got up for a moment your seat was taken before you could look round.

We bought a couple of programmes. The hall was nearly full, but there was still a quarter of an hour to go. We read the Wit and Humour pages, stories of Scotsmen, drunks and mothers-in-law clipped from some senile Joe Miller. We read the topical advertisements. FOR A KNOCK-OUT SHAVE USE BLANK'S BLADES. We scanned the list of fights – four three-round bouts, four four and one of five.

The cinema was full now, but the curtain masking the stage and the ring from the auditorium remained down. The gallery was clapping in unison, and Panama Joe, who was disqualified a while back, was fighting a young boy for his seat.

At half-past eight, amid cheers, amid stamping, thumping, shouting, the curtain rose. We saw the ring, surrounded on three sides with seats ready for the knowledgeable buttocks of West Indian fistocracy. Most of them were occupied: white fans, black fans, curry-coloured fans, grouped round an empty ring.

Behind was a backcloth, cut into by high double doors. These doors were not related to the composition of the back-cloth itself. On their left, against a faded prospect of blue sky, rose a vast semi-human figure,

6. FIGHT! FIGHT! BLACK IS WHITE

Epstein's version of the Sphinx. On their right were the simple but mysterious words: A BAR, and, underneath, PROPERTY ONLY.

This sight so dazzled us that after our first outburst of clapping, we fell into a bemused trance from which we did not rouse until ten minutes later a loud speaker began to warble forth calypso records.

For the next quarter of an hour the air grew more and more tense. Beauties sauntered down the aisles until they found sequestered ham-rests. A new type of man, striding resolutely, made a tank-line for the stage, to park pneumatic cushions on an empty rush seat. The hall, which thirty minutes back seemed full, gorged and digested more and more, as men crouched down pretending that there was a seat below theirs.

At last the calypsos stopped. Two midgets stepped into the ring. Captain Cipriani, wearing khaki with the dignity of a labour leader in whom the capitalists have the fullest confidence, led them to the microphone and announced their names and weights.

As an audience, we were predominantly Negro. The darker of the two boys was instantly our favourite. Betting ran high on him. He stepped out lithely. He was the dark champion of our race. We roared and cheered. We had waited long enough for a fight. There was no slow transition to excitement. It was like jumping into water, so sudden.

The boys were small, quick and light. They hadn't been taught to box, but fight. They lammed and ducked and clinched and sidestepped. They had no knowledge of anatomy. They aimed at the head, because that was the obvious place to aim at.

Because the head was the obvious place to hit, we cheered at a touch, roared at a glancing blow and at a real hit we flung our arms into the air and bawled. During minute rests, keeping excitement at fever pitch, we turned on each other and argued. We lost our tempers. We told one to sit down, another to take his hat off and a third he had stolen our seat.

But the instant the next round started, our eyes swivelled to the stage. The dark boy was better. To see him cop the whiteskin was a joy. That boy had guts, had pluck, had spunk, the way he coshed the whiteskin on the nose, the ears and on the back of the head.

In physique our fighters weren't much to write home about. They were the queerest shapes that malnutrition can twist the human body to. None of them weighed over eleven stone. A gangling giant, six foot four, weighed under ten.

But for all that, there was a lot of good hard battering about the head, more wild misses that sent us howling into laughter and even more deliberate clinching that enraged us. With each fight we grew more excited, because we were nearer the big fight, when our Assam would trounce the life out of snooty Alkins. Even when Kong, with his quick arms and slow, slow feet, his bull-like stance, was pounding Goddard we kept ourselves in, because we were waiting for the big fight. But in each case you could see where our sympathies lay, the light against the dark, the dark against the light, the colour-war we wage in business and our social life.

A roar went up when Alkins came into the ring, wearing little white pants and vest. The ring was wet in two corners with the seconds' sponging, so they shifted the seats over to the two other corners and Alkins sat down. There was no sign of Assam and Captain Cipriani looked around and finally came into the ring. "Where's Assam?" we shouted. "Where's Assam?"

Captain Cipriani stood in the ring and Alkins went on sitting in his corner and we shouted: "Assam! Assam! Where is Assam?" "I favour Assam," a fellow sat on the back of his seat, waving a two-dollar bill, "I favour Assam." But nobody took him. We all favoured Assam. A nightshade Negress in white satin stood up and shouted: "Fight! Fight! Black is white !"[1]

Assam came in. He was built more solidly than Alkins, though there wasn't three pounds difference between them and both were under ten stone.

As soon as we saw him, we burst out clapping and a chap climbed through a window above a side door and pushed aside the curtain to see. Captain Cipriani went and asked them their weights, and a man standing underneath the window caught sight of the chap squatting on the sill. The Captain came to the microphone and announced On my right and On my left: and they beat the legs of the chap on the sill with a long stick.

The two fighters went to their corners and they opened the side door and beat the chap over the shoulders as he scrambled down. Then they closed the doors and the two fighters stood with their hands on the ropes, rubbing their shoes in resin and somebody else climbed in through the window and they beat him down too.

They didn't go outside to beat him on the shoulders because the fight started and we were all shouting at the top of our voices and nothing existed but two boxers in a ring. Assam kept the centre with Alkins circling and then Assam drove his man against the ropes and in an instant was back in the centre, with Alkins circling.

In the gallery we began to beat on the floor with our feet, and that noise, like drums thrumming, broke through individual shouting.

Alkins began to mix it and there was no more circling. He landed a straight left to the shoulder, a right to the throat and a left and was out, leaving Assam a bit shaken.

To the rhythm of our foot-beats, we began shouting: "Ass-am. Ass-am. Ass-am." Drowning all other noise. "Beat 'im, Assam. Beat 'im, Assam."

The first three rounds were a mix-up and they never got down to real scrapping. But at the beginning of the fourth Assam sailed in with a left to

---

1. *'Black is white' is a local intensive and here just means 'like hell'.*

6. FIGHT! FIGHT! BLACK IS WHITE

the jaw and a right to the neck and a left to the jaw. We were on our feet and one of us sprang from his chair three feet in the air, legs raised, arms flung outwards. Alkins was shaken. He staggered back. Assam followed up and smashed him back against the ropes and...

The ring collapsed.

The right corner post, which had been loose, fell inwards and the ropes flopped to the floor. The two fighters stood back in their corners. The fistocrats rallied round. A hammer was brought and somebody started hitting the boards with it. He would have won, we were saying, it was a K.O. Assam. Assam. He'd got him on the run.

Three men raised the corner post and stood it on end while the fourth hammered the floor. Then they let go and the ring fell down again. This happened so many times it got monotonous. Somebody noticed that the chap was sitting on the windowsill again. He beat him on the legs, but after a time he got bored and stopped.

More and more fistocrats came forward who knew how to erect a corner post. They crowded around so thick, that if any of them had known they wouldn't have had room to do it.

At last some ropes were brought on to the stage.

Then the lights were turned on in the back of the pit and everybody in the auditorium stood up to see what was happening and the people at the sides stood on the seats to get a better view. It was a fight between someone who said something angrily which we couldn't hear and a fellow who waved his hands and said something contemptuously which was inaudible. We began to take sides.

A police corporal with protruding lips, receding chin and *retroussé* nose, came striding up the aisle. He edged his way to the centre of the crowd and waved his swagger-stick. The two fellows turned on him their combined fury. Hands waved. Voices were raised to a screech. And the dark officer, dressed in Stephens' Blue-Black uniform, became a simple shock-absorber. One took off his hat to speak and put it on when he had finished. The other flashed light palms to prove his logic.

Then the argument was over. There were no blows and no arrests. The shock-absorber suddenly became a corporal again. He turned on the people standing round and ordered them to sit down. He raised his swagger-stick and flipped them over the shoulders.

Gradually we all sat down. The two boxers were still standing in their corners, while men were tying the posts and straining ropes to the orchestra rail and fixtures offstage. At last they got everything fixed and stood back, mopping their brows. The last rope was released. And the ring fell down again.

This started a violent argument at the back of the stage. Two men, separated by half a dozen others, started to quarrel. They waved their hands and shouted, pushing all the time to get at one another. It was beginning to get interesting and people were craning forward to hear what was being said, when someone turned on the loud speaker and we had another dose of calypso music. This didn't lessen the argument, but it meant that we could only watch it as a dumb crambo.

Finally the corner post was fixed so that it didn't fall down. It had taken about twenty minutes and Assam, our champion, standing in his corner all that time, seemed to have lost some of his fire, while Alkins had regained composure. We shouted and stamped as hard as we could as they swung and battered at one another. But even we had lost our fervour. The *Trinidad Guardian,* we felt, had let us down again.

They fought the remainder of the fourth and a fifth round without much result. The judges conferred and told them to fight a sixth. They fought a sixth.

And then, and then if you please, the fight was a draw. After all that waiting, there was no decision.

We got up grumbling and went into the street. We were dark and knew that Assam won easily on points, the judges being unfair. We were light and there wasn't any doubt that Alkins had the best of it. We stood on the pavement and in the gutter, shouting and waving our hands. We moved off in disgust and then turned suddenly, shadow-boxing to illustrate our arguments.

The Empire was empty now. But the fighting had spread from the ring to us. It was in the street with us and we took it through the town. Down Duke and Frederick Streets we reboxed the bouts. We showered invective and contempt on one another. Round the savannah in the last tram, walking through Tranquillity Square, we battled, light against dark, with anger for arms, abuse for gloves. Till finally, in Belmont, John John or St. Anns, parted from opponents and lying beside our wife or paramour, we made the last reconstruction of the fight, fought it to the finish we desired and then enjoyed the fruits of victory.

7. LIBERTY COSTS EIGHTEEN POUNDS

WHEN the Blum Government came into power they abolished the practice of sending convicts to the penal settlement in Cayenne. For years 'Devil's Island' had provided material for sensational articles in the Yellow Press and a literature as lurid as the Foreign Legion. No economic reason existed for the transport of white labour to French Guinea and the system was condemned by commissions and humanitarians alike.

The penal system consists of a term of imprisonment at settlements on the mainland or on the islands. This term is followed by an equal period as a *libéré*, during which time the prisoner has to earn his living within the colony with the slender capital which he had earned during his term of imprisonment.

There was, and is, almost no work for these ex-prisoners. Posts of responsibility are filled by free white men from France, and the unskilled labour market is glutted with native labour. The period of imprisonment, which in most accounts has been the centre of horror, is in fact nothing compared to the period of 'liberation'. In prison at least food and shelter of a primitive sort are provided. The prisoner earns a small daily wage. But in 'liberation' he has to fend for himself, seeking work in a country which does not want him, living in a climate which taxes the health even of those white men who have the money to take precautions and provide themselves with comforts.

In consequence there has been in recent years an increasing number of *libérés* who have bought dug-out canoes and attempted the dangerous 600-mile journey to their nearest sanctuary, Trinidad.

The fact that Trinidad was a sanctuary to these men was due to the humanity and cleverness of a Trinidadian judge. When called on to extradite escaped *libérés*, he refused on the ground that he could only do so if their papers were sent him in proper order from their country of conviction, France. And supposing those papers were in order, he could not extradite them to Cayenne, but to the country where they were convicted.

This decision, which was legally correct, put the French Government to great inconvenience and expense. They did not feel inclined to pay the fares of these men from Trinidad to Marseilles, and then from Marseilles to Cayenne. So they let the matter drop. Trinidad became acknowledged as an unofficial sanctuary for the French *libérés*. On landing they were arrested, and sometimes, after a short period in jail, were handed over to the Salvation Army, who gave them board and lodging. When a sufficient number had collected, they were provided with an open boat and certain essential provisions, were towed out for a distance of twelve miles, and bidden Godspeed in their journey towards safety.

The judge left Trinidad, but the ex-convicts continued to arrive in larger and larger numbers. The authorities in Trinidad, who did not cherish any humanitarian sentiments towards these people, who merely cost the colony money, decided to set aside the ruling of the judge. In future, no *libérés* will be allowed to stay in the island and leave by boat to take the chance of freedom or drowning. They will be clapped into prison, and sent straight back to Cayenne by the next boat. Out of stinginess, the Trinidadians have reached the conclusion which the French Government wanted.

I went down to see the last contingent of *libérés* leave the island. Their boat was about twenty feet long, made of thick planks, caulked but not painted. Their sails were old flour sacks (the sort in which you buy seven pounds). They could not possibly withstand a violent wind. There were two crude oars, two barrels of water, biscuits and bananas.

Of the men, two had been sailors. One, the captain, told me that this was his fourth attempt at escape. They were making for Mexico, sailing up the West Indian islands. They did not dare to put ashore on the islands, however, because they would be arrested and sent back to Cayenne. They hoped that in Mexico they would find sanctuary.

"And if you don't get there?" I asked, "what then?"

"I shall escape a fifth time," he said. He had apparently no fear that he would be drowned. I wasn't so certain of the others. Some were working. Some were looking down at the keel, as they sat on the thwarts.

"Have you got a map?" I asked.

"Yes," said the captain. "Here's our map." He felt in his breast pocket and pulled out an atlas, four inches by two and a half. He showed me a map of the Caribbean and Gulf of Mexico, in which the two thousand miles between Trinidad and Vera Cruz could be covered by half a crown.

I turned to the Salvation Army officer standing by my side. "So they're going off," I said. "This is the last contingent."

"Yes," he said. "Yes. It's a fine boat, isn't it? The others never had as good a boat as this. Not by a long way."

"And you mean to say that these men are going off in this tub of their own accord," I asked.

"Of course," said the Salvation Army officer. "Quite of their own accord. Nobody's forcing them."

Tony was standing near. "Of their own accord!" he said. "You mean they'll be jailed and sent back to Devil's Island if they don't?"

7. LIBERTY COSTS EIGHTEEN POUNDS

"Yes," said the Salvation Army officer. "That's true. Sort of Hobson's choice, really. Ha! Ha!"

The boat was supposed to leave on Saturday, but it didn't. Some of the men couldn't face it. They went into hiding and the police wouldn't allow the boat to sail till they had got all the men herded in. It left instead on Sunday. I heard later that it reached Jamaica, where it had to put in. The men were arrested on the spot: and are being sent back to Cayenne. I thought of the little captain, with his plan for a fifth escape, and wondered where he'd land this time.

On Monday, Tony and I were walking down Marine Square. He stopped and spoke to a short man in a frayed white tennis shirt. It was one of the convicts. I remembered him sitting in the boat. "Why haven't you gone?" said Tony.

The man smiled. "I didn't have to go," he said. "I've been pardoned. When it came to yesterday, I decided not."

That evening Tony rang me up from the 'Kwong Tung'. "I've got that convict down here," he said. "Maybe you'd like to come along."

I went along and found Tony filling him up with Chinese food. He seemed to need it. I asked him why he hadn't gone with the others and what this stuff was about his being pardoned.

He explained that his papers and a full pardon had come through three weeks before. He had been in the boat, because the police said that if he wasn't out of the colony by June 15th, they would put him in jail and send him back to Cayenne. They wouldn't give him the money to get out, nor would the French consul. Yet he was free. He had a valid passport.

"How are we going to get him out?" asked Tony.

We asked him what he could do, what his story was. His name was André Louis Gambier. He had been born in Caen, Normandy, in 1910. He joined the Marine Militaire in 1927. In 1931, when the fleet was at Toulon, he went on a spree with one of his comrades. They went to the Seamen's Club first and got well liquored up. Afterwards they went to a café chantant and stood drinks to a lot of girls only to find suddenly that they hadn't got any more money. They felt the evening had only just begun, so they went back to the Seamen's Club to borrow some more money. When they arrived there, they found it was later than they thought. Everyone had gone home and the place was locked up.

They broke into the club, looked around and found the till, took eighteen hundred francs (then about fifteen pounds) and went back to their party.

Next day Gambier was had up before the Commander and identified as one of the men who had broken into the club. He admitted his guilt, but he wouldn't say who the other man was. His accomplice was never discovered, but he was sentenced to five years' hard in Cayenne.

I interrupted him at this point to ask what Cayenne was like, was it as terrible as it was made out to be?

"Well," he said. "In a lot of ways I like it better than the Trinidad jail. At least they do pay you there."

His five years' hard labour was nothing compared to the struggle as a *libéré*. He decided to escape. He and five others scraped together enough money to buy a dug-out canoe from the natives. They laid by some food and set out, making for Trinidad.

They crept up the coast past British Guiana and finally landed on a little island, within sight of the mainland. They did not know whether the mainland was still British Guiana, until they hailed a fisherman, who told them that they were in the mouth of the Orinoco and that the mainland opposite was Venezuela.

They decided to risk landing. They got ashore without being observed and Gambier managed to hang on, living a hand-to-mouth existence for a year. But, as he said, he hadn't escaped from Cayenne for a life like that. He crossed over to Trinidad, was imprisoned there and then released. He had been living at the Salvation Army for six months.

It took a long while to get the story out of him. The date was July 11th. His notice to leave ended in four days' time. I realised his extraordinary daring in remaining in the island and not going with the other prisoners. In four days' time he was going to be jailed and returned to the penal settlement.

"What about your father?" I said. "Can't he spare the money for you?"

"No," he answered, "I've written him and he hasn't got the money. He is a poor man."

We thought how we might get him a job on a boat. But he talked only French and Spanish. He would be very unlikely to get a job on an English boat without any papers. We discussed people we might appeal to for help. Those who were rich enough wouldn't be sympathetic: those who would be sympathetic weren't rich enough.

We had another bottle of rum. I kept thinking that I could afford the money if I wanted to, and knowing that though I had the ready cash to get him home I would be a fool to give him the money, because in a month's time I couldn't afford it.

"Well," said Tony, looking at me. He had an idea that I was much richer than I was.

I looked back at Gambier, with his shirtsleeves rolled up showing the snake, the anchor and a naked woman on his arm. On his chest was Dieu et mon droit, 'What's it got to do with me?' I thought. 'I'm always taken in by a hard-luck story. I never make any money for myself, but when anybody comes around for money I have to get it for them.' If there had been anything I could have got hold of to criticise in the man, if he had

7. LIBERTY COSTS EIGHTEEN POUNDS

André Louis Gambier (left) wonders shall he sail?

begged or whined, I'd have left him like a shot. But there was no sob stuff. He was direct. He had stated his case when we asked for it. It was we and not he who said something had got to be done.

"I've got it," I said. "I'll write a feature article in the *Chronicle*. I'll appeal for the money to get him his fare back to France."

Tony burst out laughing. "But it's not a story," said Tony. "There've been hundreds of these chaps here."

"But not pardoned," I said. "And the last batch to go out. And his not sailing. With a passport, but going back to Cayenne if he can't leave the island."

"Well," said Tony, "the only difficulty is that your article won't get there in time. He's only got four more days."

At such moments my mind works quickly, but invariably wrongly. "I'll cable straight away to get cable facilities," I said.

I sent my cable and spent the next morning checking up on Gambier's story. The Belgian consul was acting for the French consul. But he found out that the passport I had seen was perfectly in order and that the pardon had come through a month before. "But can't you do anything for him?" I asked. "He's a French citizen."

"We've given him a passport," said the acting French consul. "After that it's for the Trinidad Government to take what action they think fit."

"But they're going to send him back to Cayenne."

"It's out of my hands," said the consul.

I left him and went to the bank where I had my mail sent. There was a cable to say: "Send airmail."

There was only one thing to do, what I should have thought of the night before, to go to the police and get a prolongation.

I went to my friend Louis Wharton at his chambers, told him what the situation was and asked him for help. He had always helped me in anything I had asked, and now he rang up Detective-Inspector Liddelow and I went straight round to the detective headquarters.

Detective-Inspector Liddelow was a white-faced man with light eyelashes. He had a thin mouth and smiled when he talked, though he said nothing funny.

I explained that I had met Gambier and was interested in his case. I thought that I could do something for him but that I had to check on his story.

How did I think I could do anything for him, asked the inspector, smiling as if the idea of anybody wanting to do anything for Gambier was a joke.

I explained that if I had time for my article to get to England I was sure that the readers of the *News Chronicle* would subscribe the money. But I needed till the end of the month.

"You mean to say that the readers of the *News Chronicle* will subscribe the money for this man's passage home?" asked the inspector, smiling even more broadly.

"I'm sure they will," I said. "But I don't want to write until I've checked up on my facts."

"Well," answered the inspector, "I want you to understand that I can tell you nothing for publication."

"I don't want you to," I said. "I merely want to know whether I've got the facts right."

Inspector Liddelow agreed to this, extorting the promise once more that I would print no information which he gave me. Then I went through the story, ending up: "And you really intend to send the man back to Cayenne?"

"Yes," said the inspector.

"Even though he's been pardoned?" I asked. "It's much further to send him to Cayenne than it is to Martinique."

"M'yes," said the inspector. "Yes. Then we'd probably send him to Martinique."

I got up. I had guaranteed that even if my article failed, Gambier wouldn't be sent back to Cayenne. And yet my promise that I shouldn't reveal anything that the inspector said bound me to say that the police intended to send Gambier back to Cayenne, as they had before the interview. The point of the article was not ruined, and the money was essential, because deported even to Martinique without money Gambier would have had no chance of success.

I sent the article off. In ten days' time it was published. The same day, the *News Chronicle* received over a hundred and fifty pounds in donations, of which, unfortunately, Gambier could only get the eighteen for which I asked. The rest was returned to the donors. But the eighteen pounds was enough to send him to Martinique, his deposit of 1800 francs paid, with a new suit and four pounds to start him off.

I expected that that was the last I should see of Detective Inspector Liddelow. But it was not. Things began to happen fast.

I was collecting material for another *News Chronicle* article on the Labour Situation in Trinidad. I had contacted the unions and agreed to speak to them on the subject of trade unionism. I had had the other side of the picture put to me by various employers. But I decided that it was essential for me to interview Mr. A. V. Lyndon, the Industrial Adviser.

Mr. Lyndon had been appointed by the Colonial Office to act as arbitrator between Capital and Labour. He was a specialist in what are called Public Relations. Without any specific legal powers, it was his function to act as a social lubricant.

I had already heard a great deal about Mr. Lyndon from people in the trade union movement, both leaders and rank and file. He was regarded as a man of great persuasiveness and plausibility. But he was not entirely trusted. The type of trade unionism which he wanted to see in Trinidad was one based on the post-General Strike principles of Capital-Labour co-operation. That form of co-operation, they considered, would be the co-operation of Labour with Capital in the interests of Capital.

I rang up Mr. Lyndon and asked for an appointment. He told me that he was very busy. Perhaps later in the week. Would I ring him if he had forgotten to ring me. I told him not to worry about that.

The very next day, however, I had a call. "Mr. Lyndon speaking. I'm in bed. I hope you don't mind that. Two o'clock. Yes, I shall still be in bed."

And so he was, lying propped up with a couple of pillows, wearing cream pyjamas. While he explained that he had been ill and I said how sorry I was and he said he was really better, I had a good look at him. He had long grey hair which was swept back from the forehead and curling slightly at the ends, thin hands which played over that hair, and a soft, insinuating manner.

I had told him over the telephone why I wanted to see him, so I told him all over again. And he asked how Aylmer Vallance was, and said how well he knew the *Chronicle* and how he liked it as a paper. And I told him Aylmer Valiance had left the *Chronicle* two years ago.

"Well," he said at last, "what exactly do you want to know?"

"Firstly, I want to know how you are progressing with your work."

"Ah," he said, "excellently. Excellently. I'm very pleased indeed."

"Good progress?"

'Considering that I've only been here two months, excellent progress. I'm very satisfied."

Lyndon was handling the interview the way he wanted. I wasn't satisfied so I tried shock tactics.

"What exactly does this progress consist in? What are your positive results?"

"Results?" He laughed lightly. "It's rather premature yet to talk about results. But we're sitting. We're discussing. These things take time, you know."

"I suppose that you would say one of your major tasks was to win the sympathy of the workers, Mr. Lyndon. How are you getting on with that?"

"Remarkably well," said Mr. Lyndon. "That is one of the sides of my work with which I'm specially pleased."

"You've noticed the amount of suspicion in the island, Mr. Lyndon?"

"Yes, I'm afraid I have."

"Well," I said, "I have been mixing with people in the island quite a lot, with trade unionists and their leaders, and I can tell you that in this island riddled with suspicion there is no man more suspected than yourself."

That wasn't quite true, though nearly true. But it succeeded, as it was meant, in knocking him off his perch. "But this is most remarkable," he said. "You must be mistaken." He hesitated for words. "They speak to me so nicely."

"Don't you speak to them nicely?"

"But they keep on ringing me up and asking me what I think they ought to do."

"If you were in their position wouldn't you ring up the Industrial Adviser and ask him what to do? It's very important to know, even though you don't do it."

"But it's so... so doublefaced."

"Who isn't doublefaced?" I asked. "Do you show the same face to the employers that you do to the workers? Do you talk to them in the same way?"

At that moment a maid came in with a tray of lemonade. Mr. Lyndon took a glass and I had one. As I raised it he said: "By the way, would you like whisky in it?"

I like lemonade and I like whisky. But the mixture didn't appeal to me. "I never drink till sundown," I said.

"Nor do I," said Mr. Lyndon and he lifted his glass, "Cheerio!"

"Don't you find that in this climate you can drink much more than at home? Sweat it out or something."

"Yes, I do," said Mr. Lyndon.

For a moment we said nothing. Then I returned to the attack. "Do you find the attitude of the employers on the whole conciliatory or otherwise?"

He gave me a detailed account of different personalities among the employers, outlining very well the types which I should have expected him to find. He tried to represent himself as the instructor of the ignorant trade unionists, too young in trade union experience to know what they wanted or how to get it.

I saw that it was time for me to go. But I still wanted to get a definite expression from him of what type of unionism he thought desirable. Point by point, I got the admission of the perfection of the modern trade union movement in England today. And having succeeded in this, I rose to leave.

As I got up he suddenly said: "But how much of this are you going to print? You know I've been indiscreet at times."

"I've given you my word," I said, "that nothing you have told me in confidence will be printed. As for the article, it's on the whole labour situation in the island: and each element has to receive its due importance. You need have no fear that there will be much about you."

Soon after four that afternoon Colonel Mavrogordato, the Commissioner of Police, went to a party. He was met by his hostess, who said: "Mr. Lyndon wants you to ring him immediately. He says it's important."

The colonel went to the telephone and rang through to Kent House. "What?" he said. "Who's that? What's the name? Calder-Marshall? Right. I'll get his record from the M.I.[1] Urgent? All right."

---

1. *M.I., Military Intelligence. Not usually high.*

The next day I went down to San Fernando with Tony to interview the San Fernando Borough Councillors on the subject of their receiving stipends. After an exhausting day, beginning at five-thirty in the morning, we arrived back about five in the afternoon.

We were going to attend the meeting of the Clerks' Union, to which we had been invited. To get there we had to cross Woodford Square where a mass meeting was taking place. The mass meeting was being held by the Negro Cultural and Social Welfare Society. There were about two hundred and fifty people grouped round and listening.

Miss Françoise was talking about the Shop Hours Bill.[1] The audience consisted of men who would have been at the Square at this time anyway. They were listening, instead of sleeping or gossiping, because it was entertainment. Not very good entertainment, but entertainment all the same.

When we came up Françoise was speaking. "I want you to listen very carefully to what I am saying. Because when we are arrested, we depend upon you to give testimony for us. I am not appealing to any violence. I do not want you to resort to force. But I do implore you to protest against the Shop Hours Bill; I implore you to sign the protest and make your friends sign it. Then we will present it to the Governor."

As we came across the square, under the trees, Percival, a leader of the Negro Cultural and Social Welfare, saw me and beckoned. I thought he wanted me to speak at the meeting and I shook my head. He came to the outskirts of the crowd and I told him we were going to the Clerks' Union.

While we were talking, a coloured detective walked into the circle and went up to the chairman, Clement Payne, who had led the strike in Barbados and been deported from there. He brought Payne across to a white inspector.

As soon as they started to talk the crowd lost its lethargy. In a moment it was alive and began to move across from the meeting and regroup itself about the inspector and the detective. The speech had been pacific and immediate resentment flared up against any attempt to stop it.

---

1. The Shop Hours Bill demands the uniform closing of all shops, apart from parlours, at four o'clock. Hitherto, shops in the main street have closed at four and other shops have remained open till much later. The move for early closing originated as a progressive Bill to limit the hours of shop-assistants. But it was used by the principal merchants to hamper the competition of the small shopkeeper, who was selling at the hours when the worker returned from his work. The Bill was carried through in the Legislative Council as a Government Bill, which meant that all Government officials had to vote in its favour, whatever their opinions. In this case it was not necessary. This measure aroused great indignation on the part of the general public and the small shopkeepers, who saw their opportunities of purchase and profit respectively curtailed.

Two desperate characters – Mr. and Mrs. Percival

Percival saw this and ran back into the circle where Françoise was trying to continue her speech. "Keep around, comrades," Percival called. "Keep around. Keep to the meeting." His voice stopped the crowd, but did not draw it back to the meeting.

He and his wife and Françoise began to sing the Internationale, their voices rising up quavering through the square. Excitement was mounting. I could feel it, intangible as it was, like something liquid, like water coming suddenly to the boil. And these three standing on the grass, with their heads raised, shakily singing the Internationale, were trying to control that excitement.

I looked around and saw Payne still talking with the inspector. They were set against the background of the hideous straggling Red House, the seat of Government.

Then the chairman turned and came back to where the platform was. Françoise stepped down and he got up in her place. "Comrades," he said, "Comrades. We have been told to break up this meeting. We are law-abiding citizens and we will break up the meeting. But I want you to remember what Comrade Françoise has told you about the Shop Hours Bill. I can't explain about this meeting. I haven't got the time." He glanced at the coloured detective coming towards him. He raised his voice. "But, Comrades," he shouted in a high, clear voice that sounded across the square, "I call you to witness that this square is OUR SQUARE. I shall come back and speak to you, in this square of ours, if they throw me in the jailhouse for it. Comrades, we shall be back."

He stepped down from the platform, which was a packing-case. They took it up and carried it away. In ten minutes the temper of the crowd had been transformed. Two hundred people had been listening to Françoise as a crowd of idlers. The police action, unwarranted by the speaker's words, drew them from apathy to indignation. Their sense of fair play was outraged. Whether they agreed with her or not, they felt that here their right of free speech was challenged. And the chairman in those few words forced that lesson home.

Two hundred men walked around the square, stood in knots talking indignantly. "In Hyde Park, yes," they said. "You say what you want. Nobody stop you speakin' your mind, givin' your opinion. But Trinidad, Trinidad is different. Here you can't say nothin'. Not we coloured folk. Our colour can't talk to our colour." They walked off in groups and ones and twos. They were important now. They had seen how the police treated people who wanted to talk of their colour. They went from street to street, spreading the news, telling of the meeting that the Negro Cultural and Social Welfare were holding indoors that evening, where the police couldn't stop them.

I went up to Percival and clapped him on the back. "Congratulations,"

7. LIBERTY COSTS EIGHTEEN POUNDS

I said. "The police have done your propaganda for you. If you'd been allowed to speak for a fortnight you couldn't have done the work as well as they've done it."

Percival and Françoise were too wrought up and too indignant to see it that way. "We went to the Mayor," he said, "two days ago. We asked him permission for the meetin'. He says: 'I got no objection, but you got to submit it in writin'. So we wrote a letter to him and took it round that afternoon. Personally. But he doesn't give permission. Yesterday he done no thin'. Said he was sick when we spoke on the telephone. An' now they broke the meetin' up."

Françoise was more emotional. She had been working all day and every day for the appeal of Jim Barratt. Jim Barratt was another Negro Welfare leader and he had been jailed on a charge of 'sedition', which means what it does in Jersey City or Detroit, Michigan, rather than what it means in England. Union activity is very nearly a synonym.

Françoise was almost starving. But her devotion to Barratt engrossed her. She did not spare herself, going from place to place appealing for funds for his appeal. As a result of the prosecutions after the strike of 1937, the membership of the Negro Welfare had fallen off. Danger always causes such a fall-away; but it also brings out the heroic qualities of people like Françoise and Percival, making them capable of energy and self-sacrifice, of which they themselves had no suspicion. She was desperate, because the fire in her was so strong that she could not understand the indifference that would leave a leader to suffer for his leadership. Barratt, she knew, was fighting in prison the struggle of the workers. If his case was carried through to the Court of Appeal in England, even supposing that the decision was not reversed, it would be a triumph for the workers. It would prove that they would not desert their leaders, and it would be a costly example that would make Government think twice before bringing such charges again.

"If it hadn't been for Comrade Barratt," she said to me, "I would have made them arrest me and put me behind prison bars. We all of us would." She was tired, exhausted by the struggle.

I said: "That wouldn't do anybody any good. You've done right. You must show that the force doesn't come from your side. You must remain outside prison, and if they break up your meetings, do just as you did today. You can't lose at this game. If they let you speak, you can talk to the people and educate them. If they don't let you speak, they do the educating."

"That's right," Percival said. The indignation was going. He was beginning to feel exalted, to know his power. He laughed. "They can't win," he said.

Tony and I had been asked to attend the Clerks' Union by a member of L'Ouverture who was on the committee. It was a critical meeting. The

Clerks' Union belonged to the Trinidad Labour Party, under the leadership of Captain Cipriani. Cipriani became interested in politics after the war, as a result of the war. A parlour Socialist, he grouped round him a 'left' party. But having no political or trade union training, nor stronger connection with the working class than a vague sympathy for the underdog, he made no effort to organise trade unions on orthodox lines. His 'unions' were just associations of people in the same employment for the assistance of his political machine.

In his time Cipriani did valuable work. But when the strike broke out in 1937 he was absent from the colony. He had been to see the Coronation. The leadership of Labour had long been ready to pass out of his hands. He had consistently indulged in red-baiting and had expelled the most brilliant members of his Party for extremism.

The strike made actual the failure of Cipriani's organisation to provide the leadership which the workers wanted. And after the strike one group after another broke away from the Trinidad Labour Party and came out for straight unionism.

At this meeting the clerks were discussing secession. In Trinidad it is not customary, as elsewhere, to hold union meetings in secret. So that there was nothing unusual in Tony and myself being invited. Percival, Françoise and a dozen others had also been invited.

As soon as Tony and I went into the hall, however, proceedings were stopped. John Henry, a Cipriani henchman, got up and asked us why we had come. We looked at the L'Ouverture member who had invited us. He gave us no assistance.

So we both said that we represented the Press; Tony the *Trinidad Guardian* and I the *News Chronicle*. We were asked to leave. And we left.

Outside was a crowd of other people who had been invited to the meeting. One by one they went in. One by one they were ejected. Each time that proceedings started again some new guest arrived.

For a time it was amusing. Then we decided to go back to Woodbrook and have a drink. It had been a long and exciting day.

But it was not yet finished. As we came up to my house we saw a Negro on a bicycle staring at us. There was something extremely obvious about the stare. It was us he was looking for and no one else.

I was just puzzled, but Tony made straight for the bicycle, walked around it, said, "Eh, eh!" and came back to me. "Hasn't got a numberplate," he said.

"Well, what about it?"

"He's a dick," said Tony. "They either have a police numberplate or none at all."

I looked round at the man. He looked at us going into the house and then bicycled off.

As soon as we got into the house, Mother Ram, the landlady, said: "Mr. Wharton wants you to ring him up as soon as you get in. It's important."

I went to the 'phone and rang through to him at his house. He said "I got a call today from Liddelow, asking me if I could give him any particulars about you. He said he heard you were going to speak to a trade union. I told him if he wanted to know anything he'd better ask you himself."

"Good idea," I said.

"Well, are you going to talk to any trade unions, my dear fellow?"

"Yes," I said, "I'll give him full particulars tomorrow."

"So that's why he put the dick outside the house," said Tony. "Trustful."

8. MOSCOW AGENT

I WENT to see the Detective-Inspector next morning. Through sources of my own I had learnt of Mr. Lyndon's urgent telephone conversation with the Commissioner of Police.

Liddelow, of course, was not giving away the reason for his curiosity. He was just acting on instructions from above. I left him to open.

"Is it true," he asked me, "that you're talking to a trade union?"

"No," I said. "It's not exactly true. I'm talking to three."

"Oh!" he said. "And could you tell me which they are?" These questions, in England, I should have regarded as impertinent. In Trinidad, despite the close identification, when necessary, of trade unionism with sedition, they were quite outside the legal province of the police. But I wasn't going to give him anything that he could hold against me.

"Certainly," I said. "Seamen's Union, Sunday night. Public Works, Monday. Teachers', Thursday."

"And can you tell where the meetings are?"

I told him what I could. I only knew where one meeting was.

He made notes on a little pad. "And can you tell me what you're going to say?"

"I'm afraid I can't," I said. "I haven't written the speech out. I shall be talking for an hour and a half and I can't go through it all for you now. But in three words, it's Organization and Discipline."

"You can't say more than that?"

"If you want to hear more, why don't you come along to the meeting? I haven't got any objection to your hearing what I've got to say."

The Detective-Inspector looked very bashful. "I'm very busy," he said, "I don't think I could spare the time."

"Then why not send round a shorthand writer to take the thing down verbatim?" I knew that despite the intense police supervision this was illegal.

"But would they let him in?" he asked. "Can you guarantee that they wouldn't throw him out?"

"I'm afraid I can't," I said. "I can ask them not to. But I can't go any further than that."

"All right," he said. "You know, of course, it won't do any good talking to them."

8. MOSCOW AGENT

I smiled at that. "I'll let you know what the Seamen say about a stenographer."

He nodded.

"Before I go, I want to tell you that I know who all these inquiries were started by," I said.

"I don't know that myself," he answered.

Detective-Inspector Liddelow didn't want to talk about this.

"Another thing," I said. "Maybe your inspector reported my being at the meeting at Woodford Square yesterday. I saw your men break up that meeting, and if you're interested in preventing trouble here, I think you ought to be more careful. You're making a lot of people who aren't in the slightest bit interested militant by doing things like that."

"It was an illegal meeting," he answered. "We can't allow that."

"I know that," I said. "Technically it was illegal. But what it meant to those people in the square was that you wouldn't allow a perfectly peaceful meeting to be conducted without breaking it up."

"That's the Mayor's affair," he answered.

"Between the two of you," I said, "you're using the law to cause trouble, not to stop it. Not that it's any business of mine."

"Quite," he answered.

I came back in an hour's time. "I'm very sorry," I said. "I've asked the seamen and they're quite firm. They said they've got few enough rights in this island and they're not going to resign this one."

"Oh, well!" said the Inspector.

"I'm very sorry," I added. "I'd have liked one to be there." I was genuinely sorry, because a police shorthand writer, placed judiciously in the front of a meeting, is an infallible butt when what you want to say is innocuous.

With their elaborate system of spies, informers and plainclothes detectives, the police have fallen a victim to their own fantasies. Recruited from men of limited education but almost unlimited prejudice, their leaders have no realistic knowledge of the problems of the island. The unions they regard as potential centres of sedition. They never meet the union leaders personally unless they rope them in on a sedition charge. They see labour problems through the eyes of those spies and detectives whose main stock-in-trade is the peddling of sinister rumours.

The policing of the island presents an insoluble problem. The main personnel is recruited from the Negro population. These Negroes are poorly educated and they are trained rather as soldiers than as policemen. They are housed in barracks, taught the use of firearms. Their general education is neglected. Their methods in the detection of crime are lamentable. In East Indian villages feuds have been going on for years, in which four, five, six men have been murdered without a single murderer being brought to justice.

I attended most of the trial of two Indians for the murder of Inspector Bradburn. The police had been nearly a year in bringing the case. The murder had been in June and the trial took place during the next May. The police had been over the scene of the crime, had interviewed people on the spot, had traced the accused's movements for the next three weeks. This activity took place during July, August and September. During that time they made no notes, took no depositions, could give no documented account of the investigations. The depositions taken from witnesses were made three to six months after the shooting took place: in one or two cases even more. The main witness recanted in the middle of the trial, declaring that he had been beaten up in the San Fernando police station and made to sign a dictated confession under threats. Even before that witness gave evidence, it was plain that the case in the form in which it was presented could have no chance of success. As it was the jury threw it out without hearing the defence.

Previously to this, thirty-nine persons were brought into the box for the murder and burning of Charlie King at Fyzabad. Everyone was acquitted.

It is obvious that the task of detection in the island is more difficult than in Europe. Among the coloured people there is a union against the law. Those who give evidence for the Crown do it more often from malice than from public-spiritedness. But at the same time, the methods pursued, at any rate in an important case like the trial of Inspector Bradburn, were such as to bring both the police and the law into contempt. It is very difficult to see how a semi-military local force is capable of much improvement.

On the other hand the solution of local inefficiency by the importation of police from abroad would make clear that the government of the island is by white men in the interest of white men: the more this fact is obscured, the better. The lesser evil is to have the present inefficient local force. This force, however, will be drawn from the worst native element, because the service demands a repudiation of the Negro's natural ties of relationship and colour. When called on to shoot his own people in order to protect the dividends of British rentiers, the better element will jib. It is for this reason that the fire-brigade is the most popular branch of the service, the men feeling no conflict of loyalty in this job.

My speaking to unions was a double betrayal, of class and of colour. My friends, the Wharton, were worried. They were afraid that I would either get into trouble or start trouble. So they asked me to lunch on Sunday, before I spoke to the Seamen, and the Honourable Vernon Wharton, Member for Sangre Grande, was brought along for moral support.

The afternoon was spent in discreet tuition, what I should say, what would be bad to say, and so on. I listened, while the ball was passed from one to the other, each tactfully making a play before handing it over to the next. I didn't tell them what I intended to say, which was already quite fixed in my mind. I could see that they, too, were under the influence of the same bogy as Mr. Lyndon, the Commissioner of Police, and the Detective-Inspector. But I did not resent the interference from them, firstly because they were delightful people whose company I always enjoyed, and secondly because there was a genuine desire to help. I could not blame them for the conception they had formed of me as an irresponsible firebrand, because they had had two months in which to form an opinion. But it surprised me that they should have had the same opinion of the union leaders, whom they did not know.

There is no need to outline the various meetings at which I spoke during the next month. My theme was nearly always the same. These unions were of recent growth. They had been formed either during or after the strike of June '37. Before then, all union organisation had been very primitive. The strike, or the 'disturbances' as they were called, was a spontaneous uprising without organisation, discipline, or the means of bargaining. In Port of Spain, the waterfront workers and the men on public works came out on strike without any formulated demands. Their unions were formed as the consultative body to formulate demands. On the other hand, the oilfield workers, without having union machinery, formulated demands and struck for them.

Obviously, the most important element in such a situation was the violent transition that had been made from individualism to co-operation. The attitude of many workers prior to the strike was that they were working for that day's bread and no more. They were not planning their lives on more than a two- or three-day basis. They were not used to thinking in more distant terms. Undercutting was a common thing. Each man was for himself.

It was necessary to stress that, in forming a union, they had started a new way of living and thinking. They had started something which would last their lifetimes and longer. It was important to give them a historic and dramatic sense of what they had done: to make them realise that the discovery which they had made had been made by workers in other countries before them: to bring to them a sense that the struggle that they were making in Trinidad, was a struggle taking place in the rest of the West Indies, in England, the States, Mexico, Spain, France; to make them feel kinship with the workers building socialism in the U.S.S.R. and trying to overthrow fascism in Germany and Italy.

In Trinidad, because it was an island isolated from other countries, there was a tendency for people to think first of Trinidad and then of the rest of the world. I tried to show them what their role was in relation to the rest of the world, to give them bearings in geography as well as history.

After that I came down to the dull business of union building: the necessity for the payment of dues, for the ventilation of grievances within and not without the union, for frequent union attendance, for the democratic principle of airing views and then obeying the majority vote, the struggle for 100 per cent unionism, the need for presenting a front which the majority of members will follow, the dangers of leftism and any form of split either from right or left, the relation of women to the union, the need for education of workers, both elementary and advanced, the ultimate aims of unionism as the establishment of socialism, the possible future of a Union of West Indian Republics and finally the sinking of colour distinction between White, Negro or East Indian and the realignment of peoples according to class lines.

I varied the lecture in different places, according to what I knew of the audience. I have lectured before to different audiences in England. But in England, whether the audience was proletarian or intellectual, I have always had a sense of depression after lecturing. In Trinidad I know that I lectured better than I have ever done in my life. I ascribe that not to any sudden advance in my rhetoric, but merely to the fact that the people I was lecturing to wanted knowledge. In England or in the States, knowledge is there for anybody who takes the trouble to get it. In Trinidad, it is the prize of wealth.

I spoke to six different trade union meetings. In Port of Spain I addressed the Seamen's Union and the Public Works. In both those cases I had the impression of a wise though untrained executive with a listless rank and file.

The Seamen's Union included the Waterfront Workers who must finally take over the union. The membership was around 30 per cent. And the executive had not yet induced the membership to pay regular dues. Their struggle had been too easy. They got their concessions early in the strike and the membership had not realised the need of co-operation.

The Public Works Union was in a very similar situation. They had won their advance too easily. There was a nucleus of men with understanding, but the principles of unionism had not yet become part of the life of the rank and file. Too many still believed that they could do better for themselves individually outside the union.

The Union Executives, however, and a certain number of rank and filers had a fine spirit. They were none of them extremists. In their approach to union problems they were more temperate in their language than a number of employers I met.

Though they were not fanatical in their views, their attitude to their union work was almost religious. The victimisation to which every worker who comes out for trade unionism, is subject, had developed in them a feeling of devotion. When you are down on the starvation line, it needs great courage to come forward and oppose established authority. They talked quite a lot about death, not in a dramatic way, but because it was close to their thoughts. The violence with which the last strike was put down will be nothing compared to the next strike. The oilfield employers had a few shotguns, old rifles and revolvers during June '37. This armoury didn't cow the workers. It was the old story of the workers standing out against violence. They could have massacred the whole white population if they'd had a mind to. But now the oilfields have got their modern arsenals with machine guns and new rifles. They have their regular rifle practice and the white employees are enrolled as volunteers, company police with the authority of the Government to use arms. Some drillers get a lot of fun, talking about what they're going to give the niggers next time.

So there isn't a man at the head of a union who doesn't think about death. The fact that he has come forward to take that position means that he has faced the possibility of death this year, next year or the year after. He knows that the other side is just waiting for the shooting to start. It means that he himself is very moderate in his demands, but at the same time he is ready to give even his life for his cause.

The Teachers' Union was a different proposition. White-collared workers, they have got that little more which they don't want to lose. So when it came to the day of my speech, I got a 'phone call, not from the secretary of the union, but from some junior member, to tell me that the meeting had been unavoidably called off. I asked why, and he said he didn't know. But I learned later that all the teachers were circularised and reminded that they were not allowed, as civil servants, according to their contracts, to attend meetings of a political nature. This was taken to include trade unionism, though I could not see how the teachers could have a union, if trade unionism was political.

Trade unionism is strongest among the oilfield workers. It was they who initiated the strike of June '37, At that time, however, they had only an embryonic organisation, led by Uriah Butler.

In order to understand the formation of the Oilfield Workers' Union, it is necessary to understand something of politics in the south of Trinidad. In San Fernando, the largest town in the south, a politically advanced group had been formed. The men composing it had been expelled or resigned from the Cipriani Trinidad Labour Party. The object of this group, called the Citizens' Welfare League, was to educate and mobilise the general public along popular-front lines, to secure a progressive member in the Legislative Council, to do the same with the Municipal Council and to bring forward the grievances of the people of the south.

Uriah Butler was one of the founding members of this group, but after a time he moved into the oilfields and began to organise the workers there in what he called the British Empire Home Rule Party.

Butler was not a native Trinidadian. He had come from Grenada, a small neighbouring island in 1922, then being about thirty years of age. He was employed in the oil industry, but in 1929 sustained an injury which lamed him. He first came into prominence in 1935, when he organised a hunger march of some hundred and twenty men on Port of Spain. Expelled from the Trinidad Labour Party, he started his British Empire Workers' and Citizens' Home Rule Party in 1936. He stated that at the time of the disturbances he had about one hundred paying members and nine hundred sympathisers.

The cost of living had been rising steadily in the island. The hunger march which was stopped by the intervention of Captain Cipriani had had no positive results. Butler met Sir Murchison Fletcher in Port of Spain in October 1936. He had made an urgent appeal to the Governor to do something to assist the workers. An eyewitness of this scene told me that Butler went down on his knees literally and begged the Governor's assistance, because otherwise there would be an outbreak. The Governor himself described the scene as follows: "…It seemed to me that while he was somewhat extravagant in his views and definitely extravagant in his mode of expressing them, yet there was sincerity." The Governor promised that when he went to Fyzabad he would meet Butler's organisation provided that there was a proper introduction from the Warden. But in fact the Governor never went to Fyzabad in the eight months that elapsed between this meeting and the strike.

In January 1937 the Negro Welfare and Cultural Association sent the Governor a report of a meeting, complaining of the rise in the price of foodstuffs, especially flour and bread. The Governor called for a report, and figures were provided by the Commissioner of Customs and a member of the Legislative Council, Mr. Grant. The Governor also decided to institute a simple cost of living index, and wrote to the Secretary of State for particulars. Colonel Hickling, of Apex, Ltd., estimated that the rise in cost of living during the previous year had been 17 per cent.

There is no doubt that the Governor was trying to do something to benefit the position of the unemployed and the underpaid in the island. He was a man of liberal sympathies and was genuinely affected by the condition of the people. Nevertheless, the progress of even a beneficent officialdom is slow. Eight months after Butler had made his appeal to the Governor, nothing had been done. The condition of the people was just as bad, and it seemed likely that it would remain so unless it was made plain that the people could not be trifled with.

Butler had become more and more impatient in his speeches and written propaganda. A very small group arose within his organisation prepared to use violence as a method of calling attention to the problems facing the Negroes. There is no evidence that Butler was directly connected with this

8. MOSCOW AGENT

group, or that he approved of their tactics. Butler was not planning either an armed uprising or a strike in the sense that it is known in Europe. His meetings were reported on by police agents, and notes of his speeches were handed to the Governor, who discussed them with Colonel Hickling of the Apex Oilfields. Colonel Hickling expressed the opinion that Butler's speeches were not the cause of the unrest in the oilfields, but that the true cause was the rise in the cost of living. But nevertheless the Government decided that it was time to intervene. On May 25th a summons was issued for Butler, returnable on June 14th. Butler did not appear. A warrant was issued and Butler was arrested on the night of the 14th and bailed out on the 15th.

Meanwhile Colonel Hickling, whose proposals to the Petroleum Association of Trinidad were known to have been rejected, had been recalled. Things seemed to be going from bad to worse.

The Governor had promised to come down to Fyzabad and had not come. Colonel Hickling, who was comparatively popular among the workers, had been recalled. The police were out after Butler.

Butler, there is no doubt, was carried away at this time. He felt that a net was closing round him. He became desperate. He started talking strike. He went to Point Fortin and held a meeting. He held other meetings at Fyzabad. But when he called a strike for June 7th, the men didn't follow him.

On June 17th the Inspector-General reported to the Governor that a strike was expected in the oilfields on the 22nd. On the morning of June 18th, the Governor had a consultation with two of the senior managers, as a result of which reinforcements were sent down to the south. At 2 a.m. he received news of very slight sabotage on the oilfields. At 10 a.m. he had a meeting with the managers of seven oilfields.

The decision was taken to issue a warrant for the arrest of Butler on the charge of inciting to violence. Further contingents of police were moved to the south. And that afternoon, Inspector Power and his men tried to arrest Butler while speaking at the open-air meeting in Fyzabad.

We have seen the result of this. The repulse of the police and the death of Corporal Charlie King.

During the whole of the events leading up to the strike, hysteria can be seen growing on all sides: the Government, the employers after the recall of Colonel Hickling and Butler himself, driven further and further by the preventive measures of the police, instigated by the pressure of the oilfield managers.

It is necessary to form an estimate of the state of affairs before, during and after the strike. Before the strike, Uriah Butler was known to a large number of people as a leader who had the workers' interests at heart. The hunger march had made him famous throughout the island. What he said at meetings seemed good sense.

The Commission have written Butler down as a 'fanatic'. But the word 'fanatic' is a cliche in describing the leader of any growing labour movement, to whom the term 'opportunist' does not apply. Sir Murchison Fletcher, with better opportunities to observe, describes him as sincere, but extravagant both in his demands and his style. Even the Governor, however, must be discounted to a certain extent, if we are to understand the appeal of Butler to his audience. Sir Murchison Fletcher, a man of university education and Colonial Service training, observing Butler from the security of Government House, would listen with different ears from the men and women to whom Butler's speeches were primarily addressed. Sir Murchison Fletcher could feel genuine pity and sympathy. But Butler's audience felt indignation, bitterness at the fact that nothing was being done for them as far as they could see. Words which seem bitter and extreme to the man with a full belly may appear an understatement to the man with an empty one.

I have described above the effect of police intervention on an apathetic meeting. The attempted arrest of a leader at a meeting not of idlers but men engaged in a task for which they know they are being underpaid was even more provocative. When Butler turned to his audience and said: "Will you let them take me away?" the only answer for the audience to make was the one they did make. Such an arrest was a common outrage of justice, if the audience felt as it did that the words that Butler was speaking were true. 'Here is a man telling us the truth about our lives,' felt the audience. 'And immediately the constabulary comes along to clap him behind prison bars.'

Butler was in fact neither a fanatic nor a great leader. He was an agitator. But it is necessary to clarify the meaning of the word 'agitator'. No agitator is capable of putting into people's heads ideas that are not there already. His function is to put the ideas that are already in people's heads into words. He is the mouth of the people. He says what they know. His superiority lies in articulateness. He is capable in his speeches and on rarer occasions in his actions to give expression to the thoughts and the desires of the people. It is when the fate of one man becomes identified with the fate of a group that trouble is liable to start.

Choosing the time that they did, the police succeeded in producing this identification. Butler had been saying what people thought for a long while. But it was not enough to rouse the workers to action. The conduct on June 19th provided the symbolic action which really started things.

Butler became suddenly the leader of the coloured workers. Prior to his attempted arrest he was not. He had tried to call a strike on June 7th, but he couldn't carry his followers with him.

This does not, however, support the Governor's analysis of Butler's importance. Colonel Hickling was much nearer the truth. The real danger, the real cause of the strike was not Butler, but the oppression of the workers in face of the rising cost of living. A spark may set alight a field of hay, but the spark will die out unless the grass has been parched by drought. Butler's attempted arrest was the spark, but the true cause was the suffering brought by the high price of food and clothing.

The strike, begun in Fyzabad on June 19th, spread through the island in a couple of days. It was not confined to one field or one industry. It was not localised in one village or town. In the space of forty-eight hours it became general. And it was in each case centralised in the figure of Butler. 'On the 21st the strike was spreading,' said the Governor. 'Reports from the fields stated that it was becoming racial in character, and that, *if we made an attempt to arrest Butler, the position would become one of grave danger.*'

On the evening of the 19th a cruiser was summoned from Bermuda, and on the 21st there was the request for a second cruiser. These arrived on the 22nd and 2 3rd respectively.

This strike is in many ways unique. It was not planned as an island-wide strike. Even within the oil industry there was no organisation for holding meetings,[1] sounding the temper of the workers and sustaining their morale. The leader, whose arrest was sought by the police, remained in hiding throughout the strike. He had no direct and little indirect contact with his followers. He had no contact with the majority of workers who had struck in other industries. He had been the mouth of the people, but that mouth was silent. He remained a figurehead, the symbol of an oppressed class.

A mouth. A symbol. These things are necessary. But equally important are the planning brain and the co-ordinating limbs. Before the strike, these did not exist. As I have said, the waterfront workers struck without having formulated any demands. They had, in fact, struck for two reasons. They had struck in sympathy with Butler and the oilfield workers: and they had struck for higher wages. They got their higher wages and they went back to work. Without a union organisation, it is not surprising that their aims were confused. Yet the inevitable result of this lack of planning is that the union today is weak.

The planning mind. Where did that come from? It was necessary and it had to be found. It appeared on the seventh day of the strike. Adrian Cola Rienzi came forward as the legal representative of the Home Rule Party with a written request to the Governor for a meeting with Butler and his committee and a safe conduct.

Rienzi, of course, didn't spring out of the blue. He is a native of San Fernando. His grandfather came to the island as an indentured labourer. After the conclusion of his indenture, he became a provision merchant. He prospered and fetched his wife and child from India. When he died he was

---

1. *Barratt and Percival saw the need of building this organisation: and this was the origin of the conduct, which brought down on them the charge of 'sedition'.*

a comparatively wealthy man. Rienzi's father, however, squandered his legacy: and Rienzi left Naparima, the Government College in the south, at the age of fourteen, entered a solicitor's office as a junior clerk at 2s. 6d. a week, and after two years went as clerk to the office of Cyril Hobson, whom he served till the age of twenty-four.

During that time he organised the San Fernando branch of the Trinidad Workingman's Association, which is now the Trinidad Labour Party. In 1924, at the age of eighteen, he was chief organiser for South Trinidad, and President of the San Fernando Branch. He wrote to Saklatvala, the Communist M.P. for Battersea, and as a result of his correspondence he swung more to the left. He organized a meeting to protest against the Saccho-Vanzetti Trial. His action was censured by Cipriani, but he held the meeting all the same.

During this time, Rienzi, or, as he was then called, Krishnadeonarine, was working and planning to get away from the island to gain an education which he could not get in Trinidad. He was ambitious and he did not want to stay a lawyer's clerk all his life.

At first he thought of going to the United States, and it was for this reason that he changed his name. A visa would be difficult for a young man named Krishnadeonarine, but with the name of Rienzi, culled from Lytton's novel, he hoped with his light skin to pass as Spanish.

It was his correspondence with Saklatvala which decided him to change his mind and go to Great Britain. He had saved and borrowed sufficient money to carry him through a course in Jurisprudence. He matriculated at Trinity College, Dublin: and in the freer air of Ireland was soon swept into the Sinn Fein Movement. He went round lecturing for the I.R.A. and finally had to leave Ireland for London. In London he met his compatriot Saklatvala for the first time. The association with Saklatvala was educational, both intellectually and civilly. The young Rienzi found his ideas clarified and his movements watched by the police.

The suggestion of Saklatvala that he should go to India and study there was prevented by the refusal of passport facilities. A citizen of the British Empire, Rienzi began to find, had not the liberties of the citizen of the Roman Empire. Though the grandson of an Indian, he was not allowed to go to India, and furthermore, his rooms were arbitrarily searched by the police.

For a time he had the idea of qualifying as an optician and studied at Northampton Polytechnic, but finally he returned to law and qualified as a barrister in eighteen months. During the time that he was in England he married, and when he returned to Trinidad he was in desperate need of money to repay his debts and pay his rent. He applied to be admitted to the Bar, but he found at first that permission was refused. His police dossier had been sent by the same boat, and after these years of struggle it seemed as if he would not be allowed to practise as a barrister in his own island.

East Indian leader, the Honourable Adrian Cola Rienzi, né Krishnadeonarine

Finally, however, a promise was extorted from him that he would not indulge in agitation, and he was admitted to the Bar. He went back to San Fernando and during the next two years built up a practice in the south.

In December 1936 he helped to found the Trinidad Citizens' League. But he had no direct connection with Uriah Butler's British Empire Home Rule Party, though he seems to have assisted them with unofficial advice.

Rienzi was not in favour of a strike called at the particular time it was. But he was faced with a growing fact, and as Butler immediately came to him for advice, he had to deal with it as best he could.

Butler went into hiding. His popularity was such that he could probably have hidden anywhere in the island. But in fact, while the police were searching for him in the south, Butler was in Port of Spain.

It fell to Rienzi to act as double liaison, between Butler and his workers, and between Butler and the employers. It was Butler's strike, and to that extent the role of Rienzi was purely that of go-between. On the other hand, of course, he was working from the side of the workers rather than the employers.

It would not be diplomatic to disclose at this stage the tactics of the strike. But it seems clear that the directing mind throughout was not Butler's, but Rienzi's. Butler in his lonely hideout lost touch with the movement which he had started. If he had not been forced to a bolt-hole, he would probably have had a more realistic assessment of the situation. As it was, he stuck out for the full recognition of demands, when the morale of the workers was incapable of lasting out that length of time.[1]

As it was, the workers went back without the recognition of their demands. In certain cases, minor increases were made to the well behaved. But these increases were less than the offers turned down by Butler.

But though the results of the oilfield strike were not tangible, a tremendous lesson had been learnt, much more thoroughly than it was by the waterfront workers who got greater concessions. The oilfield workers realised that the reason for the failure was the lack of organisation. What they needed was a real trade union.

This gain in knowledge was worth any gain in wages. June 19th, 1937, means to seven thousand workers in Trinidad the beginning of a new era, the era of co-operative effort. They knew why they struck before they struck: but it was only after they went back to work that they understood how they ought to have struck.

---

1. *An amusing human sidelight on the strike is the attitude of the marines, who were called in after three days. The marines were receiving a pound a day while the strike lasted, "Get along there, get along there," they'd say, making a great show with their bayonets. And then in an undertone: "Stick it out, boys. You're making a great show. Stick it out."*

A deputation of workers from the fields approached Rienzi and asked him to help them in their organisation. This step in itself shows a change of attitude which it is difficult for anyone who does not know the West Indies to appreciate.

Another story of the strike, told me just as a joke, illustrates the difference in outlook between the coloured people and the terrified whites. At the refinery at Pointe a Pierre, the white staff was holding back the workers with shotguns and revolvers. The situation was very tense. There might be shooting any moment.

Suddenly from the crowd of workers there broke a small East Indian, who walked resolutely forward across no-man's-land to the gates. Guns were levelled at him, but still he came on. And as he got close, he took a white paper from his pocket, oblivious of the danger to his life. He flourished the paper, calling the name of one of the white staff. The man came forward and took the paper. The East Indian turned and walked away. The man opened the paper. It was a summons for the nonpayment of a bill.

Here was a group of Negro workers approaching an East Indian to ask for his help. The colour and race barrier was broken down. I have no doubt that if there had been two men who could help them equally, one a Negro and the other East Indian, the Negro would have been chosen. But here the issue was clear cut. There was only one man and he was of a different race. The race question became insignificant.

After the oilfield workers came the sugar workers. They wanted to form a trade union. They also approached Rienzi to become their president. And here, in my opinion, Rienzi made a false analysis of the situation.

There are three distinct groups of labourers in the cane industry. There are two groups of field workers, those who work for wages, and those with small holdings who are contracted to sell their product to one estate. The contract of the wage-earners is a money contract, that of the smallholders a tenancy contract for products which includes a clause that the cane of the tenant farmers should be ground after the estate canes. Now it is true that the economic status of the tenant farmer is little, if any, better than the wage-earner's, but this clause ensures that in the event of a strike, the first person to suffer will not be the estate but the tenant farmer.

The controlling factor over the lives of both wage-earners and tenant farmers is the refinery worker. If he strikes, he is capable of holding up all work on the fields, since cut canes can only last a few days before decomposing.

These three types were all grouped in one union, called the All Trinidad Sugar Estates and Factories Workers' Trade Union. Yet it should have been clear that the interests of the tenant farmers were at variance with the interests of the two wage-earner groups. It was necessary, therefore, to create two distinct associations, one of sugar workers proper, and the other of tenant farmers, each to agitate separately for the improvement of their conditions.

In the oilfields there are nine thousand workers of whom seven thousand have joined the Union. In the canefields, however, only two thousand workers have joined the union: although there are thirty-four thousand engaged in the industry.

This difference in percentage is due partly to the fact that the oilfield workers are industrialised and form the nearest approach to a proletariat in the island, whereas only the refinery workers in the sugar industry are industrialised. But it is due also to an incorrect analysis of the sugar industry in the island.

Finally Rienzi was approached by workers belonging to a number of different trades for the formation of trade unions. As these trades were in each case small, he decided to lump them together in what is called the Federated Workers' Trade Union. This union includes builders, plumbers, carpenters and a hundred other small trades. When these trades are organised 100 per cent, it is possible that they will break away from this general organisation to form their own union. Meanwhile they are able to act with more or less efficiency.

A certain amount of the workers in the oilfields are transitory. They work a few days on one field and then they move on to another. Then they go to Port of Spain or San Fernando and get work on a construction job. An arrangement has been made whereby workers leaving the fields can join the Federated Workers' Union, thereby keeping in touch with the union movement.

Rienzi is the presiding genius of these three unions. Uriah Butler, imprisoned on Carrera Island, remains a figure round whom is grouped a feeling of great reverence. He is the inspiration of the movement, almost the patron saint. But even supposing that he had never been thrown into prison, there is little doubt in my mind that effective leadership would have passed to Rienzi anyway.

As things are, the imprisonment of Butler has provided the island with a popular martyr and allowed Rienzi to consolidate his position without any of the squabbles which might have harmed the movement incalculably.[1]

---

1. *On July 6th, the day that the strike ended, a reward of $500 was offered for the arrest of Butler. A reward of this size would prove a great temptation towards betrayal. But though his whereabouts must have been known to a number of people, no one ratted on him. He was in hiding three months, two of which he spent in Venezuela. He would never have been captured if he had not voluntarily stated that he was going to give evidence to the Commission.*

He stated the date and the time when he would appear. The police were determined that he should not reach the Commission. All roads to Port of Spain were watched.

8. MOSCOW AGENT

In the oilfields the feeling of militancy among the men is strong. In certain fields, the influence of the executive has to be constantly exerted to prevent the men from striking on issues which could be settled without resort to that weapon. As in all the unions, one of the hardest problems is the enforcement of the regular payment of dues. But the fact that the union officials are men of high probity prevents any suspicion that the union funds are being diverted to wrong purposes, and in the course of time, union discipline will succeed in enforcing regular dues payments.

As a body, the trade unionists were the finest people that I met in Trinidad. They are simple, eager people, faced with a task which they knew was the biggest thing they have ever tackled. They are trustworthy and, what is even rarer in the island, efficient. In discussion, the rank and file are not complicated, but they have an intense shrewdness and ability to learn from their immediate experience. They are not fanatical in any sense. They have the love of life and the direct approach to it that all the Negroes have: and their new-found seriousness is because they want more life, more opportunities for themselves and their children.

They are suspicious of the employers, of Mr. Lyndon and of the Government. But they have every reason to be. Government has expressed a desire to see the formation of trade unions in the island. Yet wherever the union officials go they are followed by detectives. I dined with the committee of the oilfield workers after they had had a conference with the employers and Mr. Lyndon. We sat in one of the central booths of the Kwong Tung Restaurant. The restaurant swarmed with detectives. They stood on tiptoe looking over the half-doors, and one even walked through the room pretending that he was looking for somebody.

Government can't expect to get it both ways. If they want to see trade unions established and their Industrial Adviser accepted without suspi-

---

And the approaches to the Red House, where the Commission was sitting, were guarded by detachments of militia and police. An eyewitness described it to me: "You've never seen anything like it. You'd have thought there was going to be an invasion, instead of them just waiting to arrest a lame Negro." True to his word, Butler got through the police cordons right into Woodford Square, where he was surrounded and taken straight off to the police station, under a heavy guard.

In popular thought as in the calypso, "Murder at Fyzabad," he is 'the great Butler'. Opinion is very sensitive about his treatment. When the film, The Life of Emile Zola, *was shown in the island, the trial scene of Zola was immediately identified with Butler's trial. I have never sat in a cinema in which the reaction of the audience was so tense and acute to what was being shown on the screen as during that trial scene. In the popular mind, there is no doubt at all that the trial of Butler and his sentence to two years' hard labour was a monstrous frame-up.*

cion, they must stop shadowing the workers' leaders with a vigilance that they show towards no common criminal.

The union officials, however, have developed a very realistic attitude towards this behaviour. As their secretary said to me: "It's much better to have them with you all the time, because then you don't have to worry about whether you're being spied on or not. Anyway, we've got nothing to hide. And when we've got a lot of people going to a meeting, we can send some of them with the detective. He's quite a decent chap." He added: "But if they'd only realise how little we want, how moderate our demands are."

This made me think of a story which a man told me about Jamaica. While he was stopping on a plantation, there was a strike. The workers came round the house, shouting and waving machetes. During the slump in sugar the planter had been to them and asked them to take a cut from a shilling to tenpence a ton for cutting cane. They had taken the cut, and when the price of sugar rose, their wages remained at the same level. My friend had not been able to discover what the planter's total annual profit had been, but he knew that the planter had made £40,000 over and above his normal profit. The cane-workers got some idea of this and demanded a rise.

The planter refused the rise. When the strike became ugly he called in the police. Ninety men were arrested and imprisoned for rioting. And then the cut was restored.

"But why didn't you do that to start with?" asked my friend.

The planter laughed and shook his head. "If I did that, then they'd ask for one and threepence."

The oilfield workers' demands are small, but they will be resisted at every stage. The formation of unions may be encouraged halfheartedly by Government, but the managers of the fields are doing everything in their power to break the unions and spread dissension among the men. It is hoped that race division can be caused by the introduction of East Indian workers into the fields. The distinction in housing has already succeeded in splitting the clerical workers away from the union. Schemes for company unions are introduced over and over again under different names, such as the Shop Stewards' Plan.

The only one of these manoeuvres which is meeting with any success is the separation of the higher wage-level workers from the main body. Race discrimination is resisted by the union, which is the only force making for the breakdown of the colour discrimination that we saw rampant in the different dramatic groups.

The common complaint of the educated Trinidad resident is the existence of this colour distinction and the lack of responsibility of the coloured workers. But colour distinction is, in fact, deliberately encouraged in order to split the ranks of the people: and this sense of irresponsibility is the inevitable result of crown colony government, as we shall see later. The trade union movement is evidence of the combined desire of the workers to take over greater responsibility. It will result in a much higher standard of labour, a better regulated and further-sighted attitude to work, and the proper sense of the worker's place in his society. These are qualities which are essential for the adult growth of the Negro and East Indian to citizenship.

But his struggle towards that end will be resisted both by his employers and by Government. His position in the structure of the British Empire is that of a wage-slave whose labour is exploited, a consumer on whom the trash of the home market is unloaded, and a dependant who finally has no say in his own Government. The coloured workers' full demands for greater responsibility cannot be granted within the present constitution of the British Empire. Yet those demands will be repeated more and more insistently: and gradually concessions will have to be made.

The struggle of the coloured worker will not be peaceful, because force will be used to suppress each effort towards greater responsibility, in the same way that force was used in Trinidad and Barbados in 1937 and in Jamaica and British Guiana in 1938. Commissions will be appointed as they have been in the past. They will make recommendations, most of which will be ignored. But each time certain advances will be made. A definite improvement has been made in housing conditions as the result of the June strike. Trade unions have won recognition. A new spirit has arisen among the workers. They have tasted freedom; they begin to know their power. And they intend to use that power, not as the whites fear and perhaps like to think, for the stupid display of violence, but for the attainment of better education, better conditions of work and a higher standard of life.

PART III

Your colour is God's colour

SOME OBSERVATIONS ON PATRIOTISM

R. MALCOLM MACDONALD stated to the House of Commons that he had no doubt that the West Indies were loyal to the Empire. In saying that he had no doubt, he proved that he had no information.

The feeling of loyalty or respect for Great Britain is almost completely absent from the people of Trinidad. This applies not only to workers, but to people of the middle class: and the reason for this indifference is traceable to a number of causes.

Firstly, the Trinidadian is insular in his attitude to life. The island is the centre of his universe, and everything outside is slightly unreal. His knowledge of Great Britain is confined in most cases to the British people whom he has met in the island. These people are either in Government or business.

Government officials and their wives keep to themselves. They form a clique, centred on Government House and the personality of His Excellency, who is referred to as H.E. in reverent terms. They do not even mix with the local middle class (there is no upper class). Their accents are strange, their manners distant and often patronising. Many of them are people conceited at their unaccustomed power: and almost to a man the officials are thinking first of their career and secondly of their job. The dominance of local vested interests in a crown colony demands a firm and independent line in Government policy. But experience soon teaches a Government official that he will earn more credit by doing nothing modestly, for his period of service in that part of the empire, than by throwing himself vigorously into the fulfilment of his job.

Government officials, therefore, are not liked in their official capacity or socially. The emotions they inspire are mockery, contempt, and dislike.

The business men who come from home have distinguished themselves by their scrupulous attention to their own self-interest. They regard the inhabitants as niggers, and the island as a place in which to get rich by being smarter than the next guy. They have contributed nothing to the good of the island as a whole, unless it was also to their own good. They are mostly drawn from the petty *bourgeoisie,* and lack both the virtues of the better public school type and the common decency of the worker.

But perhaps the most unpopular people on the island are the white men working in the oilfields. Drillers all over the world have a reputation for toughness. They are men with a specialised training, used to a hard life. Many of them come from the Southern States of America and a few from South Africa. In both these places, the attitude of the white man to the coloured is harsher than in Trinidad. In South Africa the Negro is not allowed to ride in the same tram as a white: and in certain Southern States there are Jim Crow laws relegating Negroes to special railroad cars. Drillers are usually excellent company among their fellow whites; but Negroes resent the attitude of many of them to coloured people.[1]

The Trinidadian, whatever race he comes from, is a very touchy person. He has at the same time a feeling of inferiority because he is not allowed to govern himself, with a compensation that he is not only as good but often better than you. The whole time that I was in Trinidad, though I met quite a lot of the low types to be found in any port, I met only two Negroes who denied their own colour.[1]

Apart from the sponge, the tout and the trickster, Trinidadians take no patronage. They speak to you on equality. There is none of this 'sirring' between one class and another as in England. The coloured man knows that the white man starts with an enormous advantage at the present time. But he does not accept that as God's law. With equal chances in a country run without colour prejudice, he knows that man for man the Negro would be as good as the white. And even in Trinidad today the Negro's wit and shrewd comment on the customs and pretences of the whites show great independence and acute judgment.

---

1. In the Hotel de Paris I saw a drunken driller having some fun with a waiter. The driller was so drunk that he could scarcely stay conscious. The waiter had to stand by the table. There were other people to be served, and as soon as the driller's head sank he would start edging away. But he hadn't got five yards before the driller would lift his head, his eyes half closed; his lips sagging in a blood-red face, and shout: "Bradburn! Bradburn!" in a voice like a drill-sergeant's.

The waiter would then return and stand politely, waiting for an order. But the only order that the driller gave was to point to where the waiter was to stand. Then again the head drooped, the waiter tiptoed off and the voice bellowed: "Bradburn! Bradburn!" and a stream of foul abuse followed if the waiter didn't come back.

2. One of these was an old man living on the island of Gasparee. He had a banana plantation. His name was Seraphin and his passion was to receive postcards from abroad. "Your colour is my friends," was his slogan. "Everything I got was from your colour. I love de bosses." He was slightly crazy, had testimonials dating back for thirty years. But his love of the bosses was due, in part at least, to a desire to get tobacco. The other one was a great fat lady we picked up at the races. We called her Netti, and took her dancing. She was very tipsy, and her theme-song was: "Your colour is God's colour. Let me go down on my knees an' wash your feet."

This is what some Government officials, who have served in Rhodesia, find it hard to stomach. In Rhodesia the simple native is grateful and respectful towards an official in whose good faith he believes. But the Trinidadian has had a long history of broken promises, of cruel oppression and calculated neglect. He is a sophisticated type. His distrust is never far away. He doesn't believe until he sees, and then not always.

But though the opinion of Britishers is low, the opinion of Americans is high. I had an argument with a taxi-driver one night. "If there's another war," he said, "they can string me up, they can crucify me before I fight for England. But for the States, I'd fight tomorrow, if they wanted me."

I tried to get him to explain why. But the only argument he could give was that Americans in Trinidad took more taxis than the English did. And they never squabbled about the fare, whatever you asked. But the English took a tram whenever they could: and if they couldn't, well, they knew what the fare should be.

Secession to the United States is not practical politics but the dream of a jester rule than the British has been.[1] Most people were vague in their arguments to support this position, but on analysis I found the following reasons for Pro-Americanism.

Many of the wealthier Trinidadians have been educated in America. They admire the atmosphere, the liberty of the North. Class and racial prejudice is less acute. The people who come from the States are not so stuffy, snobbish and patronising. Their wealth and high standard of living impress them. Workers who have been to the States have come back inspired by the American labour movement, compared to which the English one seems dead. American tourists spend their money more freely and are more frequent than English tourists.

Geographically, the West Indian islands should be a unit. Native West Indians look forward to a United West Indian States. Historically they have the example of the United States, the only group that has succeeded in breaking away from the British Empire. In the distant future it is hoped that the United States might lend her power and authority to the islands of the West Indies. The example of Hawaii is remembered and Puerto Rico is ignored.

There are two important local newspapers in Trinidad, the *Trinidad Guardian* and the *Port of Spain Gazette*. Of these the former is owned by a group of powerful local importers, in whose interests the local government is often criticised. The general tone of this paper is conservative. Its circulation is around 9000. Its format is similar to the *Daily Express*. The *Port*

---

1. *By competent observers, I am told the same is true of British Honduras and Jamaica, where the negroes refer to themselves not as 'British subjects' but 'British objects'.*

of Spain Gazette has a circulation of only 2000 odd. It is owned by Mr. Ambard and represents the interests of the native-born middle class and the Catholic Church, often criticising the Government from this angle.

Inasmuch as both these papers represent the interests of capital rather than labour, at any such crisis as the Trinidad Strike of 1937, they will rally to the support of the Government. Indeed, the fate of papers which do not do so is suppression on the grounds of 'sedition'.

The economics of newspaper production in a colony like Trinidad are different from the position in England or the United States. In England the capitalist newspapers have enormous circulations and are able to hold competing papers in check by reason of the huge revenues they receive from advertising. In Trinidad this is not so. A Labour paper representing the point of view of the trade unions would be able to mobilise a circulation of ten thousand readers immediately. Negro and East Indian business men would be prepared to support such a paper with advertisements, and the hegemony of the *Guardian* could be challenged in the first month of publication. This is the reason of the frequent Government prosecutions of progressive papers.

The Labour movement has a greater belief in the *Port of Spain Gazette* than in its rival, because Mr. Ambard has shown willingness to give Labour a hearing in his paper. But it would be incorrect to think that either of these papers has much influence on the majority of Trinidadians. The most influential papers in the colony are the *New Statesman and Nation* from England and *Time* from the United States. Though *Time* is more Conservative in outlook than the *New Statesman,* its reporting of the Simpson affair has given rise to the general belief that America's papers are more reliable about British affairs than even the progressive papers of the Empire.

In the second of three articles on the West Indies in *The Times*, Harold Stannard wrote recently:

> "The screen now belongs to America, and America probably has the lion's share of the air. The Empire broadcasts from Daventry are, however, growing in popularity, and more than once a wish was expressed for an expansion of the Empire news bulletin. The news itself is excellent, but does not convey anything of the British atmosphere. If the B.B.C. could take the principal London and provincial papers and add to the news bulletin every night extracts from the leading articles of two or three of them West Indian listeners would be grateful. Educated West Indians strain after England, try to appreciate her and find her inaccessible. An organization has been set up to improve British cultural relations with foreign countries; it would do a good day's work if it extended its activities to the colonies."

Mr. Stannard is writing, of course, of the West Indies as a whole. This may account for the difference between his experience and mine. I found that West Indians, who had been educated in England, had great love and loyalty for England. But those educated West Indians, who had not been educated in England, did not feel this love or the need 'to strain after England'; the majority of educated West Indians had not been to England, and numerically the small percentage of educated population counted little in relation to the great mass of illiterate or semiliterate workers.

I found, furthermore, that no one had a high opinion of the English news bulletins; they thought it absurd that football scores should be related at length; the actual news items were slight, uninformative and one-sided. When they wanted to hear news, they tuned in to the United States, because they knew that though even here the news would be one-sided, it would not have been edited in the interests of British Imperialism.

No one told me that he thought that the Daventry programmes had improved. The invariable complaints were that the reception from Daventry was so bad that even if the material broadcast was good, it would be impossible to listen to it; and that as it was, the programmes were composed without any understanding of what the West Indians wanted, and that the conception of the programme director was obviously of a homesick Empire builder sitting in the jungle, pining for the old country. Broadcasts like 'half an hour in an English pub,' may give ease to the nostalgia of the exile, but they give the West Indian, who is turned out of his pub at seven o'clock, a bellyache.

People listen to the American stations when they listen in at all: firstly, because the reception is better; and secondly, because they like the programmes more.

Suggestions on the lines laid down by Mr. Stannard would be futile for Trinidad, and, I suspect, for the rest of the West Indies. At the moment there is no broadcasting station in the British West Indies. Programmes are re-broadcast by a relaying company, which selects partly from England and partly from the States.

While this scheme is pursued, the hegemony of radio propaganda will remain with America. There is only one way in which this can be overcome. A West Indian broadcasting station must be set up in Jamaica, Bermuda or Trinidad.

The men selected to run this station must be given great discretion in their choice of programmes and they must be men with the imagination and creative talent to understand what programmes are needed and the best way for the material to be presented.

This work should not be confined to the presentation of propaganda bolstering up the British Empire. There are plenty of other things to do. Though Great Britain has ruled the island for over a hundred and forty years, educational facilities are scandalously backward. Compulsory education exists only in San Fernando and Port of Spain, and the all-over percentage of illiteracy is 43.1 per cent.

The work of the educational authorities is proceeding with lamentable slowness. The desire to read and write, the desire for knowledge and for music exists far in advance of the supply of facilities. Radio education, both in the juvenile and adult fields, could supply this demand, and in so supplying it give a material reason for gratitude and loyalty to the Empire much more powerful than any propaganda talks.

The Colonial Office is beginning to realise the strategical importance of Trinidad. Trinidad supplies 62.8 per cent of the Empire's petrol – though this is only 0.92 per cent of the world supply. It is capable of doubling production when the need arises. The refineries at Pointe a Pierre and Point Forth provide targets which a couple of raiding planes could destroy with the greatest ease. There are no anti-aircraft guns, in fact no fortifications of any sort. The only move which has been made towards the fortification of the island has been the New Harbour scheme, which will enable warships to be stationed close in to Port of Spain.

The Colonial Office does not, however, seem to be aware of the, propaganda which the Fascist States are pumping into Central and South America. During the last war the States of South America were kept in dangerous neutrality, German agents, however, succeeding in carrying on important anti-Allied propaganda even after the German fleet was driven from Latin-American waters.

At the moment a radio campaign is being waged by the Germans, countered by a new American short-wave station, for the possession of the sympathies of Latin-America. An English station in the West Indies, in addition to the valuable work that it could do in the West Indies themselves, would be important for the broadcasting of propaganda to counter the German attacks on Great Britain and the democratic States.

These are a number of the reasons why the Trinidadian feel a greater loyalty to the United States than they do to Great Britain. But I have left the two most important reasons to the end.

What reason is there why the West Indian should have any feeling of loyalty to the British Empire? After a hundred and forty years of British rule the Trinidad worker lives in houses which successive commissions condemn in the strongest terms, he receives wages which are admittedly insufficient to keep him in a state of health, much less of happiness. The efforts which he makes to call attention to his grievances are suppressed with violence. There are not enough schools, and what schools there are are badly equipped. The same applies to the hospitals. The government of his country is in the grasp of a few powerful vested interests and the Colonial Service seems to consider its first job not to run foul of these interests. Why, therefore, should the West Indians have any feeling of loyalty to any British Empire under any British Government?

The West Indian is more politically minded than the Englishman. He follows the policy of the British Government in foreign affairs with intelligence and eager interest, though his knowledge of actual facts may be limited. That interest and intelligence can be seen in the popular calypso songs, quoted in an earlier chapter.

The role that Great Britain has played in foreign politics during the last three years has finally obliterated any belief in the old slogan that the British Empire has a sense of justice or feeling for the oppressed. While that belief persisted, and it was always a belief founded more firmly on faith than fact – it was possible for the British Imperialist to get away with a lot of local oppression. But since the Baldwin-Chamberlain Government have made clear what the true foreign policy of the Empire is, they have destroyed that illusion. "This Empire," says the West Indian, "is not our Empire. We don't want to have anything to do with it. At home it oppresses us. It resists all our attempts to get a straight deal as sedition. It jails our leaders, shadows our representatives with detectives, admits our grievances and then does nothing about them. Abroad its policy is the same. In Ethiopia, Spain, China and Czechoslovakia England has aided the oppressor, not the oppressed. That is not the policy that our Empire would pursue."

Since the troubles in the West Indies there has been a lot of talk about 'using a strong hand'. The phrase is meant to imply that a strong hand ought to be used against the West Indian peoples, in order to impress them of the strength of the British Empire. The West Indian peoples would like to see England ' using the strong hand', but not in the West Indies. They would consider that the display not of strength, but tyranny. They want to see that strength used in the enforcement of justice.

This attitude is clear in the works of a Negro poet like Alfred Cruickshank.

> Hast thou grown weak,
> O England, thou – thou who went once most strong
> To guard the Right, to curb – to scourge the Wrong?
> Oh, I would rather die than know that thou
> Hast lost that English pride that scorns to bow
> Or bend the knee to aught unholy! See!
> The Church is mute as only stone can be!
> An utter failure in the hour of need,
> When deed alone must test the worth of creed.
> Thine, therefore, now – thine is the Chastening Rod
> To do the right in service of thy God!
> Thy million million subjects call to thee!
> Thy million million children call to thee!
> Arise, Britannia, in thy Chivalry!
> Stretch forth thy hand and keep the peoples free!

That was the cry of thousands of Negroes besides Alfred Cruickshank, in the early stages of the Abyssinian War. It changed later:

"My trusting friend! Oh, tell me, tell me, pray,
For our dear England do you weep today?"

Alfred Cruickshank's attitude here is the kindest that a Negro can arrive at. At his most forgiving, he can only feel pity of the weakness and cowardice of his Government. No display of warships in the Caribbean will change that pity to respect. The next emotions in that scale are contempt and hatred.

The folly of British foreign policy in relation to Imperial trade routes has often been emphasised. The sacrifice of Gibraltar and the threat levied on the Cape of Good Hope route to India by the Canary Islands have been made the centre of the attack on the National Government's shortsightedness in Imperial affairs.

But a much more important factor has been almost ignored. The psychological effect of British foreign policy on the subjects of the Empire has been to break any bond that existed before. Britain's betrayal of Abyssinia is nearly as much to blame for the riots in Trinidad and Jamaica as the high cost of living. The politicians and the diplomats are engrossed in the fascinating game of *realpolitik*, of shady bargaining, the partitioning of spheres of influence, the exchange of concessions. They do not realise that these games, fascinating as they are in their intellectual subtleties, and dramatic manoeuvres, are being watched by millions of people whose minds are tuned to simpler concepts of Right and Wrong, Justice, Cowardice and Treachery. And to these millions of simple onlookers, the real politicians present the pathetic likeness of cardsharpers who are losing, however hard they cheat. 'Twist the Lion's Tail and he bares his false teeth.' Millions of people who would rally to the support of the British Empire, if it was pursuing a policy in support of international justice, are turning away in sorrow and disgust.

Yet even now the loyalty of the West Indies is not finally alienated. It can be won back, but only by a fundamental change of policy all round. The overthrow of Chamberlain *realpolitik* is necessary, but that is a job which must be done in England and not in the West Indies. A popular front Government at home would rally the Negro people to its support. The islands are 95 per cent solid in opposition to Fascism and Nazism. They have come too close to it in their own administration to have any illusions about it.

But at the same time, before peace comes to the West Indies, certain things must be done. I do not say that they will be done, but I know that unless they are, troubles such as have occurred in Barbados, Trinidad, Jamaica and British Guiana will become more and more frequent.

In the remaining two chapters I will try to show what these changes must be.

ON TRINIDAD'S INDUSTRIES

TRINIDAD differs from the other West Indian islands in one important respect. In all the islands the majority of the population is engaged in agriculture. But in Trinidad the greatest percentage of exports is contributed by the oilfields and asphalt industry. There are only 9000 workers employed in the oilfields and at the Pitch Lake, with an estimated 27,000 dependent on the industry. Whereas the figures for agriculture are 72,000 workers or 212,000 dependants.'

In the colony, as all over the capitalist world, the position of agriculture is depressed. The cocoa industry enjoyed a period of fifty years' unbounded prosperity from 1870-1920. During this time cultivation and production rose, the young fields gave high yields, labour was cheap and plentiful, capital was ready to hand and large profits were made. In 1898 the export of cocoa for the first time exceeded that of sugar and sugar products in value. And cocoa, because of the area devoted to its growth, the labour it employed and the economic hold it had on the lives of most of the Trinidadian, came to be regarded as the index of the colony's prosperity.

During this period fortunes were made in cocoa. But those fortunes were not spent either in the improvement of the workers' conditions or in the accumulation of reserves for the improvement of estates or combat of disease.

In 1921 the price of cocoa slumped and the cracks in the structure of the industry split wide open. Capital had been raised on mortgages to bring into cultivation land which could only yield a profit while cocoa prices were high and the fields young. The mortgages were not redeemed, because the continued extension of cultivation proved very profitable, and the mortgagees themselves considered their investments as gilt-edged.

As soon as prices slumped many estate owners found that they could not pay the interest on their mortgages. In 1921 Government restricted the right of mortgagees to foreclose and introduced a scheme of financial assistance to the estate owners. In 1924 they founded the Agricultural Bank of Trinidad with the primary object of providing for the redemption of mortgages.

---

1. *Distributed roughly as 34,000 in both sugar and cocoa, 4000 in coconuts. There are also small subsidiary industries, growing grapefruit, limes, coffee, bananas, tonka beans and rubber.*

Things got worse instead of better, because the short-sightedness of the planters was coming back on them. Under ordinary cultivation, a field of cocoa shows a rising yield for the first fifteen to twenty-five years, after which it declines. This tendency was partly obscured by the fact that more and more land was being brought under cultivation, so that while the yield of individual fields decreased, the total yield of the estates had been increasing. But in 1920, when the price slumped, no new areas were brought under cultivation. The estate owners, who had spent their money as fast as they earned it, were not even able to pay proper attention to the cultivation of their existent fields, which were automatically declining in yield with age.

For the last eighteen years the cocoa industry has declined. Prices rose during the period 1924-5, 1929-30, and Government assistance was withdrawn and payment on mortgages resumed. But during 1930-31, prices slumped again and stayed low for the next five years. The workers, who had benefited little by the boom, lost by the slump. Wages were cut, tasks were increased and labour was reduced. The estates fell into decay through neglect of cultivation and interest payments on mortgages fell hopelessly in arrears.

In 1928 witchbroom disease appeared in the island, and since then has spread to most of the districts in the island. Few planters are sufficiently prosperous to keep the disease under control, and each year heavy losses of crop are recorded in certain districts. In the south and south-west portions of the island production was further reduced by the hurricane of 1933.

In 1935 Government introduced the 'Cacao Industry Relief Ordinance', whereby a sum equivalent to the value of a halfpenny per pound of cocoa produced by each estate during the crop year 1935-6 should be granted for the purpose of rehabilitating cocoa estates or converting them to other crops. This subsidy comes under review annually, though it was originally anticipated that the scheme would remain in force for four years. As certain of the alternative crops take four to five years to reach maturity, planters have been hesitant of making long-term plans under an annually renewed subsidy.

During the comparatively prosperous years 1923-4 to 1929-30, the average price for cocoa was £2 11s. 4d. a fanega (110 lb.). In the analysis made by the Imperial College of Tropical Agriculture, of a hundred and twenty-six cocoa estates, producing approximately one-quarter of the island's cocoa, it was found that 25 per cent of the estates operated at a loss, another 25 per cent had produced at a cost of only £1 5s. a fanega and the remainder were midway between.

The average price for the next seven years was £1 11s. 7d. The bottom 25 per cent of estates have obviously only the chance of surviving as cocoa producers on their richest fields. The top 25 per cent have a good chance of survival, while the remainder hang in the balance.

The Commission recommends as the best prospect of survival that they should be subdivided among small peasant proprietors. But the method of subdivision is not outlined. Are the lands to be bought over by Government and distributed as small holdings with a nominal rent and assistance in the treatment of the best fields and the planting of other fields with new crops? Are the estate owners to divide up their estates into small holdings and try to find the suckers who will operate economically estates that the owners cannot? Or is there to be some system of tenant farming, such as obtains on the sugar estates?

Any or all of these schemes are open to objections so considerable that this is probably the reason why the Commission tossed the suggestion lightly into the air and left it to fall into the oblivion in which nearly all the suggestions of all the Commissions have fallen.

Alternative crops have been suggested for the uneconomic cocoa districts: citrus, coconuts, tonka beans and sugar. Sugar, says the Commission, would ordinarily offer by far the best prospect of success, but since the production of the island's sugar is limited by quota, and that quota has already been fixed too high, there is no possibility for development in that direction. The market for tonka beans is small. The price of copra is down so low that the existing estates are operating at very small profit, and a special warning has been issued by the Colonial Office not to extend the crop of grapefruit, because of the extensive cultivation in Palestine.

The conclusion of the Commission is, therefore, that nothing can be done with this land.

The sugar industry is now once more the most important agricultural industry in the island. But the plight of the workers in that industry is little better than in the cocoa industry.

In March, 1930, a report made by the Olivier Commission was presented to the Houses of Parliament. The four most important recommendations of the Commission can be summarised as follows:

(1) The preference on Imperial sugar should be raised to 4s. 8d. a cwt. (£4 13s. 4d. a ton).

(2) Pending the conclusion of an international agreement on the subject of tariffs and subsidies, and the establishment of a single purchasing agency to buy Imperial sugar at about £15 a ton c.i.f. (and other sugar at the market price), duty on sugar should not be reduced below 4s. 8d. a cwt. under which tariff Imperial sugar would be admitted free, provided that the total price did not exceed £15 a ton.

(3) Alternative industries should be encouraged wherever possible, and peasant settlement and co-operation among peasants should be developed; and

(4) Labourers' houses upon estates should be improved and greater attention paid by Colonial Governments to sanitation and to the provision

of facilities of access for labourers to their work on estates and to their own provision grounds.

The most important recommendation of the Commission was the stabilisation of the price of sugar produced in all non-self-governing Colonies by fixing it for the British market at a figure which had regard for the reasonable cost of production. The figure recommended was round £15 a ton c.i.f. (equivalent to £13 10s. f.o.b.) for 96 degrees sugar. This figure was arrived at having a 'reasonable regard' for decent living conditions in the industry. The recommendation was refused, however, though the preference on Imperial-grown sugar was increased to £4 15s.

World prices have no regard for the reasonable conditions of living in an industry. In 1929 the f.o.b. value of sugar in London was not £13 10s., including preference, but £10 10s. By 1936 it was as low as £7 14s. 7d.

To meet the competition in the world market the sugar producers introduced new machinery in the refineries and improved mechanical cultivation in the fields, at the same time keeping labour costs as low as possible. As a result of this, the export of sugar has leapt from 41,805 tons in 1927 to 142,672 tons in 1936; molasses exports have risen from 1,188,840 to 3,909,009 gallons during the same period, and rum from 35,699 gallons to 90,185.

During this period of rationalisation the two other recommendations of the Olivier Commission were either completely or partially ignored. The workers 'contributed their share by continuing to accept a standard of wage and living conditions far below what is desirable': and though one or two companies made some effort in improving housing conditions, the majority let the matter slide. 'Some indeed,' adds the Commission, 'have allowed the housing of their labour to deteriorate to such an extent as to become a discredit to the industry.'

Conversation with sugar, as with cocoa planters, is not illuminating. It is impossible, judging from their conversation, to understand why they continue to waste their time and capital on producing so little profit at such enormous cost. No figures are obtainable to show what their actual profits are, but some slight indication can be obtained even from the figures which the Commissioners give.

Sugar, as we have said above, is farmed by wage-earners and by tenant farmers, It is estimated that there are 34,000 workers in the sugar industry, of whom some 3000 work in the refineries. There are approximately 19,500 cane farmers and 11,500 field workers, paid on a wage basis.

In 1936 the value of the exports of sugar and its by-products amounted to £1,338,651. Fifty-six per cent of the cane was grown by the companies who have the advantage in their production of up-to-date field machinery. The remaining percentage was grown by the cane farmers. For this 44 per cent of the crop, 600,000 tons of cane, the cane farmers were paid the sum of £326,000. The average income of each cane farmer was therefore under £17 10s. per annum. That is to say that the daily allowance to feed what the Commission estimates at three people was under elevenpence, less than fourpence per person per day.

The cane farmer, of course, is able to set aside a small portion of his land to the growth of his own vegetables, so that his income from crop does not represent the entirety of his resources. He probably grows bananas and eggplants, has a mango-tree and perhaps a breadfruit. But he is not allowed to use his land for the production of vegetables for the local market. He is tied to the production of sugar and he is tied much more effectively than the sugar worker, because the estates advance him money on his crop and he remains permanently slightly in their debt.

He is not a competitor in an open market. He has to produce for the estate specified in his contract, taking his sugar to specified scales, where it is weighed. These scales are often a long way from the cane farmer's field. The poorer farmer has to hire a cart or in certain cases carries it on his back. At the scales there is an overseer appointed by the estate to judge the quality of the canes. If the overseer says that the canes are not properly cleaned of trash, the cane farmer is given the option of taking a lower price nominated by the overseer, returning home with his canes a distance often of some miles and cleaning them, or having them dumped, that is to say, tilted out of the cart on to the ground, which is usually a morass of mud round the scales, and further examined. Any dispute between overseer and cane farmer can only be referred to a court of law, a procedure involving loss of time and money. Even supposing that the cane farmer took his case to court, as his contract stipulates that he must always go to the same scales, he would be open to reprisals from the overseer whose judgment he had challenged.

The cleaning of canes is a laborious process. There is a hard cane from which the trash can be burnt without damage to the cane. But though this is grown on the estates, the cane farmers are not allowed to produce it. The great fires that during the cutting season one sees all down the coast, pillars of smoke by day, red glows by night, all come from the estates.

The most inequitable clause of all is the clause which exempts the estate from taking the cane of the cane farmers till after the estate cane has been cut. As we saw above, this means that the first people to be penalised by a strike are the cane farmers. But it means more than this. It means firstly that if the season is curtailed for any other reason, the cane farmers will suffer first again. And it means, now that a quota has been fixed for Trinidad sugar, that when that quota is filled, the cane farmers are left with the surplus, a sheer loss. This situation has not yet arisen, because the quota has only just come into operation, but it is a situation liable to arise in any high-yielding year.

The cane farmers maintain that the profit of the sugar industry is being annexed inequitably by the refineries. And they argue that if this is not the case, the refineries would be prepared to show them the figures of production, with the exact statement of profits.

The sugar workers, as opposed to the cane farmers, earn higher wages per day, but their labour is not constant. The fields require attention only at certain times of the year. During the rest of the time only a skeleton staff is necessary. In consequence, their annual income is even lower than that of the cane farmers.

Their position could be improved if land were allotted to them for the growth of vegetables. But though land is set aside for this purpose, it is the estate's land, and the produce is sold to the estate labourers.

Complaints are made on the other side by the employers, and this applies to every industry in the country. The coloured worker, it is stated, thinks only of the day. He wants to get enough food, just enough, to keep his home together. The rest of the day he will spend in idleness. A copra planter complained to me that he could not get the labour that he wanted though it abounded in the neighbouring village. Manufacturers told me of accidents happening through laziness or blind neglect of the elementary precautions with regard to machinery. On the oilfields, a man told to test the quality of the oil in a tank, went down into the tank and was overpowered by the fumes. His mate went down after him and died by his side. A third man, a white driller, tried to rescue them from above, and losing consciousness, fell in on top of them.

There seems to be little doubt that many accidents do occur through stupid laziness, that labourers do not work as hard or as efficiently as they do in other more temperate countries. But the conclusion that was always drawn from these arguments seemed open to suspicion. It was always meant to be conclusive and triumphant proof that coloured labour was no good and didn't deserve a higher wage.

I reached the conclusion that this condition, which certainly exists though on not such a vicious scale as employers maintain, was due to a complex of circumstances of which all but one can be remedied.

The irremediable factor is the climate. The efficiency of anyone, however good his health, however perfect his relation to his work, automatically declines in the tropics. In England I can write fourteen hours a day. In Mexico City, where I am, writing this book, eight hours is my capacity. But in Trinidad two hours of writing left me exhausted.

It is said that the Negroes are adapted to the climate; that they came from Africa and are used to intense tropical heat. But, in fact, their wearing of European clothes more than cancels this native adaptation. Their dark pigmentation resists the sun's rays. Naked they would receive their quota of rays. But in European clothes they are starved of light. Their health suffers as a European's would if he went naked in the tropics.

Among the agricultural population it is generally admitted that the prevalence of hookworm has reduced efficiency enormously. It is not laziness in most cases that makes a labourer refuse a task, but sheer exhaustion. The Government campaign, which should be supported by all employers, will increase the resources of energy both for the better execution of present work and of more work.

But when all these physical factors have been taken into account, there remains an even more important psychological one, the disposition to sabotage. Sabotage is the natural weapon of all workers who feel that they aren't getting a square deal. It is used in European factories in the deliberate tactics of the 'slow-up'. With the coloured workers, conditions have been so constantly against him that it has become almost second nature. To do things with the least possible effort rather than the greatest possible efficiency has become a rule of life. The stories of appalling deaths and injuries through carelessness are the chronicles of the martyrs of this philosophy.

To the manufacturer, sabotage is contemptible, especially when it is not directed towards the achievement of a definite aim, but has become the chronic withholding of labour. But the manufacturer is mistaken in thinking that this tendency to sabotage is an immutable part of the Negro temperament. It was formerly his only type of resistance to exploitation, the most invincible and least constructive form of protest.

The leaders of the newly formed trade unions are quite aware of this. They are substituting the constructive and articulate form of protest, collective bargaining and the withholding of labour for a definite purpose. But the trade unions will have to give the workers the conviction that they are fighting for better conditions and that they can win them, if they are to succeed either in establishing unionism or eradicating temperamental sabotage. Temperamental sabotage is the attitude of the man who has no hope of bettering his own conditions; the only happiness that he can see for himself is the avoidance of unnecessary effort. That attitude disappears as soon as the worker realises that he has an interest in the wealth that he is creating. Hitherto this has not been true. He has borne the slumps, but not enjoyed the booms.

Trinidad has not suffered from depression in the way that other countries have. Always there has been some industry in the ascendant. Cocoa, sugar, and now oil. Oil has come to rank as the chief export from the island and will do so for many years. There are five main oil companies, producing 87 per cent of the island's oil. Of these, in 1936, Apex produced 29 per cent, Trinidad Leaseholds 28 per cent, United British 50 per cent, Petroleum Development 10 per cent and British Controlled 10 per cent.

The oil is treated at two main refineries, one owned by Trinidad Leaseholds at Pointe a Pierre, the other by United British at Pointe Fortin.

These two companies arrange to refine for the other fields and take only so much of their own oil as is needed to keep the plant working at capacity.

The latest returns of British Controlled (a Canadian Company) are not available. But the issued capital of the other four big companies at the date of their last balance sheets was £4,040,000 pounds. Add in reserves and profit and loss balances of £2,730,000 and the shareholders total interest is raised to £6,770,000. Profits for the year 1936-37 totalled £1,540,000, which after allowing for taxation and amortisation leaves a 23 per cent interest on the total. The Apex company declared a dividend of 45 per cent, and Leaseholds 30 per cent.

In 1936 wages paid amounted only to £473,000, less than a third of the profits.[1]

It is in the question of wages that the Commission shows itself in its worst light. Throughout the report the principle is accepted that irrespective of the vaguely definable 'value' of work done,[2] if an industry is doing badly, the workers ought to bear a share of its failure by taking a cut. This implies conversely that they ought to receive a share of its prosperity. As the agricultural industries were able to make out a good case for their depression, this implication was allowed to stand. But in the case of the oilfields, it was necessary to have recourse to the old idea of the fixed value of a man's labour.

Before quoting the Commission's memorandum on wages, it is necessary to explain the reasons for the different prosperity of various companies. The big five companies are operating in rich fields which have been fully surveyed. There are other companies, most of them subsidiaries of the big five, which are engaged on exploratory work. A number of 'wildcat' wells are being sunk on favourable ground. About the usual percentage of successes, one in five, has been recorded. But even when oil is struck, there is no guarantee that it will be worked. In a number of cases it is more profitable to cap the well and explain to the owner that it is unfortunate but no oil has been found. Then a suggestion is made that though the property is no use for oil, it could be used to house oil-workers. If the owner can be induced to sell out on these much lower terms, the wells are then worked. Otherwise the oil remains unworked, until a more convenient time. At the

---

1. *For these figures I am indebted to an article in* Empire, *June* 1938, *called 'Trinidad on Strike'. The figures given by the Commissioners are presented in block, the twenty-two oil companies operating in the island being treated as a group.*
2. *Work done has no fixed 'value' in fact. The value of a man's labour is purely and simply what he can get for it. This is determined by four factors: what the employer is prepared to pay, what other competitive employers are prepared to pay, what most labourers will accept, and by the estimated skill of an individual worker.*

present moment the refineries are handling about as much oil as they can conveniently take. They are expanding their plant rapidly, but until the extensions have gone much further, the production of existent wells cannot be handled at maximum output.

The game is, of course, very much more complex than this. It stretches from the fully worked field, throughout a network to those fields which are being surveyed by air-and field-geologists. Lawyers are employed on a commission basis to approach peasants and buy in the mineral rights of their land at a figure which seems attractive to them at the time, but is not worth a tithe of the royalties if oil is discovered.

The Companies working closely together in the Petroleum Association are able to plan what fields should be developed and what retarded, in a manner most profitable to themselves.

The Commission's report runs as follows:

> ...there are a few oil companies which are meeting with financial success and which therefore are in a position to offer their labour more favourable conditions of work than the less-successful companies. The question here arises whether the more successful companies should use their financial advantages in part in the payment of wages at higher rates than the poorer companies, according to the capacity of each. At present, standard rates of wages for the various grades of work are laid down by the Petroleum Association of Trinidad, and these rates are paid by the constituent companies. In our opinion this system of standard rates should continue, subject to our general recommendations (which are contained in Chapter VII) for the establishment of negotiating machinery for the settlement of differences between employers and workers as to the exact rates payable. We feel that any arrangement under which different wages were paid for the same class of work and occupation by different companies would tend to dislocate the industry and would probably lead to further discontent among those workers who were unable to secure work with the companies which paid the higher wages. *In any case the wage is paid for the value of the work done, and if in any given industry the standard of work required is the same, there is no logical reason for a differentiation in the standard rates paid within that industry.*"

When it is remembered that many of the twenty-two oil companies are in fact subsidiary companies of the big five, and also that the 'few successful' companies are in fact producing 87 per cent of the island's oil and employing the majority of the industry's workers, it can be seen the extent to which the Petroleum Association succeeded in foisting its views on the Commission. On the plea that the remaining seventeen companies were unsuccessful, the wage rates must be kept down near their present level. When in other industries the demand for higher wages is met by the argument that the industry cannot pay more, for the oil companies the new principle is established that the value of the work does not justify a rise. The value of the work can, however, be seen in the 45 per cent dividend paid by Apex and the 30 per cent paid by the Leaseholds.

The argument used for the payment of a standard rate has been disproved over and over again in other countries. Where a minimum trade union wage is fixed, employers find that by paying wages above trade union rates they get more work and better work from the men. Workers are not fools. A man employed in an English motor factory may wish that he was working for Morris Motors, because they pay higher wages. He may struggle to get higher wages in his own factory, fired by the example. But if those wages cannot be paid, most workers are willing to work at the wage which the industry can afford. A certain percentage of workers argue, perhaps correctly, that if the industry cannot pay them decent wages, it must be re-organised according to a plan which can. But this is not the view of the majority at the moment in the capitalist countries. If workers are able to understand the argument for the cutting of their wages in times of depression, they are quite capable of understanding the argument of raising their wages in prosperous plants.

On the other hand an issue is raised by this question which was carefully avoided by the Commission. It is obvious that the enormous profits enjoyed by the development of Trinidad's oil should be enjoyed not only by the workers in the oilfields, but by the community at large. Taxes on such enormous profits should be heavy.

The taxation of Trinidad, however, is designed to spare the rich man and soak the poor. The scale of rates of income-tax payable on net chargeable income is as follows:

> For every dollar of the
> first 1,000 dollars 1 and a half cents $1,000
> next 1,000 dollars 2 and a half cents $2,000
> next 1,000 dollars 4 and a half cents $3,000
> next 1,000 dollars 5 and a half cents $4,000
> next 1,000 dollars 7 and a half cents $6,000
> next 1,000 dollars 9 and a half cents $8,000
> next 1,000 dollars 12 and a half cents $12,000
> next 1,000 dollars 15 and a half cents $18,000
> next 1,000 dollars 18 and a half cents $21,000
> next 1,000 dollars 21 and a half cents $24,000
> next 1,000 dollars 27 and a half cents $29,000
> next 1,000 dollars 32 and a half cents $38,000
> Remainder of the chargeable income 38 cents.

Every individual resident in the colony shall be allowed a deduction of $1200; also every nonresident British subject, provided that he makes a return of his total income, including income not liable to tax in the colony.

The tax upon the chargeable income of a company shall be charged at the rate of 12.5 per cent of the chargeable income thereof, and in the case of Life Insurance Companies at the rate of 2.5 per cent.

The list of articles liable to customs tariff occupies eight pages in *Franklin's Year Book;* there are a hundred and four sub-headings. There are tariffs on practically all building material, on timber, metal sheeting, asbestos boards, cement, bricks and tiles. There are tariffs on all meats, except fresh meat from the Empire: on all vegetables, excluding fresh vegetables from the Empire other than potatoes, onions and garlic. On every sort of grain, meal, flour, pulse and farinaceous preparations such as macaroni. On tea, coffee, cheese, biscuits, butter and butter substitutes, lard and lard substitutes. On jams, jellies, preserved, canned, dried and bottled fruits. On condensed milk, pickles, condiments, sugar, spices and unnamed provisions. Household utensils such as china, earthenware, hardware, glass, brooms, brushes, baskets, cutlery, are liable to duty. Tax must be paid on cotton goods, woollen goods, silks and linens. Hats, shoes, boots, umbrellas and neckties are dutiable. Oil of every kind, soap, the majority of medicines, beers, wines and spirits, tobacco, candles, electrical apparatus, chemicals, leather, jewellery, musical instruments, stationery, paper, perfumery, watches and the parts of watches all figure in the list along with vinegar and games, starch and linoleum, hay, lime, cider and perry.

There are exemptions. Books and some drugs, eggs in the shell of British Empire origin, artificial limbs, cups, shields and medals of British Empire origin, radium and wine for public worship. Quebracho extract and cylinders for the transport of compressed gas. Bees and sand, shocks, staves and headings of white oak for the manufacture of rum puncheons, tierces, hogsheads, barrels and casks. Articles imported for the use of the Constabulary Sports Club and Prisons Sports Club, not including articles intended for sale or exchange, whether to members of the Club or otherwise, on the signed declaration of the Inspector-General of Constabulary and Superintendent of Prisons respectively.

In *Franklin's Yearbook* there are four and a half pages of exemptions. But the exemptions are for the Colonial Government, the blind and the Church, for consuls, returning athletes and privileged trades rather than for the ordinary people. The ordinary people pay tariffs on their food and the pans they cook it in; on the clothes they wear, when they are fit; and the drugs they take when they are ill. On their drink, on their smokes, on the oil and sugar which many produce with their own labour. In the year 1936 they paid $5,405,713.85 in indirect taxation. Licenses (and even bicyclists have to pay a licence fee of five shillings a year), together with other Internal Revenue not otherwise specified, raised another $1,253,675.71 . This totals $6,659,489.56. Set against it the income-tax contribution $878,322.38.

The General Manager of Apex estimated that from 1935 to 1936 the cost of living rose 17 per cent. The local population had to pay 10 to 20 per cent *ad valorem* duty on most articles purchased. And in addition to this on December 13th, 1935, a surtax of 15 per cent was added to a great number of articles. On the other hand, the wealth produced in the colony was exported to shareholders with an income-tax deduction of only two shillings and sixpence in the pound.

The excessive profits earned by the big five oil companies could be passed on to the community as a whole by means of a graded income-tax scale for companies. The gains in revenue through direct taxation could be passed on to the public by the reduction of indirect taxes on foodstuffs not produced by the colony but generally used by the poorer classes, on the cheaper grades of clothing, cotton goods, etc., and on building material used for workmen's houses. Legislation would have to be passed at the same time to ensure that the benefit was passed on to the public and not retained by the merchant.

Such an income-tax would draw on those companies making a profit, without harming those running near the margin line. It would distribute the benefits of Trinidad wealth not only among the workers in the oil industry but also among the population as a whole. It would ease the pressure caused by the rising cost of living. And it would make plain, what crown colony government affirms but nobody living in a crown colony believes, that Government wishes to rule in the interest of the native population and not in the interest of exploiting capitalists.

This revision of the incidence of taxation would, of course meet with strong resistance from the employers' association and powerful local and foreign interests. For this is the central point in the conflict between the interests of big business and of the people as a whole. A strong man is needed in Government House to carry through such a scheme against the pressure that certainly would be exerted against it The present Governor, Sir Hubert Young, has the reputation of being such a strong man. He can also have the assurance that if he disregards the opposition of a minority he will have the solid support of the majority behind him.

ON CROWN COLONY GOVERNMENT

THE hub of Government is the Red House, a remarkable building stretching the whole of the west side of Woodford Square. As so often no better words can be found to describe it than those chosen by Mr. Franklin in his *Yearbook*. "Externally the stucco embellishments of the ground floor are of the Doric Order, while those above being [sic] of the Corinthian Order. The lofty dome whose pinnacle is 110 feet from the base, is carried out *in four orders of architecture.* The Council Hall is an ornate chamber where the Legislative Council meets; and in which the rich entablature is entirely of the Corinthian Order, the flooring being of native hard wood."

This erection is called the Red House, not for political reasons, but because stucco embellishments and all have been washed a terra-cotta red, which is as distinctive as it is hideous.

At the south end of the Red House are the Courts of Justice. Around the central courtyard on the ground flood are the Education Office, the Mines Department and the offices of the Sub-Intendant of Crown Lands, Registrar General, Administrator General and Crown Solicitor; above them sit the Colonial Secretary, His Excellency the Governor, the Attorney-General and the Solicitor-General.

These can be studied at their best in the Ornate Chamber at the northern end of the pile. But a word must be added to the description of that Chamber, given by Mr. Franklin.

An architectural note of originality has been struck by the introduction of a number of plaster of paris columns of the Corinthian Order, placed projecting from the walls and supporting nothing. The western end is filled with some twenty benches made from native very hard wood. These benches are open to the public. In front of these benches there are four chairs and a table large enough for two. This table is the Press table and the chairs are the Press chairs.

At the extreme east end there is a mass of dark wood, elaborately carved and looking like a mutilated reredos looted from a decadent baroque church. It forms a sort of canopy over a chair whose last occupant was the Duke of Windsor when he visited the island in September, 1920.

Between reredos and Press table sit the Legislative Council. They are arranged in a double horseshoe. The Governor or Acting Governor sits at the head of the horseshoe at floor-level. The wings of the shoe to his right seat thirteen elected and nominated members of the Council in order .of seniority, junior members sitting on a raised platform, seniors on floor-level. On the left are opposed twelve Government officials, representing different departments.

Of the unofficial members of the Council, six are nominated and seven are elected. The six nominated members represent the vested interests of the colony: banking, oil, sugar, the law, property. The seven elected members include the Cipriani group, the khaki captain himself, the Hon. Sarran Teelucksingh, elected for Caroni on the East Indian vote; the Hon. Timothy Roodal, another East Indian candidate and the owner of several cinemas; the Hon. Vernon Wharton, head of the Coconut Growers' Association; the Hon. Michael Aldwin Mallard, ex-storekeeper; the Hon. George de Nobriga, member for Tobago; and the Hon. Adrian Cola Rienzi, union president.

The term 'elected member' needs a slight explanation. Though there are 440,000 people living in Trinidad and Tobago, only 26,000 of these are allowed to vote. And in order to stand for membership in the Council it is necessary to prove an income of four hundred pounds a year at least.

The fact that there are twelve official members apart from the Governor, and thirteen unofficial members, does not mean that the unofficial members have a majority. The Governor has an original and a casting vote which gives Government a final majority of one. This means that the business of the Legislative Council is in fact a farce since Government is able to carry any measure that it wants. It is an elaborate game in which the opposition is allowed from time to time to win a point or two so that they may not feel too sore.

Game though it is, it is worth studying. Even something can be learnt from watching a crap-game, played with loaded dice.

I attended the Legislative Council on several occasions. Knowing the constitution of the Council, I had expected the smooth passage of laws without a hitch. I argued that where the Government had a solid majority and the opposition had no common bond of unity the Council would be easy to control.

I found, however, that a parliamentary procedure new to me was followed. The Acting Governor would sit back in his chair, his hand over his eyes, while speeches were made upon some controversial point. In the course of discussion, an amendment would be proposed. This amendment would be amended in its turn by some member who had got up apparently to second the first amendment. A third amendment would then be proposed either separate from or supplementary to the two preceding amendments.

At this stage His Excellency would look up and say: "Government will not countenance Amendments one and two. Will the Honourable Member repeat Amendment three?" Quite likely Amendment three would bear an entirely different significance, separated from the two previous amendments. The Honourable Member would be flustered, would repeat his amendment, trying at the same time to realise its new implications. These new implications would not be discussed. The amendment would be put to the vote. Members would plump this way or that and then spend the next three hours after adjournment trying to discover the exact significance of what they had voted.

Another interesting point of Council procedure was the use of the Rule Book. There was only one copy of this rule book extant: and that lay on the table before His Excellency. At any point in the procedure, the Acting Governor might look down and say, "That is not in my rule book. If you refer to Paragraph so and so, subsection whatnot, you'll see what I mean." The argument was unanswerable.

The architect, who so ingeniously combined four styles of architecture in the Red House, had achieved an interesting acoustic effect in the construction of the Council Chamber. Though the general public was admitted to sessions of the Council, the voices of most speakers were almost inaudible even at the Press table twelve feet away. In the body of the hall you were able to watch the hands and lips of the speakers, but if you wanted to know what was happening you had to read the paper next day. This system was well adapted to crown colony government. For just as the Council itself gives the appearance of self-government with the reality of dictatorship, so the admission of the public gives the appearance of openness with the advantage of secrecy.

The acoustic properties of the Council could be, and were, put to a variety of uses. With a little training, the voice could be thrown so that either a section or the whole of the Council could hear what was being said without the Press knowing. Or again, the Press could be brought within hearing, without the audience hearing anything.

In this hall, of course, it was possible for a speaker to make himself audible to everybody. Rienzi made deliberate use of this fact. Knowing that an unofficial member of the Council has more power to voice grievances than to remedy them, he would speak in a voice that could be heard all over the hall, deliberately digress from the point at issue and enlarge the scope of the question under debate. Whenever asked by the Acting Governor how this was relevant to the discussion, he would come back to the main point again, before wandering off in another digression. In this way the Council Chamber became a platform for the dissemination of ideas that might not have been tolerated elsewhere.

It was very amusing to watch these passages between the Acting Governor and Rienzi. Rienzi succeeded so well in disguising his intentions that many members of the Council merely believed that he was incapable of sticking to the point. "I really cannot see the relevance", the Acting Governor would break in. "In a moment, Your Excellency will," Rienzi would answer. During this, Colonel Mavrogordato would sit with one little leg crossed over the other, leaning back in his chair and quizzing the mob through his precarious monocle. The Hon. Vernon Wharton would indulge in a deep-throated snort of laughter as the Governor became particularly restive. Sir Lennox O'Reilly would look at his nails and Dr. Rankine would stifle a yawn.

Sir Lennox O'Reilly, 'Trinidad's most distinguished K. C.', was himself an excellent study. I heard him speak against the Government Shop Hours Bill, which, while being framed ostensibly as a Bill to prevent the sweating of labour, entrenched the large shops against the small by making hours of opening identical for all shops, except parlours.[1] The Bill had come in for a great deal of opposition from the Press, from unions and from the unofficial and even official members of the Council. Government, however, without giving any valid answer to the criticisms made of the Bill, were prepared to railroad it through. The Government members were instructed to vote not according to conscience but *en bloc.*

As soon as the Acting Governor had announced that Government would vote *en bloc,* all further discussion was valueless. It was at this point that Sir Lennox rose to make his contribution. He is a tall, distinguished-looking man, with grizzled curly hair and horn-rimmed spectacles. He began his speech in the traditional manner. Leaning forward on the tips of his fingers, he opened his mouth and a vague murmur of sounds came softly to the Press table. The gestures with the hands, the taking off and putting on of spectacles, all these were in the fine tradition of Anglo-Saxon oratory. The Council might have been a meeting of creditors being staved off, it was done with such facility.

And then suddenly, Sir Lennox stopped being the old English squire turned company promoter. He dropped the carefully nurtured English accent which was too careful and too nurtured to be English. He raised his voice, speaking with his native Trinidad accent loud enough for everybody to hear. He turned towards the Press table. The reporters began scribbling. And for half an hour he made a powerful attack on the Government, repeating with powerful eloquence the arguments which had already been made by the opponents of the Bill. It was a fine piece of oratory. It raised the issues on to a higher plane than before. Here was no longer the question of vested interest succeeding once again in distorting labour legislation to its own advantage. It was a question of a fair deal for everyone. It involved

---

1. *All shops, according to this Bill, must close at 4 p.m., up to which hour all workers are employed.*

the issue of democracy. It... it ... well, it proved in fact that Sir Lennox was a greater champion of the people than any of the others who had opposed the Bill.

The Legislative Council is a farce. I have devoted the last few pages to showing in what way it is a farce. But now a much more important question arises, and that is, Why is crown colony government a failure?

The theory behind crown colony government is that the people are not yet sufficiently advanced for self-government. They must be led to it gradually, by paedeutic means such as the Legislative Council and by the grant of municipal self-government. Step by step self-government will come.

"Will it come soon?" you ask.

"Well," says the Government official, "how can it? In Port of Spain, for example, they have complete municipal self-government. We can't do anything about it. Everything is in their hands. And what sort of a job do they make of it? Nepotism, corruption, the distortion of public measures to private ends. Look at housing. Look at the sewerage scheme for Woodbrook, which doesn't need it, and the neglect of Piccadilly and St. James."

At first this sounds convincing. The municipal government of Port of Spain is certainly corrupt and certainly inefficient. But why?

The population is 76,384. But in order to elect a councillor you must be a burgess. To be a burgess you must be either the occupying owner of a house or business place in the city assessed at an annual rental of at least £10, or the tenant of such house or business place for which you have paid one year's rent at least to the amount of £12 10s., or pay not less than £62 1 0s. for board and lodging combined. The number of burgesses thus qualified is 7881.

In order to be a councillor there are higher property qualifications. Ownership of a house assessed at £50 annual rental, tenancy of a house with minimum rental of £62 10s. or an income of at least £312 10s. per annum.

It is ambiguous to talk about Port of Spain being self-governing. Port of Spain is governed by men selected from a small propertied class by the votes of a rather wider propertied class, which represents about a third of the adult male population of the city. The population whose need for expression is greatest live in barracks. They are debarred from standing for office and from electing their representatives. The misgovernment blamed on the municipal council by Government officials is due to the fact that there exists no check on legislation made in the interests of a propertied oligarchy. The 'self-government' of Port of Spain is a failure because it is not 'self-government' in the true sense of that term, that is to say the democratic election of representatives from any class by the adult members of all classes.

As things are, the depressed classes are exploited by the local vested interests in exactly the same way as they are by foreign capitalist concerns. As we saw in the slum tour with Dr. Marcano, insanitary property was owned by local property owners, commercial companies with foreign capital and by the Church.

The natural check on class legislation and administration is not, as I have heard suggested, a curtailment of the rights of the Council, but an extension of the franchise and abolition of the property qualification for councillors. The bogy that is always raised – that irresponsible demagogues will stand for office – is nothing but a bogy. Irresponsible demagogues may stand for office, but they will not get elected, or at least they will not get re-elected. And the election of one or two irresponsible demagogues does not seem to me more dangerous than the continued re-election of several chisellers.

There is no doubt that the municipal government has a poor record for the reasons I have given. The administration of the colony under the crown colony government has, if anything, a worse record. And for that there are no excuses. The Government, despite the Legislative Council, is all-powerful. It can carry through any measure which it sees fit to carry through. It can stand superior to the vested interests of foreign and local capital. A tyranny, it can be benevolent. And it has had over a hundred and forty years to show what it can do.

Every Commission which has come to the island has been appalled at the conditions. Every committee has made recommendations, most of which are repeated from the Commission before. But nothing has been done.

The forces warring in the island unite sometimes this way, sometimes that. Strange alliances are formed for one purpose and dissolved for another. But the three types of force and interest are simple. There is the interest of the Imperial Government, to whom Trinidad is not an isolated unit but part of a vast empire. When the Colonial Office warns the Trinidadian not to plant grapefruit because grapefruit is being planted in Palestine, Trinidad is being controlled in its development not so much for its own interest as for the Empire's. The strategic importance of Trinidad is not important to Trinidad but to the Empire. When the million pound deep-water harbour scheme was initiated its primary aim was strategic, though it may also bring great benefit to the colony.

Secondly, there is the interest of capital. This capital may come from abroad or from the island itself. On certain issues there will be competition and conflict between rival capitalists. But in face of larger threats these differences will be settled for the moment and a common front formed.

The third force is the force of labour, the largest numerical group in the island and finally the most powerful. At the present, the most oppressed and the least united of the three forces, it represents the creative force that alone can bring the island from that darkness and unhappiness which has been its lot since white men came to the island. Glory dead when white man come. But the force of labour can bring about the resurrection of glory.

The theory of crown colony government is that of benevolent despotism. The colonial official, with his public school and university training, is supposed to have a patriarchal impartiality. He is supposed to have the true interests of the native population at heart, to be superior to the power of vested interests. There are many colonial officials who believe in this themselves, in so far as their class training allows them to. But if Trinidad is a true example of crown colony government the theory is a myth, covering a history of savage exploitation. Trinidad has never been a poor island. Since the English seizure of it, wealth has constantly been drained from the island, a toll taken from the various peoples imported there to be exploited. A rich island, with 90 per cent of the population impoverished.

The benevolent tyranny, which is supposed to be superior to the interests of the exploiting capitalist, has in fact legislated throughout in the interest of that class. It has been the political side of capitalism, with a different personnel but a common aim. Its police are summoned to defend the employers against the threat of the workers, but not to defend the workers against the employers. The volunteer corps is the extension of this alliance, the endowment of the rich with police and military powers to shoot to preserve their position of ascendancy.

During the last hundred and forty years there have been advances in the conditions of the people of Trinidad. But those advances have been given either as freedom from slavery in order to overthrow an entrenched economic body or as a concession to appease the widespread discontent. These concessions have been gained not as a result of reasonable demand, because reasonable demand has been ignored, but at the cost of human life, when conditions have grown so bad that men have become desperate.

The fact that these outbreaks have taken place is because the native people have been given no means of expression. The benevolent tyranny, close to the demands of big business but distant from the workers, has blundered on, deaf to the cries of distress because it has not tried to listen.

Trade unionism is the beginning of the constructive, articulate struggle of the workers. But trade unionism does not go far enough. Just as the Port of Spain Municipal Council must be democratised, so the Legislative Council must be elected by a truly representative body, the property qualification must be lowered and the number of nominated members reduced.

The recommendations of Commissions will always fall into oblivion when the political power remains in the hands of the representatives of big business. Government still retains its majority. But supposing that instead of having twelve representatives of capitalism in the opposition to one representative of the workers the proportion was reduced only to seven and six, Government would get a fairer understanding of the thoughts and temperament of the majority of the people they govern.

As it is, Rienzi speaks for 90 per cent of the population, and appears a freak, a red, an agitator. The twelve others, representing a fraction of the remaining tenth and their shareholders abroad, give the appearance of being the opinion of the majority of the colony. It is small wonder that a Government, each member of which is naturally swayed towards his own class and colour, should turn from being the benevolent dictator of a colony into the obedient tool of business interests. And it is smaller wonder still that such a Government commands not loyalty but contempt, not pride but sense of Glory Dead.

ABOUT THE AUTHOR

Arthur Calder-Marshall was a novelist, playwright, travel writer and essayist. At the time of writing *Glory Dead* he was a member of the British Communist Party and a member of the left-wing Readers & Writers Group along with writers such as Mulk Raj Anand. He was born in 1908 and died in 1992.

Bridget Brereton is Emerita Professor of History at UWI, St Augustine, Trinidad & Tobago. She is the author of several books on the history of the Caribbean and of Trinidad, including standard works such as *Race Relations in Colonial Trinidad, 1870-1900* and *A History of Modern Trinidad, 1783-1962*. She is the editor or co-editor of several more (including Volume V of the UNESCO *General History of the Caribbean*), and the author of many journal articles, book chapters and book reviews. She is a former Head of the Department of History, Deputy Principal, and Interim Principal, all at the St Augustine Campus of UWI. She has also served as Chair of the Board of NALIS, Chair of the Trinidad & Tobago Nominating Committee for the ANSAMcAL Caribbean Awards for Excellence, and Chair of the Cabinet-appointed Committee to consider the Trinity Cross and other National Symbols and Observances, among other public service positions.